D1204705

## VISIT Spanish100.com TO ACCESS ONLINE CONTENT AND DOWNLOAD THE APP.

Spanish in 100 Days

Second Edition: January 2020

© 2019, TRIALTEA USA
© 2019, of this edition, Penguin Random House Grupo Editorial USA, LLC.,
8950 SW 74th Court, Suite 2010
Miami, FL 33156

Cover images: © Paffy1969 / © Vadymvdrobot | Dreamstime.com

All other images © Dreamtime
(visit Spanish100.com for detailed copyright information)

ISBN: 978-1-949061-97-0

The publisher is not responsible for the websites (or their content) that are
not owned by the publisher.

Printed in the USA.

Penguin
Random House
Grupo Editorial

# INTRODUCTION

You can learn Spanish and it can be fast, easy and fun! With the *Spanish in 100 Days* proven method we will teach you how to understand, speak, read and write in Spanish in only 100 days. This is a practical, modern and mobile method that enables you to learn on-the-go and get results!

You are invited to join the almost 1 million people who have learned a language with the proven *100 Day Method*. Organized into concise and easy-to-understand sections you will learn the most common expressions used, easy grammar with step-by-step examples, and the most used vocabulary for both Spain and Latin America via fun dialogues.

You can learn anytime and anywhere! Enjoy unlimited free access to our www. Spanish100.com website to download updated content anytime so that you can keep on learning.

Make the most of your time and get results quickly and easily! With *Spanish in 100 Days* you will learn only the Spanish you need, and learn it fast. Whether you are on business or pleasure you will know the correct words, expressions and grammar for any situation.

Get started now, and you can quickly learn anytime and anywhere. With *Spanish in 100 Days* you will soon be speaking Spanish! Felicidades!

# SPANISH IN 100 DAYS

## TABLE OF CONTENTS

**UNIT 1** ............................................................................................................... **13**
. Use of question and exclamation marks ........................................................... 13
. Greetings: "hola" and "adiós" (hello and goodbye) ...................................... 14
. Identification of people and things: Subject pronouns (singular). ............... 15
. Formal and informal treatment: "Tú" and "Usted" (you)............................... 16
. The alphabet. Pronunciation............................................................................. 16

**UNIT 2** ............................................................................................................... **18**
. Thanking and responding expressions ............................................................. 19
. Identification of people and things: Subject pronouns (plural). .................. 20
. The verb "to be"................................................................................................... 21
. The verb "estar". Present simple ...................................................................... 22

**UNIT 3** ............................................................................................................... **23**
. Asking and answering about how people are ................................................. 24
. The use of "estar" in questions and negative sentences............................... 25
. Adverbs of place: Aquí, acá, allí, allá and ahí (here and there). ................. 26

**UNIT 4** ............................................................................................................... **27**
. Asking for and giving personal information. .................................................... 28
. Possessive adjectives (singular): mi, tu, su (my, your, his/her/its) ............. 29
. The present simple of the verb "ser"................................................................ 30

**UNIT 5** ............................................................................................................... **31**
. Asking where things are...................................................................................... 32
. Vocabulary: Household objects.......................................................................... 32
. The definite article: "el, la, los, las" (the)...................................................... 33
. The use of "¿dónde?" (where?) and the preposition "en" (in, on, at)........... 34
. Yes-No answers .................................................................................................... 35
. The conjunctions "y" (and) and "e" (and) ...................................................... 35

**UNIT 6** ............................................................................................................... **36**
. Introducing oneself and others ......................................................................... 37
. Expressions: apologizing .................................................................................... 38
. Vocabulary: the Family........................................................................................ 39

**UNIT 7** ............................................................................................................... **40**
. Asking where people or things are from............................................................ 41
. Vocabulary: countries and nationalities. .......................................................... 42
. Possessive adjectives (plural): nuestro/a, su (our, your, their)...................... 43
. Asking for repetition............................................................................................ 44
. Asking how something is said in another language ......................................... 44

**UNIT 8** .......................................................................................................**45**
. Nouns: gender and number..............................................................................46
. Vocabulary: Animals.........................................................................................47
. Written accents ...............................................................................................48
. Diphthongs ......................................................................................................48

**UNIT 9** .......................................................................................................**49**
. Spelling and expressions when spelling............................................................50
. Cardinal numbers (0-19) ..................................................................................51
. Telephone numbers..........................................................................................51

**UNIT 10** .....................................................................................................**52**
. Differences between the vebs "ser" and "estar"................................................53
. Expressions with "ser" and "estar"...................................................................55
. Adjectives used with "ser" and "estar" .............................................................56

**UNIT 11** .....................................................................................................**57**
. Asking questions...............................................................................................58
. Interrogative pronouns (Questioning words) .....................................................58
. Questions to ask and answer when filling out a form .......................................61

**UNIT 12** .....................................................................................................**62**
. Asking questions with prepositions. Prepositions + interrogative....? ...............63
. Vocabulary: Rooms and objects at home...........................................................64
. Verbs in Spanish ..............................................................................................65
. Regular and irregular verbs .............................................................................65

**UNIT 13** .....................................................................................................**66**
. The present simple: uses .................................................................................67
. The present tense of regular verbs (ending with "-ar").....................................68

**UNIT 14** .....................................................................................................**71**
. The present tense of regular verbs (ending with "-er" and "-ir") ......................72
. Vocabulary: Colors............................................................................................74

**UNIT 15** .....................................................................................................**75**
. Time markers of the present tense ...................................................................76
. The days of the week (I)....................................................................................77
. Vocabulary: Jobs and occupations....................................................................77
. Asking and answering about jobs and occupations ...........................................78
. Irregular verbs. Present simple of irregular verbs (I) ........................................78

**UNIT 16** .....................................................................................................**81**
. The present tense of "tener" ............................................................................82
. Expressions with the verb "tener"....................................................................83

# SPANISH IN 100 DAYS

. The indefinite article .................................................................................................................... 84
. Vocabulary: Clothes ...................................................................................................................... 85
. The verb "llevar puesto" ............................................................................................................. 85

**UNIT 17** .............................................................................................................................................. **86**
. The present simple of irregular verbs (II) ............................................................................... 87
. Spelling changes to maintain the pronunciation of some verbs ...................................... 91

**UNIT 18** .............................................................................................................................................. **92**
. The present simple of "poder" ................................................................................................... 93
. "Poder" versus "can" .................................................................................................................... 93
. The verbs "saber" and "conocer" ............................................................................................. 94
. También (also/too) and tampoco (neither/not...either) .................................................... 95
. Cardinal numbers (20-99) ......................................................................................................... 96

**UNIT 19** .............................................................................................................................................. **97**
. The verb "hacer" ............................................................................................................................ 98
. Expressions with "hacer" ........................................................................................................... 99
. Vocabulary: the weather ........................................................................................................... 100
. Differences among "bueno","malo", "bien" and "mal" ...................................................... 102

**UNIT 20** ............................................................................................................................................ **103**
. Reflexive verbs .............................................................................................................................. 104
. Adverbs of frequency. How often? ......................................................................................... 106
. The verb "soler" ............................................................................................................................ 107
. How to express habitual actions ............................................................................................. 108
. Vocabulary: Routines ................................................................................................................... 108

**UNIT 21** ............................................................................................................................................ **109**
. Demonstrative adjectives and pronouns .............................................................................. 110
. The indirect object ...................................................................................................................... 112
. Expressing likes or dislikes: the verb "gustar" ................................................................... 113

**UNIT 22** ............................................................................................................................................ **115**
. Describing people. Adjectives: position and agreement with the noun ...................... 116
. "Ser" and "estar" + adjective .................................................................................................... 118
. "Parecer" + adjective .................................................................................................................. 118
. Vocabulary: Adjectives (physical appearance) .................................................................... 119

**UNIT 23** ............................................................................................................................................ **120**
. The time: Asking and telling the time .................................................................................... 121
. ¿Qué hora es? versus ¿A qué hora es? ................................................................................. 123
. The verb "venir" ........................................................................................................................... 123
. Vocabulary: Banking ................................................................................................................... 124

**UNIT 24** ............................................................... **125**
. The present participle (gerund)....................................... 126
. Uses of the gerund..................................................... 127
. The present progressive. Form and uses............................. 128
. "Todavía", "aún" and "ya" ("still", "yet" and "already") ............ 129

**UNIT 25** ............................................................... **130**
. The impersonal form "hay" ........................................... 131
. Indefinite pronouns.................................................... 131
. Prepositions and adverbs of place.................................... 133
. Vocabulary: Personal items ........................................... 134

**UNIT 26** ............................................................... **135**
. Describing people physically.......................................... 136
. Vocabulary: The face .................................................. 137
. Describing someone's personality .................................... 138
. Adjectives for descriptions ........................................... 138
. Cardinal numbers (100- 999)........................................... 139

**UNIT 27** ............................................................... **140**
. Direct objects pronouns............................................... 141
. The use of no quantifiers for uncountable and plural nouns......... 143
. Vocabulary: The shopping list........................................ 143

**UNIT 28** ............................................................... **146**
. Adverbs of quantity ................................................... 147
. ¿Cuánto? and ¿Cuántos?............................................... 148
. Asking for prices, quantities, weights and measures................ 149
. "Muy" and "mucho".................................................... 149
. Expressions of quantity................................................ 150

**UNIT 29** ............................................................... **153**
. Asking for and borrowing things ..................................... 154
. Asking for a favor..................................................... 155
. Expressions to confirm and excuse .................................. 156
. Cardinal numbers (1000-millions)..................................... 157

**UNIT 30** ............................................................... **158**
. Expressions on the telephone ........................................ 159
. Leaving and taking messages on the phone.......................... 160
. Vocabulary: The telephone ........................................... 161
. The past simple in Spanish........................................... 161
. The preterite. The preterite of regular verbs ....................... 162
. Time markers in the past.............................................. 163

# SPANISH IN 100 DAYS

**UNIT 31** ........................................................................................................ **164**
. The preterite of irregular verbs ...................................................................................... 165
. "Desde", "hasta" and "durante" ...................................................................................... 168
. Question tags in Spanish (¿no?, ¿verdad?) ...................................................................... 169

**UNIT 32** ........................................................................................................ **170**
. Expressing actions that started and finished in the past:
  verbs "ser" and "estar" ................................................................................................ 171
. The verb "dar" .............................................................................................................. 172
. The verb "tener" .......................................................................................................... 173
. Use of "¿Cuándo fue la primera/última vez que...?" .................................................... 173
. Vocabulary: Crimes...................................................................................................... 174

**UNIT 33** ........................................................................................................ **175**
. The past imperfect: forms and uses .............................................................................. 176
. Elements to join sentences: "mientras" (while) and "cuando" (when) ......................... 179
. Vocabulary: Objects on the street................................................................................. 180

**UNIT 34** ........................................................................................................ **181**
. Expressing durative actions in the past ......................................................................... 182
. Different meanings of the same words in different
  Spanish-speaking countries ......................................................................................... 185

**UNIT 35** ........................................................................................................ **187**
. Expressing past actions: the preterite versus the imperfect ......................................... 189
. Expressions when asking someone out on a date and impressing
  the other person........................................................................................................... 191

**UNIT 36** ........................................................................................................ **192**
. To say the date ............................................................................................................. 193
. Vocabulary: the days of the week (II) ............................................................................ 194
. The conjunctions "pero" and "sino" (but) .................................................................... 196

**UNIT 37** ........................................................................................................ **197**
. To ask for details about people, things and places ........................................................ 198
. Diacritical signs............................................................................................................ 201
. Vocabulary: Months and seasons ................................................................................. 202

**UNIT 38** ........................................................................................................ **203**
. The preposition "de" .................................................................................................... 204
. Describing objects: materials and utilities..................................................................... 206
. "Ser" de + material....................................................................................................... 206
. "Servir" para + infinitive .............................................................................................. 206
. Vocabulary: Materials and shapes ................................................................................ 207

# SPANISH IN 100 DAYS

**UNIT 39** ...........................................................................................**209**
. Expressing opinions ...................................................................210
. Verbs that introduce opinions: creer, pensar.........................210
. Adverbs of time: después (de), antes (de)..............................211
. Vocabulary: Natural disasters ..................................................213

**UNIT 40** ...........................................................................................**214**
. Uses of the preposition "en" .....................................................215
. The past participle .....................................................................217
. Participles as adjectives ...........................................................217
. Vocabulary: Food and drinks .....................................................218

**UNIT 41** ...........................................................................................**219**
. The present simple of the verb "haber"....................................220
. The present perfect....................................................................220
. Vocabulary: Leisure activities....................................................224

**UNIT 42** ...........................................................................................**225**
. To express unfinished actions ...................................................226
. Use of "desde", "desde que", "desde hace" and "durante" ......227
. Verbs commonly followed by "de" .............................................228
. The verb "acabar (de)" ...............................................................229
. Vocabulary: Sitting at the table.................................................230

**UNIT 43** ...........................................................................................**231**
. Expressing past and recent actions..........................................232
. The present perfect + "alguna vez"/ adverbs of frequency.........232
. The present perfect + "ya", "todavía" and "aún" .......................233
. Vocabulary: Celebrations............................................................235

**UNIT 44** ...........................................................................................**236**
. The present perfect continuous .................................................237
. Form and uses.............................................................................237
. Use of pronouns and reflexive verbs in the present perfect continuous .....................239
. Vocabulary: Dwellings.................................................................240

**UNIT 45** ...........................................................................................**241**
. Time expressions with the present perfect continuous ............242
. The verb "llevar".........................................................................243
. "Hace + period of time + que" ...................................................244
. Vocabulary: The garden .............................................................245

**UNIT 46** ...........................................................................................**246**
. Present perfect or preterite?......................................................247

. "Ha habido" and "hubo" ........................................................................................248
. Expressions showing disgust and repugnance ..........................................................249

**UNIT 47** ...............................................................................................................**250**
. Expressing obligation and prohibition .....................................................................251
. Use of "deber", "tener que", "estar obligado a", "hay que", "no se puede" ................252
. Vocabulary: Health and illnesses ...........................................................................253

**UNIT 48** ...............................................................................................................**255**
. Joining sentences: Relative pronouns ......................................................................256
. The relative pronouns "que" ..................................................................................256
. The relative pronouns "quien" ...............................................................................258
. Vocabulary: Horoscopes and superstitions ..............................................................259

**UNIT 49** ...............................................................................................................**261**
. Relative pronouns when adding information ............................................................262
. The relative pronouns "el que, la que, los que, las que" and "lo que" .......................263
. The relative "donde" ............................................................................................264
. The relative adjectives "cuyo, cuya, cuyos, cuyas" ..................................................264
. Vocabulary: Recreation and hobbies .......................................................................265

**UNIT 50** ...............................................................................................................**266**
. Comparing things..................................................................................................267
. The comparative of equality ..................................................................................267
. Vocabulary: Means of transport .............................................................................270

**VERBS AT A GLANCE** .........................................................................................**271**

**In this unit we will learn:**

. To say **hola** and **adiós** *(hello and goodbye)*.
. Use of question and exclamation marks.
. Identification of people and things: Subject pronouns (singular).
. Formal and informal treatment: "Tú" and "Usted" (you).
. The alphabet. Pronunciation.

## Diálogo / *Dialog*

---

**Remember!**

In Spanish, exclamation and question marks are used both at the beginning and end of the sentence. They are inverted when used at the beginning (¡...!, ¿...?). **¡Hola!** **¿Qué tal?**

---

María ve a Juan en el parque, mientras él estaba mirando unas fotos que tenía en sus manos.

*María sees John at the park, while he was looking at some photos he had in his hands.*

| | |
|---|---|
| M: | ¡Buenos días! |
| J: | ¡Buenos días, María! |
| M: | ¿Qué tal? |
| J: | Bien, gracias, ¿y tú? ¿Cómo estás? |
| M: | Muy bien, gracias. ¿Qué haces? |
| J: | [Señalando una foto] Estoy mirando unas fotos. Tú no conoces a mi familia. Mira. Él es Rafael, mi hijo. |
| M: | ¿Y ella? |
| J: | Ella es Oriana, mi esposa. [Mientras le muestra el anillo] |
| M: | Yo estoy soltera. [Muestra la mano sin anillo] Mira, yo tengo otra foto. Está por aquí. [Busca en el bolso]. ¡Aquí está! Él es Miguel, mi hermano, y ella es Gladys, mi madre. |
| J: | Es una foto bonita. |
| M: | Sí. |
| J: | Bueno, María, es tarde y he de irme. |
| M: | Sí, yo también tengo prisa. |
| J: | Pues, ¡hasta pronto, María! |
| M: | ¡Adiós, Juan! ¡Cuídate! |

| | |
|---|---|
| M: | Good morning! |
| J: | Good morning, María! |
| M: | How are you? |
| J: | I'm fine, thank you, and you? How are you? |
| M: | Very well, thank you. What are you doing? |
| J: | [Pointing at a picture] I'm looking at some pictures. You don't know my family. Look. He is Rafael, my son. |
| M: | And she? |
| J: | She is Oriana, my wife. [He shows his ring] |
| M: | I am single. [She shows her fingers with no rings] Look, I have another picture. It's over here. [She is looking for it in her purse]. Here it is! He is Miguel, my brother, and she is Gladys, my mother. |
| J: | It is a nice picture. |
| M: | Yes. |
| J: | Well, María, it is late and I have to leave. |
| M: | Yes, I am also in a hurry. |
| J: | Okay, see you soon, María! |
| M: | Goodbye, Juan! Take care! |

## TOP VOCABULARY AND EXPRESSIONS

### Saying "hola" *(hello)* and "adiós" *(goodbye)*

**a)** When you want to say hello to someone, you can use:

| | |
|---|---|
| **Hola** | *Hello / Hi* |
| **Buenas** | *Hello / Hi* |
| **¿Qué tal?** | *How are you? / How do you do?* |
| | *How are things?* |
| **¿Cómo estás?** | *How are you?* |

Depending on the part of the day when we use the greeting expression, we can also say:

| | |
|---|---|
| **Buenos días** | *Good morning* |
| **Buenas tardes** | *Good afternoon / Good evening* |
| **Buenas noches** | *Good evening* |

**b)** When you want to say goodbye:

| | |
|---|---|
| **Adiós** | *Goodbye* |
| **Hasta pronto** | *See you soon* |
| **Hasta luego** | *See you later* |
| **Hasta mañana** | *See you tomorrow* |
| **Buenas noches** | *Good night* |
| **¡Cuídate!** | *Take care!* |

## IDENTIFYING PEOPLE AND THINGS: Subject Pronouns (Singular)

Subjects pronouns are used to replace names and nouns when you refer to a person, a thing or a place as the subject of a sentence, that is, as the doer of the action.
In this unit you will learn the singular forms.

| | |
|---|---|
| **yo** | I |
| **tú** | you |
| **él** | he |
| **ella** | she |
| **-** | it |
| **usted** | you (formal) |

Roberto es alto. **Él** es alto.

¿Cómo está Susana? **Ella** está bien, gracias.

*Roberto is tall.* ***He*** *is tall.*

*How is Susana?* ***She*** *is fine, thanks.*

The neuter pronoun **"it"** has no equivalent in Spanish. When you refer to animals, things or places don't use any pronoun, but the verb alone conjugated as for "él" or "ella".

| | |
|---|---|
| **El libro** es azul | ***The book*** *is blue* |
| **Es** azul | ***It*** *is blue* |

– ¿Dónde está Cancún

– **Está** en México

– *Where is Cancun?*

– ***It*** *is in Mexico.*

## FORMAL AND INFORMAL TREATMENT IN SPANISH: Tú and Usted *(you)*

In Spanish there are two main ways to say *"you"* in singular: **"tú"** and **"usted"**.

**"Tú"** is the informal form and is normally used when we talk to someone of the same age, same status, when speaking with a child, or when we want to express a certain level of intimacy with someone.
In some countries, like Argentina or Uruguay, "vos" is used instead of "tú".

**Tú** eres mi amigo.
*You are my friend.*

**"Usted"** is used to show respect, as well as to put a little bit of distance between you and the person you are addressing as **"usted"** (abbreviated as **Ud.**). We use it when addressing someone much older, or someone in position of authority or higher rank. In many cases it is also used when you are speaking to someone for the first time.
After using the formal treatment "usted", we can be asked to use "tú". That is what in Spanish is called "tu-tearse" (to address each other as "tú").

**Usted** es el director.
*You are the director.*

## EL ABECEDARIO (*THE ALPHABET*)

Now let's have a look at the alphabet and learn the sounds of the Spanish letters.

| A | B | C | D | E | F | G | H | I | J |
|---|---|---|---|---|---|---|---|---|---|
| a | be | se | de | e | efe | he | ache | ee | hota |

| K | L | M | N | Ñ | O | P | Q | R | S |
|---|---|---|---|---|---|---|---|---|---|
| ka | ele | eme | ene | enye | o | pe | ku | ere | ese |

| T | U | V | W | X | Y | Z |
|---|---|---|---|---|---|---|
| te | oo | ube | ube doble | ekis | i griega | seta |

Double letters:

| ch | ll | rr |
|---|---|---|
| (che) | (elle) | (erre) |

## PRONUNCIATION

In Spanish there are some sounds that may be different from English. They are detailed here for your review.

| | |
|---|---|
| **"b" and "v"** | are pronounced the same (as a "b"), so "baca" (roof rack) and "vaca" (cow) sound the same. |
| **"c"** | is pronounced as an "s" before "e" and "i" (in Latin American countries and some areas in Spain) but as a "k" before "a", "o" and "u". Ex: cocina /koséena/ (kitchen). |
| **"g"** | sounds like a heavily aspirated "h" before "e" and "i". Ex: ágil /áheel/ (agile); but, to make it sound the same as in "get"or "give", we need a "u" between the "g" and the"e" or "i", that doesn't sound. Ex: guerra (war), guitarra (guitar). When marked by a diaeresis (¨), this "u" is pronounced. Ex: antigüedad (antiquity), cigüeña (stork). |
| **"h"** | is a silent letter. It never sounds. |
| **"j"** | sounds like a heavily aspirated "h". Ex: José /hosé/, jirafa /heeráfa/ (giraffe). |
| **"ñ"** | is a typical Spanish letter that sounds like "in" in "onion" or "ny" in "canyon". |
| **"q"** | always precedes "ue" or "ui", sounding /ke/ or /ki/. Ex: queso /késo/ (cheese), aquí /aki/ (here). |
| **"r"** | is pronounced stronger than in English. It's similar to the American pronunciation of "tt" in "better". Ex: cara /kára/ (face). But after "l", "n", "s" or at the start of a word, it sounds stronger (the same as "rr" – see below). |
| **"w"** | usually sounds like a "u". |
| **"y"** | is pronounced as the "y" in "yes". |
| **"z"** | is pronounced as an "s" (in Latin American countries and some areas in Spain. In other parts it sounds like the "th" in "thin"). Ex: cereza / serésa/ (cherry). |
| | **Double letters:** |
| **"ch"** | sounds like "ch" in "church". |
| **"ll"** | sounds like the "y" in "you". |
| **"rr"** | is a strong trill of the tip of the tongue against the front part of the palate. |

## Unit

# 2

**Days 3 & 4**

**In this unit we will learn:**
. Thanking and responding expressions.
. Identification of people and things: Subject pronouns (plural).
. The verb "to be".
. The verb "estar". Present simple.

### Diálogo / Dialog

Luisa se encuentra en la calle a don Manuel, un señor mayor que es vecino suyo.

*Luisa runs into don Manuel, an elderly gentleman who is a neighbor of hers, in the street.*

| | |
|---|---|
| L: | ¡Hola, don Manuel! |
| M: | ¡Hola, Luisa! |
| L: | ¿Cómo **está** usted? |
| M: | **Bien, gracias.** ¿Y tú? |
| L: | **Bien**, también. **Muchas gracias.** ¿**Está** usted solo? ¿Dónde **están** sus amigos? **Ustedes están** siempre juntos. |
| M: | Sí, siempre **estamos** juntos por las tardes, pero **ellos están** ahora en el trabajo. Tú también **estás** sola. |
| L: | Sí, ahora **estoy** sola, pero voy a ver a Teresa, una amiga mía. Vamos a ir a pasear por el parque. |
| M: | ¿**Están ustedes** de vacaciones? |
| L: | Sí, **nosotras estamos** de vacaciones. ¿Le gustaría venir a pasear con nosotras? |
| M: | Es una buena idea. **Muchas gracias.** Así conoceré a Teresa. |
| L: | **De nada.** Entonces, acompáñeme. |
| M: | Muy bien. **Muchas gracias, de nuevo.** |
| L: | **No hay de qué**, don Manuel. |

| | |
|---|---|
| L: | Hello, don Manuel! |
| M: | Hello, Luisa! |
| L: | How are you? |
| M: | Fine, thank you. And you? |
| L: | Fine, too. Thank you very much. Are you alone? Where are your friends? You are always together. |
| M: | Yes, we are always together in the afternoons, but they are at work now. You are also alone. |
| L: | Yes, I am alone now, but I am meeting Teresa, a friend of mine. We are going to walk through the park. |
| M: | Are you on vacation? |
| L: | Yes, we are on vacation. Would you like to come and walk with us? |
| M: | That's a good idea. Thank you very much. This way I can meet Teresa. |
| L: | You are welcome. Then, come with me. |
| M: | Okay, thank you very much, indeed. |
| L: | Don't mention it, don Manuel. |

## TOP VOCABULARY AND EXPRESSIONS

### Agradecimientos *(Thanking and responding)*

**a)** When you want to give thanks (for something), use any of these expressions:

| | |
|---|---|
| **Gracias** | *Thank you* |
| **Muchas gracias** | *Thank you very much / Thanks a lot* |
| **Muchísimas gracias** | *Thank you very much indeed* |
| **Muchas gracias por (tu invitación)** | *Thank you very much for (your invitation)* |

**b)** To respond, say:

| | |
|---|---|
| **De nada** | *You're welcome* |
| **No hay de qué** | *Don't mention it / Not at all* |

## IDENTIFYING PEOPLE AND THINGS: Subject Pronouns (plural)

In Unit 1 we studied subject pronouns in singular and now we will see the plural forms:

| | |
|---|---|
| **nosotros, nosotras** | *we* |
| **ustedes\*** | *you* |
| **ellos, ellas** | *they* |

**\*Ustedes** is used for both formal and informal treatment. In Spain, for informal treatment, it is better to use **vosotros/vosotras**.

| | |
|---|---|
| <u>Tú y yo</u> somos mejicanos. | *<u>You and I</u> are Mexican.* |
| **Nosotros** somos mejicanos. | ***We*** *are Mexican.* |

| | |
|---|---|
| <u>Tú y Juan</u> son hermanos. | *<u>You and Juan</u> are brothers.* |
| **Ustedes** son hermanos. | ***You*** *are brothers.* |

| | |
|---|---|
| <u>Lorenzo y Pedro</u> son estudiantes. | *<u>Lorenzo and Pedro</u> are students.* |
| **Ellos** son estudiantes. | ***They*** *are students.* |

In Spanish, the 1st and 3rd person in plural have both masculine and feminine forms:

| | |
|---|---|
| **nosotros, ellos** (masc.) | **nosotras, ellas** (fem.) |

The masculine forms **nosotros** and **ellos** are used when the people or things that we refer to are <u>all masculine or if the group is mixed</u>.

| | |
|---|---|
| **Nosotros** somos Francisco y Ricardo. | *We are Francisco and Ricardo.* |
| **Ellos** son Lidia y Rafael. | *They are Lidia and Rafael.* |

We will only use **nosotras** and **ellas** when the people or things that we are referring to are <u>all feminine</u>.

| | |
|---|---|
| **Nosotras** somos hermanas. | *We are sisters.* |
| **Ellas** son Susana y Mercedes. | *They are Susana and Mercedes.* |

## THE VERB "TO BE"

The verb *to be* means **estar** (non-permanent state) and **ser** (permanent state).

| | |
|---|---|
| Él **está** en casa | Él **es** colombiano |
| ↓ | ↓ |
| *He **is** at home* | *He **is** Colombian* |

## PRESENT SIMPLE OF THE VERB "ESTAR"

In this unit we will work on the verb **estar**, that is, when we refer to locations or states that are temporary, not permanent. In present, it is used as follows:

| | | | | | |
|---|---|---|---|---|---|
| yo | **estoy** | *I am* | nosotros/nosotras **estamos** | | *we are* |
| tú | **estás** | *you are* | ustedes | **están*** | *you are* |
| usted | **está*** | *you are* | | | |
| él | **está** | *he is* | ellos/ellas | **están** | *they are* |
| ella | **está** | *she is* | | | |
| (-) | **está** | *it is* | | | |

| | | |
|---|---|---|
| **Ella está** en casa | ➤ | ***She is*** *at home* |
| **Yo estoy** en Bogotá | ➤ | ***I am*** *in Bogota* |
| ¿Cómo **estás (tú)?** | ➤ | *How **are you**?* |

| | | |
|---|---|---|
| **Nosotras estamos** bien | ➤ | ***We are*** *fine* |
| **Ustedes están** en los EEUU | ➤ | ***You are*** *in the USA* |
| **Ellos están** en la escuela | ➤ | ***They*** *are at school* |

(*) It is important to notice that, although **usted (Ud.)** and **ustedes (Uds.)** are equivalent to **you**, the verb they go with conjugates as for **he** and **they**, respectively.

¿Cómo <u>está</u> **usted**?         *How <u>are</u> **you**?*

¿<u>Están</u> **ustedes** bien?         *<u>Are</u> **you** ok?*

## In this unit we will learn:
. To ask and answer about how people are.
. The use of "estar" in questions and negative sentences.
. Adverbs of place: Aquí, acá, allí, allá and ahí (here and there).

# Unit

# 3

**Days 5 & 6**

## Diálogo / Dialog

Ricardo y Graciela se encuentran en la calle.

*Ricardo and Graciela meet each other on the street.*

R: ¡Buenas!
G: ¡Buenas! ¿**Cómo estás**, Ricardo?
R: **No estoy muy bien. Estoy** cansado. ¿Y tú? ¿**Cómo estás?**
G: Yo **estoy bien**, pero **estoy** preocupada por Teco, mi perro. Él **está mal. Está** enfermo.
R: ¿**Está** enfermo? ¿Dónde **está?**
G: **Está** en la clínica veterinaria.
R: Hay una clínica veterinaria **por allí** [señalando con el dedo]. ¿**Está allá?**
G: Sí, **allí está**. Por cierto, tú **estás** siempre **por aquí.**
R: Sí, vivo cerca de **aquí** y mis amigos **están por aquí** también.
G: ¿Y Juan? ¿**Cómo está?**
R: ¿Juan? ¿Qué Juan? ¡Ah! Juan Álvarez. **Está bien.** Ahora está en México.
G: Es un hombre muy simpático.
R: Y **está** soltero....
G: ¡Ricardo! ¿En qué **estás** pensando?
R: [Risas] Tú también **estás** soltera....
G: ¿**Estás** loco? Bueno, es hora de recoger a Teco. ¡Hasta pronto, Ricardo!
R: [Risas] ¡Hasta pronto, Graciela!

R: Hello!
G: Hello! How are you, Ricardo?
R: I am not very well. I am tired. And you? How are you?
G: I am fine, but I am worried about Teco, my dog. He is doing badly. He is ill.
R: Is he ill? Where is he?
G: He is at the veterinary clinic.
R: There is a veterinary clinic over there [pointing with his finger]. Is he there?
G: Yes, there he is. By the way, you are always over here.
R: Yes, I live near here and my friends are also over here.
G: And Juan? How is he?
R: Juan? What Juan? Ah! Juan Álvarez. He is fine. He is now in Mexico.
G: He is a very friendly man.
R: And he is single....
G: Ricardo! What are you thinking?
R: [Laughs] You are also single....
G: Are you crazy? Well, it's time to pick Teco up. See you soon, Ricardo!
R: [Laughs] See you soon, Graciela!

Don't forget that verbs have a different ending for each person (both in singular and plural). That is why subject pronouns are not always used, as they are obvious.

| | |
|---|---|
| ¿Cómo **estás** (tú)? | How are you? |
| (Yo) **Estoy** enojado | I am angry |
| (Nosotros) **Estamos** aquí | We are here |

## Remember!

The neuter pronoun **"it"** has no equivalent in Spanish. When you refer to it, use the verb alone, conjugated as you would for **él** (he) or **ella** (she).

| | |
|---|---|
| **Está** aquí ⟶ | **It is** here |
| **Está** bien ⟶ | **It is** ok |

## TOP VOCABULARY AND EXPRESSIONS

### To ask and answer about how people are

**a)** To ask about how people are, use the interrogative pronoun "**¿Cómo?**" *(How?)*:

| | |
|---|---|
| **¿Cómo estás?** | How are you? |
| **¿Cómo está ella?** | How is she? |

**b)** To answer, you can use these expressions:

| | |
|---|---|
| **(yo) Estoy muy bien** | I am very well |
| **(yo) Estoy bien** | I am well (fine, ok) |
| **(yo) No estoy muy bien** | I am not very well |

And also:

| | |
|---|---|
| **(yo) Estoy regular*** | I am ok |
| **(yo) Estoy así así** | I am so-so |
| **(yo) Estoy mal** | I am in a bad way |
| **(yo) Estoy fatal** | I feel terrible |

(*) The expression **"Estoy regular"** is equivalent to **"I am well"** in many Spanish-speaking countries, but in Spain it means that something is wrong with me.

## Things to take into account when structuring sentences:

**a)** In many cases the subject does not appear in the sentence:

| | |
|---|---|
| ¿Cómo estás **(tú)**? | How are you? |
| **(Yo)** Estoy bien | I am fine |

**b)** When you want to form negative sentences, simply add "no" before the verb:

| | |
|---|---|
| **No** estoy muy bien | I am not very well |
| Ustedes **no** están en la escuela | You are not at school |

**c)** When you ask questions, the position of the subject and verb may change, but not necessarily:

| | | |
|---|---|---|
| | Ella **está** bien | She is fine |
| | ¿**Está** ella bien? | Is she fine? |
| But also: | ¿Ella **está** bien?* | Is she fine? |

(*)You can ask a question simply by altering the tone of your voice. Unlike in English, you don't need to change the order of the words.

## SAYING WHERE PEOPLE AND THINGS ARE
### Adverbs of place: aquí, acá, allí, allá and ahí *(here and there)*

**a) Aquí** and **acá** *(here)* are used to indicate a place near the speaker:

Él está **aquí**

Él está **acá**

*He is **here***

**b) Allí**, **allá** and **ahí** *(there)* are used to indicate a place away from the speaker:

María y Lidia están **allí**

María y Lidia están **allá**

María y Lidia están **ahí**

*María and Lidia are **there***

**c)** These adverbs can also be used in other expressions:

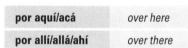

| por aquí/acá | *over here* |
|---|---|
| por allí/allá/ahí | *over there* |

El libro está **por aquí**    *The book is **over here***

Ellos están **por allá**    *They are **over there***

## In this unit we will learn:
. To ask for and give personal information.
. Present simple of the verb "ser".
. Possessive adjectives (singular): mi, tu, su *(my, your, his/her/its)*.

### Unit
# 4
**Days 7 & 8**

### Diálogo / *Dialog*

Marina quiere tener la tarjeta de acceso a la biblioteca y habla con el encargado.

*Marina wants to get a library card and she is speaking to the librarian on duty.*

M: ¡Buenos días!
E: ¡Buenos días!
M: Quiero sacar la tarjeta de la biblioteca.
E: Muy bien. **¿Cuál es su nombre?**
M: **Me llamo** Marina.
E: **¿Y cuáles son sus apellidos\*?**
M: **Mis apellidos son** García Rueca.
E: **¿Cuál es su dirección?**
M: Avenida Bolívar, número 3.
E: ¿Ciudad?
M: Guadalajara.
E: Ya está. Eso **es** todo. Aquí está **su** tarjeta.
M: Muy bien. Muchas gracias.
E: Ahora puede ir a cualquier biblioteca pública sin problemas.

M: *Good morning!*
E: *Good morning!*
M: *I want to get a library card.*
E: *Okay, what is your name?*
M: *My name is Marina.*
E: *And what is your last name?*
M: *My last name is García Rueca.*
E: *What is your address?*
M: *3 Avenida Bolívar.*
E: *City?*
M: *Guadalajara.*
E: *Okay, that's all. Here is your card.*
M: *Very well. Thank you very much.*
E: *Now you can go to any public library without any problem.*

(*) In Spanish-speaking countries people usually have two last names or surnames. They take the first last name of their father and their mother in that order. Take a look at the example below.

Roberto **Sánchez** García *(father)*     Margarita **Fernández** Ruiz *(mother)*

Luis **Sánchez Fernández** *(son)*

## TOP VOCABULARY AND EXPRESSIONS

### Pedir y dar información personal
*(Asking for and giving personal information)*

**a)** When you ask for someone's name or address, you can say:

**¿Cuál es tu nombre?**
**dirección?**

*What's your* name?
address?

And also:   **¿Cómo te llamas?**   *What's your name?*
**¿Cuáles son tus apellidos?**   *What are your last names?*

If you are talking to someone formally, it is better to say:

**¿Cuál es su nombre/dirección?**   *What's your name/address?*

**b)** To answer, say:

**Mi nombre**
**Mi dirección** **es...**

*My name*
*My address* *is...*

And also:   **Me llamo...**   *My name is...*

## ADJETIVOS POSESIVOS (POSSESSIVE ADJECTIVES)

To indicate that something belongs to somebody we use possessive adjectives. The singular forms are:

| | |
|---|---|
| **mi** | *my* |
| **tu** | *your* |
| **su (de usted)** | *your* |
| **su (de él)** | *his* |
| **su (de ella)** | *her* |
| **su (de ello)\*** | *its* |

(\*) **Su** is the possessive adjective for animals, things or places.

These possessive adjectives are always followed by a noun.

| | |
|---|---|
| **Mi** nombre es Rafael. | **My** name is Rafael |
| **Su** dirección es .... | **His/her/your** address is.... |
| **Sus** calles (de Nueva York) son largas. | **Its** streets (of New York) are long |

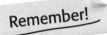

**Remember!**

Do not mistake the possessive **tu** *(your)* for the personal pronoun **tú** *(you)*. The accent mark is used on the personal pronoun to stress this difference.

| | |
|---|---|
| **Tu** nombre es Miguel. | **Your** name is Miguel. |
| **Tú** eres Miguel. | **You** are Miguel. |

If a plural noun follows the possessive, you need a plural possessive: **mis, tus, sus**.

| | |
|---|---|
| **Mis** padres son Roberto y Marta. | *My parents are Roberto and Marta.* |
| **Tus** apellidos son López Pimentel. | *Your last names are López Pimentel* |
| **Sus** hijos son altos. | *His/her/your children are tall.* |

## THE VERB "SER"

In this unit we will also learn to use the verb "**ser**". As mentioned, it is equivalent to the verb "**to be**", when you refer to permanent states.

### PRESENT SIMPLE OF THE VERB "SER"

| | | | |
|---|---|---|---|
| yo **soy** | *I am* | nosotros/as **somos** | *we are* |
| tú **eres** | *you are* | ustedes **son** | *you are* |
| usted **es** | *you are* | | |
| él **es** | *he is* | | |
| ella **es** | *she is* | ellos/as **son** | *they are* |
| (-) **es** | *it is* | | |

The verb **ser** can be used to give names, nationalities, jobs, personal features, etc.

| | |
|---|---|
| Yo **soy** estudiante. | *I **am** a student.* |
| Tú **eres** italiano. | *You **are** Italian.* |
| Ellos **son** Francisco y Rafael. | *They **are** Francisco and Rafael.* |
| Mi nombre **es** Gregorio. | *My name **is** Gregorio.* |
| Ella no **es** tu esposa. | *She **is** not your wife.* |
| Tu apellido no **es** Sánchez. | *Your last name **is**n't Sánchez.* |
| ¿Cuál **es** tu dirección? | *What **is** your address?* |
| Nosotros **somos** españoles. | *We **are** Spanish.* |

# SPANISH IN 100 DAYS

## In this unit we will learn:
. To ask where things are.
. The use of "¿dónde?" (where?) and the preposition "en" (in, on, at).
. The definite article: el, la, los, las (the).
. Vocabulary: Household objects.
. Yes-No answers.
. The conjunctions "y" (and) and "e" (and).

## Unit
# 5
**Days 9 & 10**

### Diálogo / Dialog

Francisco y Lina están en casa.

*Francisco and Lina are at home.*

| | |
|---|---|
| F: Lina, ¿**dónde** están **las** fotos? | F: Lina, where are the pictures? |
| L: **En la mesa.** | L: On the table. |
| F: **No**, no están **en la mesa.** | F: No, they aren't on the table. |
| L: Entonces, **en el cajón.** | L: In the drawer, then. |
| F: ¿**En** qué **cajón?** | F: Which drawer? |
| L: **En el cajón del armario.** | L: In the drawer of the closet. |
| F: ¡Ah! **Sí,** aquí están. Mira, Carlos **e** Isabel están muy bien **en** esta foto. | F: Ah! Yes, here they are. Look, Carlos and Isabel look good in this picture. |
| L: **No.** Esa foto es horrible. | L: No. This picture is horrible. |
| F: Bueno, no está mal, pero están mejor en **el cuadro.** | F: Well, it isn't bad, but they look better in the framed picture. |
| L: ¿Y **el cuadro?** ¿**Dónde** está **el cuadro?** | L: And the framed picture? Where is the picture? |
| F: Lina, **el** cuadro está en **la pared.** Lo colgué antes. | F: Lina, the picture is on the wall. I hung it before. |
| L: Perdona. No sé dónde están **las** cosas. Por cierto, ¿**dónde** está **el** perro? | L: Sorry. I don't know where things are. By the way, where is the dog? |
| F: Está **en la alfombra.** Es su lugar favorito. | F: He is on the carpet. It is his favorite place. |
| L: Pues ahora **el perro** y tú debéis salir a pasear. | L: Well, the dog and you have to go for a walk now. |
| F: Muy bien pero....¿**dónde** está su **correa?** | F: Alright but.... where is his leash? |
| L: [Resignada] **La** correa está **encima** de **la silla** Mira, allí. | L: [Resigned] His leash is on the chair. Look, there. |
| F: Bueno, pues ¡hasta luego! | F: Well, see you later! |
| L: ¡Hasta luego! | L: See you later! |

## TOP VOCABULARY AND EXPRESSIONS

### Preguntar y decir dónde están las cosas
*(Asking and saying where things are)*

**a)** When you want to ask where things are, use this question:

| | |
|---|---|
| **¿Dónde está** + nombre singular? | ***Where is*** + *singular noun?* |
| **¿Dónde están** + nombre plural? | ***Where are*** + *plural noun?* |
| **¿Dónde está** el diccionario? | ***Where is*** *the dictionary?* |
| **¿Dónde están** las sillas? | ***Where are*** *the chairs?* |

**b)** To say where things are, we can use the preposition **en** *(in, on, at)*.
*In, on* and *at* are equivalent to **en**. But *in* can also be translated as **dentro** and *on* as **sobre**.

| | |
|---|---|
| Las fotos están **en** la gaveta. | *The photos are **in** the drawer.* |
| Los cuadros están **en** la pared. | *The pictures are **on** the wall.* |
| La lámpara está **en** el rincón. | *The lamp is **at** the corner.* |

### VOCABULARIO:

**Muebles y objetos de casa** *(household objects).*

| | |
|---|---|
| **mesa:** *table* **alfombra:** *carpet* | |
| **piso:** *floor* | **silla:** *chair* |
| **cuadro:** *picture* | **bañera:** *bathtub* |
| **sillón:** *armchair* | **armario:** *closet* |
| **refrigerador:** *refrigerator* | **sofá:** *sofa, couch* |
| **lámpara:** *lamp* | **foto:** *photo / picture* |
| **librero:** *bookcase* | **gaveta / cajón:** *drawer* |
| **espejo:** *mirror* | **estante:** *shelf* |
| **pared:** *wall* | **cortina:** *curtain* |

Nouns are almost always preceded by articles. In this unit we will study the definite articles: **el, la, los, las** *(the).*

## LOS ARTÍCULOS DETERMINADOS: EL, LA, LOS, LAS
### [THE DEFINITE ARTICLES "EL", "LA", "LOS", "LAS" (THE)]

The definite article is used when we mention something specific, already quoted, or understood. In Spanish it has two forms in singular and another two in plural. In English it is always "**the**".

|            | Singular | Plural |
|------------|----------|--------|
| Masculine  | **el**   | **los** |
| Feminine   | **la**   | **las** |

All Spanish nouns have a gender: they are either masculine or feminine. The articles must agree with the noun they come before in gender and number.

**el** armari**o** *(**the** closet)*       **los** armari**os** *(**the** closets)*
**la** mes**a** *(**the** table)*       **las** mes**as** *(**the** tables)*

When a feminine noun begins with a stressed "a" or "ha", the article changes into masculine in singular.

**el** ave *(the bird)*       **las** aves *(the birds)*
**el** hacha *(the ax)*       **las** hachas *(the axes)*

**Remember!**

Do not mistake the subject pronoun **él** (he) for the article **el** (the). The accent mark on the personal pronoun is used to denote this difference.

**El** niño está en la escuela.       ***The** boy is at school.*
**Él** está en la escuela.       ***He** is at school.*

**USES: Apart from the cases already seen, the definite article is used:**

- before names of languages except after the preposition "en" (and sometimes "de") and the verbs "hablar" *(to speak)*, "enseñar" *(to teach)* or "aprender" *(to learn)*:
  | | |
  |---|---|
  | **El** español no es difícil. | *Spanish is not difficult.* |
  | **Ella** habla español. | *She speaks Spanish.* |

- before most titles:
  | | |
  |---|---|
  | **El** señor García está en la oficina. | *Mr. García is in the office.* |
  | **El** profesor Vives es famoso. | *Professor Vives is famous.* |

- with the parts of the body and clothing, instead of the possessive adjective:
  | | |
  |---|---|
  | Me lavo **las** manos. | *I wash my hands.* |
  | Ponte **el** abrigo. | *Put on your coat.* |

- before the names of the days of the week and dates except after the verb "ser", in some cases:
  | | |
  |---|---|
  | Hoy es jueves. | *It's Thursday today.* |
  | Hoy es 3 de abril. | *Today is April 3rd.* |
  | Mi cumpleaños es **el** 5 de mayo. | *My birthday is on May 5th.* |
  | Juego un partido **el** martes. | *I'm playing a match on Tuesday.* |

  The plural of the days of the week is shown in the article:
  | | |
  |---|---|
  | Juego un partido **los** martes. | *I play a match on Tuesdays.* |

- when we refer to the time:
  | | |
  |---|---|
  | El programa es a **las** 9. | *The program is at 9:00.* |
  | Son **las** 2 en punto. | *It's 2 o'clock.* |

- before nouns of a general or abstract nature, whereas in English the noun stands alone.
  | | |
  |---|---|
  | **La** vida es maravillosa. | *Life is wonderful.* |
  | Me gusta **el** baloncesto. | *I like basketball.* |

We have to keep in mind that the definite article is used more often in Spanish than in English.

## Contractions

If the article "**el**" is preceded by the prepositions "**a**" *(to)* or "**de**" *(of, from)*, we have to use two contractions:

| | |
|---|---|
| a + el ⟶ **al** | de + el ⟶ **del** |
| *(to + the)* | *(of, from + the)* |

| | |
|---|---|
| Voy **al** cine    *I am going **to the** cinema* | Vengo **del** cine    *I am coming **from the** cinema* |

## YES-NO ANSWERS

We have already seen how questions are formed in Spanish. Many of them are answered by simply saying "**sí**" *(yes)* or "**no**" *(no)*, or we can give longer answers.

| | |
|---|---|
| ¿Está Miguel en Perú? **Sí.** | *Is Miguel in Peru?* **Yes.** |
| ¿Están los libros en el piso? **No,** están en los estantes. | *Are the books on the floor?* **No,** *they are on the shelves* |
| Eres tú Rafael? **Sí,** lo soy. | *Are you Rafael?* **Yes,** *I am* |

The affirmative adverb "**sí**" *(yes)* is written with an accent not to be confused with the condicional "**si**" *(if)*.

## LAS CONJUNCIONES "Y" Y "E" *[THE CONJUNCTIONS "Y" AND "E" (AND)].*

The conjunction "**y**" *(and)* is used to list things or join some elements:

| | |
|---|---|
| Ellos son Francisco **y** Carlos. | *They are Francisco **and** Carlos.* |
| La mesa **y** las sillas están sobre la alfombra. | *The table **and** the chairs are on the carpet.* |

When the conjunction "**y**" is followed by a word that begins with "i" or "hi", it changes into "**e**".

| | |
|---|---|
| Ricardo **e** Iván están aquí. | *Ricardo **and** Iván are here.* |
| Es un problema de padres **e** hijos. | *It's a problem of parents **and** children.* |

## Unit

# 6

**Days 11 & 12**

### In this unit we will learn:

.To introduce oneself and others.

. Expressions: apologizing.

. Vocabulary: The family.

**Dialogo /** *Dialog*

Manuel se presenta a Victoria. Ella es la hermana de su amigo Juan. Él está detrás de ella, que está viendo algo en el monitor de una computadora.

*Manuel introduces himself to Victoria. She is his friend Juan's sister. He is behind her, looking at something on a computer screen.*

M: ¡Hola! **Me llamo** Manuel. Soy un amigo de Juan.

V: ¡Hola! **Yo soy** Victoria, la **hermana** de Juan.

M: **¡Encantado de conocerte! Perdona,** ¿dónde está el baño?

V: Es la puerta siguiente. ¿Conoces a mi **familia**?

M: Bueno, conozco a tu **hermano.**

V: Mira, aquí están [señala al monitor de la computadora]. Él es mi **padre**, ella es mi **madre**, aquí están mis **primos**, esta mujer rubia es mi **tía** Ingrid...

M: ¿Qué están celebrando?

V: Están celebrando la graduación de mi **prima** Susana.

M: Sí, la están pasando bien. Es una **familia** grande.

V: ¿Y tú? ¿Tienes una **familia** grande?

M: Sí. Mi **esposa**, Rosa, y yo tenemos dos **hijos**: un **hijo** y una **hija**. Mis **padres** están ahora en Europa. Aquí tengo un **hermano**, una **cuñada** y un **sobrino**. Mis **tíos**, **tías** y **primos** también están aquí.

V: **¿Cómo?**

M: Digo que toda la **familia** está aquí, excepto mis **padres**, que están en Europa en este momento.

V: ¡Ah! Y **te presento a** "Sunny", nuestra mascota.

M: **¡Encantado de conocerte,** "Sunny"!

M: *Hello! My name is Manuel. I am a friend of Juan's.*

V: *Hello! I am Victoria, Juan's sister.*

M: *Nice to meet you! Excuse me, where is the bathroom?*

V: *It's next door. Do you know my family?*

M: *Well, I know your brother.*

V: *Look, here they are [pointing at the computer screen]. He is my father, she is my mother, here are my cousins, this blonde woman is my aunt Ingrid...*

M: *What are they celebrating?*

V: *They are celebrating my cousin Susana's graduation.*

M: *Yes, they are having a great time. It is a big family.*

V: *And you? Do you have a big family?*

M: *Yes. My wife, Rosa, and I have two children: a son and a daughter. My parents are in Europe now. Here I have a brother, a sister-in-law and a nephew. My uncles, aunts and cousins are also here.*

V: *What?*

M: *I am saying that all my family is here, except my parents, who are in Europe in this moment.*

V: *Ah! And let me introduce you to "Sunny", our pet.*

M: *Nice to meet you, "Sunny"!*

## TOP VOCABULARY AND EXPRESSIONS

**Presentarse uno mismo y a otras personas.**
*(Introducing oneself and others)*

**a)** When we want to introduce ourselves to other people we can say:

| | |
|---|---|
| **Soy** ........................................... | *I'm* ........................................... |
| **Me llamo** ................................... | *My name is* .............................. |
| **Mi nombre es** ......................... | *My name is* .............................. |

**b)** And when we introduce other people:

| | |
|---|---|
| **(Éste, él) es** ............................. | *This is* ....................................... |
| **(Ésta, ella) es** ......................... | *This is* ....................................... |
| **¿Conoces a** .............................. **?** | *Do you know* ............................? |
| **Te/le presento a** ..................... | *Let me introduce you to* .......... |

The typical sentence said by those who are introduced is:

| | |
|---|---|
| **Encantado/a (de conocerte/le).** | *Nice to meet you.* |
| **¡Mucho gusto!** | *Pleased to meet you.* |
| **Un placer (conocerte/le).** | *Pleased to meet you.* |
| **Igualmente.** | *Nice to meet you, too.* |

| | |
|---|---|
| Paco: Luis, éste es Pedro. | *Paco: Luis, this is Pedro.* |
| Luis: Hola, Pedro. Encantado de conocerte. | *Luis: Hello, Pedro. Nice to meet you.* |
| Pedro: Igualmente. ¿Cómo estás? | *Pedro: Nice to meet you, too.How are you?* |

## EXPRESSIONS: PEDIR DISCULPAS *(APOLOGIZING)*

Now we will work on some very common expressions that could be confusing. They are used when we apologize for something.

> **Perdón**
> **Perdona** (informal) - **Perdone** (formal)          *Excuse me*
> **Disculpa** (informal) - **Disculpe** (formal)

These expressions are also used when we mean "**Sorry**", but, apart from them, we can also say "**Lo siento**" or "**Lo lamento**".

| **Suena el teléfono:** | *The telephone rings:* |
|---|---|
| - Hola. ¿Está José? | *- Hello. Is José in?* |
| - No. Tiene el número equivocado. | *- No. You've got the wrong number.* |
| - ¡Oh! **Lo siento***. | *- Oh! I'm sorry.* |

(*) You could also say "**lo lamento**", "**perdón**", "**perdone**" or "**disculpe**" in this situation.

When there is something we don't understand in a conversation and we want the speaker to repeat it, we say: **¿qué?, ¿cómo?** or **¿perdón?**  All these expressions are equivalent to "**pardon?**" or "**what?**"

| - Los libros están en la mesa | *– The books are on the table.* |
|---|---|
| - ¿Qué? (¿Cómo? / ¿Perdón?) | *– What? (Pardon?)* |
| - Digo que los libros están en la mesa. | *– I'm saying the books are on the table.* |

## VOCABULARIO: La familia *(The family)*

| Fernando **abuelo**/*grandfather* | Luisa **abuela**/*grandmother* |
|---|---|

| María **tía**/*aunt* | Rafael **tío**/*uncle* | Ricardo **padre**/*father* | Davinia **madre**/*mother* | Carlos **tío**/*uncle* |
|---|---|---|---|---|

| Ana **prima**/*cousin* | Jaime **primo**/*cousin* | **YO** | Enrique **hermano**/*brother* | Berta **hermana**/*sister* |
|---|---|---|---|---|
| | | | Paula **cuñada** *sister-in-law* | Miguel **cuñado** *brother-in-law* |

And also:

**padres:** *parents*
**hijo:** *son*
**abuelos:** *grandparents*
**nieto:** *grandson*
**sobrino:** *nephew*
**suegro:** *father-in-law*
**novio:** *boyfriend*

**hijos/as:** *children*
**hija:** *daughter*
**nietos:** *grandchildren*
**nieta:** *granddaughter*
**sobrina:** *niece*
**suegra:** *mother-in-law*
**novia:** *girlfriend*

Carlos y Rafael son mis **tíos.**
Mi padre tiene una **hermana** y un **hermano.**
Mi **cuñada** es Paula.
¿Conoces a mi **prima**?
Le presento a mi **novia.**

*Carlos and Rafael are my **uncles**.*
*My father has a **sister** and a **brother**.*
*My **sister-in-law** is Paula.*
*Do you know my **cousin**?*
*Let me introduce you to my **girlfriend**.*

The father and mother are colloquially called **"papá"** *(dad, daddy)* and **"mamá"** *(mom, mommy)*.

## Unit

# 7

**Days 13 & 14**

**In this unit we will learn:**

. To ask where people or things are from.

. Vocabulary: countries and nationalities.

. Possessive adjectives (plural): nuestro/a, su (*our, your, their*).

. To ask for repetition.

. To ask how something is said in another language.

## Diálogo / *Dialog*

Anthony y Carolina se conocen antes de entrar a clase. Hoy es el primer día del curso.

*Anthony and Carolina meet each other before entering the class. Today is the first day of the course.*

A: ¡Hola! Me llamo Anthony.
C: ¡Hola! Yo soy Carolina.
A: **¿De dónde eres?**
C: Soy **venezolana**.
A: **¿Qué?**
C: Soy **venezolana**, ¿y usted?
A: Bueno, puedes tutearme. Yo soy **estadounidense**. De Nueva York.
C: ¡Ah! Me gustan **los Estados Unidos**. Es un país muy grande y tiene una historia interesante.
A: Gracias. Bueno, en clase hay gente de muchos países. **Nuestros** compañeros son **mejicanos, chilenos, argentinos, brasileños, dominicanos**....
C: Sí, e **ingleses, canadienses** y **cubanos. Sus nacionalidades** son muy diferentes.
A: ¡Ah!, ya los conoces. Y, **¿de dónde es nuestra** profesora? ¿Lo sabes?
C: **¿Cómo?¿Puedes repetir?**
A: No sé **de dónde es nuestra** profesora. ¿Lo sabes tú?
C: Sí. **Su** profesora soy yo y, como ya sabes, soy **venezolana. ¿Cómo se dice** "¡Vamos! Es hora de empezar la clase" en inglés?

A: *Hello! My name is Anthony.*
C: *Hello! I am Carolina.*
A: *Where are you from?*
C: *I am Venezuelan*
A: *What?*
C: *I am Venezuelan, and you?*
A: *Well, you can address me using "tú". I am American. From New York.*
C: *Ah! I like the United States. It is a very big country and has an interesting history.*
A: *Thank you. Well, in class there are people from many countries. Our classmates are Mexican, Chilean, Argentinian, Brazilian, Dominican...*
C: *Yes, and English, Canadian and Cuban. Your nationalities are very different.*
A: *Ah!, you already know them. And, where is our teacher from? Do you know?*
C: *What? Can you repeat that?*
A: *I don't know where our teacher is from. Do you know?*
C: *Yes. Your teacher is me and, as you already know, I am Venezuelan. How do you say "Come on! It's time to start the class" in English?.*

## TOP VOCABULARY AND EXPRESSIONS

**Preguntar de dónde son las personas o cosas.**
*(Asking where people or things are from).*

**a)** To ask about the place of origin of people or things you can use the following expression:

**¿De dónde + present of "to be" + (subject)?**
*Where + present of "to be" + subject + from?*

You have to take into account that the preposition "**de**" is used before the interrogative "dónde", whereas in English it (*from*) is used at the end of the sentence.

| | |
|---|---|
| **¿De dónde** eres (tú)? | *Where are you from?* |
| **¿De dónde** es ella? | *Where is she from?* |
| **¿De dónde** es tu madre? | *Where is your mother from?* |
| **¿De dónde** son ellos? | *Where are they from?* |

**b)** And the answers to these questions could be:

| | |
|---|---|
| Soy **de** México. | *I'm from Mexico.* |
| Ella es **de** Colombia. | *She's from Colombia.* |
| Mi madre es **de** España. | *My mother is from Spain.* |
| Ellos son **de** Nueva York. | *They're from New York.* |

In order to ask and answer where people or things are from, it is important to know some vocabulary about countries and nationalities.

## VOCABULARIO:

**Países y nacionalidades** *(countries and nationalities).*

| Países *(Countries)* | Nacionalidades *(Nationalities)* |
|---|---|
| México | *mejicano-mejicana* |
| Colombia | *colombiano-colombiana* |
| Panamá | *panameño-panameña* |
| República Dominicana | *dominicano-dominicana* |
| Cuba | *cubano-cubana* |
| Argentina | *argentino-argentina* |
| Chile | *chileno-chilena* |
| Venezuela | *venezolano-venezolana* |
| Brasil | *brasileño-brasileña* |
| Estados Unidos (United States) | *estadounidense (American)* |
| España (Spain) | *español-española (Spanish)* |
| Francia (France) | *francés-francesa (French)* |
| Inglaterra (England) | *inglés-inglesa (English)* |
| Alemania (Germany) | *alemán-alemana (German)* |
| China | *chino-china* |
| Japón | *japonés-japonesa* |

## Remember!

Nationalities (and languages) are always written in lowercase letters. In Spanish there are masculine and feminine forms to express nationalities, except for those ending with "-e" (estadounidense, canadiense, etc.), and some others (belga, iraní, etc.).
So, you can say:

> **¿De dónde** eres? Soy de **Brasil**. Soy **brasileño**.
> *Where are you from? I'm from Brazil. I'm Brazilian.*

> **¿De dónde** es tu profesor? Es de **Argentina**. Es **argentino**.
> *Where is your teacher from? He's from Argentina. He's Argentinian.*

> Su madre (de él) es **francesa**.  His mother is French.
> Yo soy **de Miami**. Soy **estadounidense**.  I'm from Miami. I'm American.

## ADJETIVOS POSESIVOS *(POSSESSIVE ADJECTIVES)*

As we learned in unit 4, these adjectives indicate possession and always go before a noun. In this unit we are going to study the plural forms.

| | |
|---|---|
| **nuestro-nuestra** | *our* |
| **su (de ustedes)*** | *your* |
| **su (de ellos/as)** | *their* |

(*) In Spain this possessive is **vuestro-vuestra**, but **su** is the one used in Latin American countries.

| | |
|---|---|
| **Nuestro** idioma es el español. | *Our language is Spanish.* |
| ¿**Su** habitación (de ustedes) está cerrada?. | *Is your room closed?* |
| Daniel no es **su** hijo (de ellos). | *Daniel isn't their son.* |

As we can see, the possessive "our" has two forms "nuestro" (masculine) and "nuestra" (feminine), depending on the gender of the noun they precede.

| | |
|---|---|
| **Nuestro auto** es grande. | *Our car is big.* |
| Estamos en **nuestra casa.** | *We are in our house.* |

If a plural noun follows the possessive adjective, you need the plural possessive:
**nuestros/nuestras, sus**.

| | |
|---|---|
| **Nuestros** libros son interesantes. | *Our books are interesting.* |
| **Nuestras** madres están en **sus** casas. | *Our mothers are in their houses.* |
| No son **sus** llaves (de ustedes). | *They aren't your keys.* |
| ¿Dónde están **sus** autos (de ellos)? | *Where are their cars?* |

## PEDIR QUE ALGUIEN REPITA ALGO Y QUE HABLE MÁS DESPACIO
### (ASKING SOMEONE TO REPEAT SOMETHING AND TO SPEAK MORE SLOWLY)

When we don't understand someone and want them to repeat what they said or to speak more slowly, we can use any of the following expressions.

Colloquially we can say:

| | |
|---|---|
| **¿Qué?, ¿Cómo?** | *What?* |
| **¿Puedes repetir?** | *Can you repeat that?* |
| **No te entiendo.** | *I don't understand you/I didn't catch that.* |
| **¿Puedes hablar más despacio?** | *Can you speak more slowly?* |
| **¿Qué significa ....?** | *What does...... mean?* |

But in a formal situation we use:

| | |
|---|---|
| **¿Perdón?** | *I beg you pardon?* |
| **¿Podría hablar más despacio, por favor?** | *Could you speak more slowly, please?* |
| **Perdone, pero no entiendo.** | *Sorry, I don't understand.* |

## ¿CÓMO SE DICE...? (HOW DO YOU SAY...?)

In case we want to know how a word or expression is said in another language we say:

| | |
|---|---|
| **¿Cómo se dice........ en........?** | *How do you say........ in........?* |
| **¿Qué significa ...... (en......)?** | *What does....... mean in........?* |
| | |
| **¿Cómo se dice** "table" **en** español**?** | *How do you say "table" in Spanish?* |
| **¿Qué significa** "calabaza" (**en** inglés)**?** | *What does "calabaza" mean (in English)?* |

<table>
<tr><td>

**In this unit we will learn:**

. Nouns: gender and number.

. Vocabulary: Animals.

. Written accents.

. Diphthongs.

</td><td>

**Unit**

# 8

**Days 15 & 16**

</td></tr>
</table>

**Diálogo / Dialog**

Javier y Rosa hablan sobre animales.

*Javier and Rosa are talking about animals.*

| | |
|---|---|
| J: Rosa, ¿te gustan **los animales**? | J: Rosa, do you like animals? |
| R: Sí, mucho. | R: Yes, a lot. |
| J: ¿Cuál es tu **animal** favorito? | J: What is your favorite animal? |
| R: **El caballo.** Es muy inteligente. | R: The horse. It is very intelligent. |
| J: Mi abuelo tenía **una granja**. Allí estaban **los cerdos, las ovejas, las cabras, las vacas, las gallinas** y **los conejos** en **un lugar** maravilloso. | J: My grandfather had a farm. There the pigs, the sheep, the goats, the cows, the hens and the rabbits were in a marvelous place. |
| R: **La vida** en **el campo** es bonita. | R: Life in the country is nice. |
| J: Sí, allí son importantes **el sol** y **la lluvia**. | J: Yes, the sun and the rain are important there. |
| R: En **la ciudad**, también. | R: In the city, too. |
| J: Es cierto, pero **la vida** en **el campo** es muy diferente a **la vida** en **la ciudad. Las personas** son diferentes, también. | J: Sure, but life in the country is very different from life in the city. People are different, as well. |
| R: ¿Dices que había **conejos** en **la granja**? | R: Did you say that there were rabbits on the farm? |
| J: Sí, había muchos. | J: Yes, there were a lot. |
| R: **Los conejos** son lindos. | R: Rabbits are sweet. |
| J: Y están deliciosos. | J: And they are delicious. |
| R: ¡Javier! | R: Javier! |
| J: ¿Qué pasa? A mí me gustan. | J: What's the matter? I like them. |

## LOS NOMBRES: GÉNERO Y NÚMERO *(NOUNS: GENDER AND NUMBER)*

All Spanish nouns have a gender and are either masculine or feminine.

| | |
|---|---|
| el **hermano** (masc.) | *the brother* |
| la **hermana** (fem.) | *the sister* |

## Regarding the gender of nouns (the article has been added in order to stress the difference):

- Words ending in **"-o"** are usually masculine: But there are some exceptions:

  el **gato** (*cat*), el **amigo** (*friend*). la **mano** (*hand*), la **foto** (*photo*), etc.

- Words ending in **"-a"** are usually feminine: But there are also some exceptions:

  la **gata** (*cat*), la **amiga** (*friend*). el **día** (*day*), el **atleta** (*male athlete*), etc.

- Words ending in **"-e"** or in a consonant can be either masculine or feminine:

  el **hombre** (*man*), la **mujer** (*woman*), el **padre** *(father),* la **madre** *(mother),* el **calor** (*heat*), la **flor** (*flower*).

- Words ending in **"-ema"** are masculine:

  el **tema** (*topic*), el **problema** (*problem*).

- Words ending in **"-dad"** are feminine:

  la **amistad** (*friendship*), la **verdad** (*truth*).

- Words ending in **"-ción"** and **"-sión"** are also feminine:

  la **solución** (*solution*), la **información** (*information*), la **televisión** (*television*).

- Words that describe people and end in **"-ista"** can be either masculine or feminine:

  el **periodista** (*male journalist*), la **periodista** (*female journalist*), el **especialista** (*male specialist*), la **especialista** (*female specialist*).

## Regarding the number of nouns, to make the plural forms:

- If the singular noun ends in a vowel, simply add an "**-s**":
  Except when the word ends with a stressed "**-í**" or "**-ú**", that we add "**-es**":

  casa – casa**s** (*house – houses*)
  hombre – hombre**s** (*man – men*)
  jabalí - jabalí**es** [*wild boar(s)*]
  hindú – hindú**es** [*Hindu(s)*]

- If a noun ends in a consonant, make it plural by adding "**-es**":

  profesor – profesor**es** (*teacher – teachers*)
  árbol – árbol**es** (*tree – trees*)

- If a noun ends in a "**-z**", change the "**z**" to "**c**" before adding "**-es**":

  lápiz – lápi**ces** (*pencil – pencils*)
  pez – pe**ces** (*fish – fish*)

- If the plural refers to a mixed group, use the masculine form:

  2 gat**os** + 5 gat**as** = 7 gat**os**

- There are some nouns normally used in plural, although they refer to a single object:

  las lente**s** (*a pair of glasses*),
  las tijera**s** (*a pair of scissors*),
  los pantalon**es** (*a pair of trousers*), etc.

## Remember!

Articles must agree with the noun they go with in gender and number:

**el** perro – **los** perro**s**     (*the dog – the dogs*)
**la** mujer – **las** mujer**es**     (*the woman – the women*)

## TOP VOCABULARY AND EXPRESSIONS

### Animales (Animals)

The following nouns are preceded by the definite article in order to show their gender, and it's a good practice to learn them.

| | | | |
|---|---|---|---|
| la **araña**: *spider* | la **ballena**: *whale* | el **burro**: *donkey* | el **caballo**: *horse* |
| la **cabra**: *goat* | el **cerdo**: *pig* | el **conejo**: *rabbit* | el **delfín**: *dolphin* |
| el **elefante**: *elephant* | la **gallina**: *hen* | el **gato**: *cat* | el **insecto**: *insect* |
| la **jirafa**: *giraffe* | el **león**: *lion* | el **mono**: *monkey* | el **perro**: *dog* |

| | | | |
|---|---|---|---|
| la **oveja**: *sheep* | el **oso**: *bear* | el **pájaro/ave**: *bird* | el **pato**: *duck* |
| el **pavo**: *turkey* | el **pez**: *fish* | la **rana**: *frog* | la **rata**: *rat* |
| el **ratón**: *mouse* | la **serpiente**: *snake* | el **toro**: *bull* | la **vaca**: *cow* |

## WRITTEN ACCENTS

In the previous units we have seen some words with written accents. Let's learn when we need to use them.

- Written accent on the last syllable: when the last syllable of a word is stressed and ends with a vowel, "-n", or "-s":

  **café** (*coffee*)
  **Cancún** (*Cancun*)
  **estás** (*you are*)

- Written accent on the second-to-last syllable: when the second-to-last syllable is stressed and the word doesn't end with a vowel, "-n", or "-s":

  **árbol** (*tree*)
  **lápiz** (*pencil*)
  **fácil** (*easy*)

- Written accent on any stressed syllable before the second-to-last one: in every case:

  **gramática** (*grammar*)
  **médico** (*doctor*)
  **teléfono** (*telephone*)

There are also some other cases where the written accent is necessary, but they will be seen in other units.

## DIPTONGOS (*DIPHTHONGS*)

If the vowels "i", "u" or a "y" appear together with a strong vowel ("a", "e", "o") or with each other (no matter the order), they form a diphthong. Both vowels belong to a single syllable. For example: famil**ia**, **ai**re, h**ay**, b**ie**n, **rey**, rad**io**, h**oy**, s**ua**ve, **au**to, **Eu**ropa, h**ue**vo, c**ui**dado, c**iu**dad, etc.

But if the "i" or "u" are stressed, they are written with an accent. In these cases they do not form a diphthong but they are pronounced in two different syllables. That's what we call a hiatus. For example: r**ío**, d**úo**, pa**ís**, ba**úl**, re**ír**, etc.

## In this unit we will learn:
. To spell and expressions when spelling.
. Cardinal numbers (0-19).
. Telephone numbers.

## Unit
# 9
**Days 17 & 18**

### Diálogo / Dialog

Rubén y Cristina se intercambian sus direcciones y números de teléfono.

*Rubén and Cristina are giving their addresses and telephone numbers to each other.*

| | |
|---|---|
| R: Bueno, Cristina, ¿cuál es tu dirección? | R: Well, Cristina, what is your address? |
| C: Calle Veluti, número **17 (diecisiete)**. | C: 17, Calle Veluti. |
| R: ¿Cómo? **¿Puedes deletrear** el nombre de la calle? | R: What? Can you spell the name of the street? |
| C: **V de Venecia, E de España, L de Londres, U de Ucrania, T de Toronto, I de India.** | C: V for Venice, E for elephant, L for London, U for Ukraine, T for Toronto, I for India. |
| R: Veluti. No la conozco. | R: Veluti. I don't know it. |
| C: Es **una** calle pequeña. Está por aquí. No está lejos. | C: It is a small street. It is over here. It isn't far. |
| R: ¿Y cuál es tu número de teléfono? | R: And what is your telephone number? |
| C: Mi número de teléfono es el **769 853001 (siete-seis-nueve-ocho-cinco-tres-cero-cero-uno)**. | C: My telephone number is 769 853001. |
| R: Yo tengo **un** número de teléfono nuevo. | R: I have a new phone number. |
| C: ¿Sí? ¿Cuál es? | C: Yes? What is it? |
| R: Es el **769 120458 (siete-seis-nueve-uno-dos-cero-cuatro-cinco-ocho)**. | R: 769 120458. |
| C: ....**458**. Ya está. | C: ...458. That's it. |
| R: Mira, allí está Kica. | R: Look, there is Kica. |
| C: ¿Kica? **¿Cómo se deletrea** "Kica"? ¿Con "k" o con "q"? | C: Kica? How do you spell "Kica"? With a "k" or a "q"? |
| R: Con "k". **K de kilo, I de India, C de Colombia, A de América.** | R: With a "k". K for kilo, I for India, C for Colombia, A for America. |
| C: Bueno, "Kica" es un apodo. ¿Cuál es su nombre? | C: Well, "Kica" is a nickname. What is her name? |
| R: Se llama Joaquina. **Con "q", de queso.** | R: Her name is Joaquina. With a "q" for quarter. |

In unit 1 we learned the alphabet and now we will learn how to spell and different expressions related to spelling.

## TOP VOCABULARY AND EXPRESSIONS

### Deletreo *(Spelling)*.

[**deletrear**: *to spell*]

**a)** When we want someone to spell a word, their name, etc., we can ask:

| | |
|---|---|
| **¿Cómo se deletrea........?** | *How do you spell.................?* |
| **¿Puedes deletrear.........?** | *Can you spell.......................?* |
| **¿Cómo se deletrea** "mesa"? | *How do you spell "mesa"?* |
| M-E-S-A (eme-e-ese-a) | *M-E-S-A* |
| **¿Cómo se deletrea** tu nombre? | *How do you spell your name?* |
| **¿Puedes deletrear** tu apellido? | *Can you spell your last name?* |

**b)** When answering, we will repeat letter by letter, even though there may be two same letters together:

**¿Cómo se deletrea** "acción"?     *How do you spell "acción"? A-C-C-I-O-N*
A-C-C-I-O-N *(a-se-se-ee-o-ene)*
Not (a-doble se-ee-o-ene)

The only case when we have two options is with "ch" (se-ache, che), "ll" (ele-ele, elle) and "rr" (ere-ere, erre).

**c)** When spelling (especially on the phone) we can emphasize the letters to avoid any confusion by means of expressions like:

D-A-N-I-E-L: "D" **de** "Dinamarca", "A" **de** "Alemania", "N" **de** "Navarra", "I" **de** "Italia", "E" **de** "España", "L" **de** "Londres".

*D-A-N-I-E-L: "D"* **for** *"Dakota", "A"* **for** *"Alabama", "N"* **for** *"Nebraska", "I"* **for** *"Italy", "E"* **for** *"Elephant", "L"* **for** *"London". (You can choose the reference words you prefer).*

## NÚMEROS CARDINALES 0-19 *(CARDINAL NUMBERS 0-19)*

| | | 11 to 15 all end in "-ce": | 16 to 19 all start with "dieci-": |
|---|---|---|---|
| **0 – cero** | **6 – seis** | **11 – once** | **16 – dieciséis** |
| **1 – uno** | **7 – siete** | **12 – doce** | **17 – diecisiete** |
| **2 – dos** | **8 – ocho** | **13 – trece** | **18 – dieciocho** |
| **3 – tres** | **9 – nueve** | **14 – catorce** | **19 – diecinueve** |
| **4 – cuatro** | **10 – diez** | **15 – quince** | |
| **5 – cinco** | | | |

The number **"uno"** (1) changes into **"un"** when it goes before a noun:

> Tengo **un** hermano y tres hermanas.   *I have **one** brother and three sisters.*

**"Uno"** and **"un"** have a feminine form: **"una"**. Remember that these numbers have to agree with the gender of the noun they go with:

> Tengo **una** <u>casa</u> y **un** <u>auto</u>.   *I have **a** house and **a** car*
> *(one house and one car).*

## NÚMEROS DE TELÉFONO *(TELEPHONE NUMBERS)*

Telephone numbers in Spanish are expressed digit by digit or, sometimes, combining single numbers and pairs of numbers (this option will be studied further on).

**958283412:   nueve-cinco-ocho-dos-ocho-tres-cuatro-uno-dos**

When two of the same numbers are together, they are said one by one, not using the word "doble....." *(double......)*

**600987115:   seis-cero-cero-nueve-ocho-siete-uno-uno-cinco**

**a)** To ask for a telephone number you say:

**¿Cuál es tu número de teléfono?**   *What's your (tele)phone number?*

**b)** And to answer:

**Mi número de teléfono es (el) 509274831**   *My (tele)phone number is 509274831*

## Unit

# 10

**Days 19 & 20**

### In this unit we will learn:
. Differences between the vebs "ser" and "estar".
. Expressions with "ser" and "estar".
. Adjectives used with "ser" and "estar".

**Diálogo / Dialog**

Felipe y Nuria hablan sobre su vecina Zenobia.

*Felipe and Nuria are talking about their neighbor Zenobia.*

N: Zenobia **es** un nombre raro.
F: Sí, no **es** común.
N: ¿De dónde **es** ella?
F: **Es** de Manaos.
N: ¿Dónde **está** Manaos?
F: **Está** en Brasil. Zenobia **es** brasileña, pero sus padres **son** argentinos.
N: ¿**Está** casada?
F: No, **está** soltera.
N: Ahora **está** muy delgada.
F: Bueno, ella **es** delgada. Siempre lo ha sido. Ahora **estoy** un poco preocupado por ella. **Es** una muchacha alegre e inteligente, pero **está** triste.
N: ¿Crees que **está** mal?
F: **Está** mal, preocupada, cansada, aburrida o deprimida, porque **está** muy seria.
N: ¿Por qué no hablas con ella?
F: Sí, lo haré. Bueno, ¿quieres palomitas? [le ofrece el paquete del que está comiendo]
N: Gracias. Mmmm. ¡**Están** muy buenas!

N: *Zenobia is a strange name.*
F: *Yes, it isn't very common.*
N: *Where is she from?*
F: *She is from Manaus.*
N: *Where is Manaus?*
F: *It is in Brazil. Zenobia is Brazilian, but her parents are Argentinian.*
N: *Is she married?*
F: *No, she is single.*
N: *She is very thin now.*
F: *Well, she is thin. She has always been. Now I am a little worried about her. She is a cheerful and intelligent girl, but she is sad.*
N: *Do you think she feels bad?*
F: *She feels bad, worried, tired, bored or depressed, because she is very serious.*
N: *Why don't you talk to her?*
F: *Yes, I will. Well, would you like some popcorn? [he offers the bag he is eating from]*
F: *Thank you. Mmmm. They are delicious!*

As we have already seen, both the verbs **"ser"** and **"estar"** are equivalent to *"to be"* in English, but these verbs are very different in Spanish. Let's see some differences.

We know that **"ser"** is used for permanent situations whereas **"estar"** refers to temporary situations:

| | |
|---|---|
| Yo **soy** italiano. | *I **am** Italian. (permanently)* |
| Yo **estoy** en Italia. | *I **am** in Italy. (at present)* |

## We use the verb "ser" to:

**a) Define words or concepts:**
El auto **es** un medio de transporte.     *The car **is** a means of transport.*

**b) Classify objects or people:**
Los elefantes **son** animales salvajes.     *Elephants **are** wild animals.*
María **es** mi hermana.     *Maria **is** my sister.*

**c) Express identity:**
Él **es** Pedro.     *He **is** Pedro.*

**d) Express characteristics (what people or things are like):**
Ellos **son** altos.     *They **are** tall.*
Su casa **es** bonita.     *His house **is** nice.*

**e) Refer to somebody's character:**
Elena **es** extrovertida y habladora.     *Elena **is** extroverted and talkative.*

**f) Professions:**
Ruth y Víctor **son** médicos.     *Ruth and Victor **are** doctors.*

**g) Dates, times, etc.**
**Son** las tres en punto.     *It**'s** three o'clock.*
Mi cumpleaños **es** el 12 de marzo.     *My birthday **is** on March 12th.*

**h) Origin:**
Susana **es** colombiana.     *Susana **is** Colombian.*

**i) Color:**
Mi auto **es** rojo.     *My car **is** red.*

**j) Shape:**
La mesas **son** redondas.     *The tables **are** round.*

**h) Material:**
La caja **es** de plástico.     *It**'s** a plastic box.*

## We use the verb "estar" when:

We speak about **where somebody or something is located or how somebody or something is**.

| | |
|---|---|
| Miguel **está** en Brasil. | *Miguel is in Brazil.* |
| ¿Dónde **está** mi celular? **Está** en la mesa. | *Where is my cell phone? It's on the table.* |
| Mi madre **está** bien, gracias. | *My mother is fine, thank you.* |
| Las ventanas **están** cerradas. | *The windows are closed.* |

Thus, we will use the verb **"estar"** in the following cases, among others:

**estar +**
- bien, mal *(fine, badly)*
- alegre, triste *(happy, sad)*
- aburrido, cansado *(bored, tired)*
- sano, enfermo *(sane, ill)*
- vivo, muerto *(alive, dead)*

As we know the verb **"ser"** shows permanent characteristics and **"estar"** shows temporary ones, that is, states. Notice that there is a big difference between these pairs of sentences:

| | |
|---|---|
| Juan **es** nervioso. | *Juan is a nervous person.* |
| Juan **está** nervioso. | *Juan is nervous. (now)* |
| | |
| Gloria **es** delgada. | *Gloria is thin. (She is a thin person)* |
| Gloria **está** delgada ahora. | *Gloria is thin now. (She was heavier before)* |

## TOP VOCABULARY AND EXPRESSIONS

### Adjetivos y expresiones con "ser" y "estar".
*(Adjectives and expressions with "ser" and "estar").*

There are some adjectives with which we only use the verb "ser": inteligente *(intelligent)*, responsable *(responsible)*, trabajador *(hard-working)*, etc.

> Mercedes **es** <u>inteligente</u> y <u>responsable</u>.
> *Mercedes **is** intelligent and responsible.*

There are some others only used with the verb "estar": contento *(happy)*, enfermo *(ill)*, ocupado *(busy)*, preocupado *(worried)*, avergonzado *(embarrassed)*, etc.

> **Estoy** <u>contento</u>.     *I am happy.*
> **¿Estás** <u>preocupado</u>?     *Are you worried?*

And there are adjectives with different meanings depending on the verb they go with:

| | | | | |
|---|---|---|---|---|
| **ser abierto** | *to be extroverted* | | **estar abierto** | *not to be closed* |
| **ser aburrido** | *to be boring* | ≠ | **estar aburrido** | *to be bored* |
| **ser cansado** | *to be tiring* | | **estar cansado** | *to be tired* |
| **ser listo** | *to be clever* | | **estar listo** | *to be ready* |

Some of them are often used:

| | |
|---|---|
| **ser bueno** | *to be good (or a good person)* |
| **estar bueno** | *to be tasty or to be in good health* |
| **ser malo** | *to be bad (or a bad person)* |
| **estar malo** | *to be disgusting or to be ill* |

The verb "estar" can also be used with "bien" or "mal":

| | |
|---|---|
| **estar bien** | *to feel fine or to be correct* |
| **estar mal** | *to feel badly or to be incorrect* |

Although the verb "*to be*" means "ser" and "estar", there are some expressions with this verb in English that are equivalent to the verb "tener" in Spanish:

| **tener** | ........años<br>calor/frío<br>hambre/sed<br>suerte | *to be* | .......years old<br>hot/cold<br>hungry/thirsty<br>lucky |
|---|---|---|---|

# SPANISH IN 100 DAYS

## In this unit we will learn:

. To ask questions.

. Interrogative pronouns (Questioning words).

. To ask and answer when filling out a form.

# Unit
# 11
**Days 21 & 22**

## Diálogo / Dialog

Wellington quiere apuntarse en el gimnasio y la encargada le solicita datos personales.

*Wellington wants to join the gym and the person in charge asks him for personal information.*

W: ¡Hola! Ya estoy decidido. Quiero venir a este gimnasio. Ya conozco las condiciones.
E: Estupendo. Necesito algunos datos suyos. **¿Cómo se llama usted?**
W: Me llamo Wellington.
E: ¿Puede deletrearlo?
W: W-E-L-L-I-N-G-T-O-N.
E: **¿Y sus apellidos?**
W: Gómez López.
E: **¿Cuál es su dirección?**
W: **¿Cómo?**
E: **¿Dónde** vive?
W: ¡Ah! Calle Nueva, número 19.
E: **¿Cuál es su número de teléfono,** Wellington?
W: Mi teléfono es el 761039845.
E: **¿Tiene dirección de correo electrónico?**
W: ¡Sí, claro! welgo@pitimail.com
E: **¿De qué nacionalidad es?**
W: Soy panameño.
E: **¿Puede firmar aquí, por favor?**
W: ¡Claro!
E: Pues ya está todo. Puede venir cuando quiera.
W: Gracias. Vendré esta misma tarde.

*W: Hello! I've made up my mind. I want to come to this gym. I already know the conditions.*
*E: Great. I need some of your personal information. What is your name?*
*W: My name is Wellington.*
*E: Can you spell it?*
*W: W-E-L-L-I-N-G-T-O-N.*
*E: And your last name?*
*W: Gómez López.*
*E: What's your address?*
*W: Pardon?*
*E: Where do you live?*
*W: Ah! 19 Calle Nueva.*
*E: What's your telephone number, Wellington?*
*W: My telephone number is 761039845.*
*E: Do you have an email address?*
*W: Yes, of course! welgo@pitimail.com*
*E: What nationality are you?*
*W: I am Panamanian.*
*E: Can you sign here, please?*
*W: Sure!*
*E: That's all. You can come when you want.*
*W: Thank you. I'll come this afternoon.*

## TOP VOCABULARY AND EXPRESSIONS

### Hacer preguntas *(Asking questions)*

Asking questions in Spanish is easy. We have already learned that a question may start with a subject or a verb:

¿**Ella** está en Italia?
¿Está **ella** en Italia?  }  *Is she in Italy?*

¿**Ellos** son tus hijos?
¿Son **ellos** tus hijos?  }  *Are they your children?*

But this also happens when the verb is not "ser" or "estar":

¿**Ustedes** viven en México?
¿Viven **ustedes** en México?  }  *Do you live in Mexico?*

¿**Tú** tienes novia?
¿Tienes (**tú**) novia?  }  *Do you have a girlfriend?*

If a question starts with a verb, we can usually omit the subject, as we can see in the previous example.
But questions may also be introduced by an interrogative pronoun (questioning words).

## PRONOMBRES INTERROGATIVOS *(INTERROGATIVE PRONOUNS)*

They are used to ask about something or someone and placed at the beginning of the question. They are the following:

| | | | |
|---|---|---|---|
| **¿Qué?** | *What?* | **¿Quién? ¿Quiénes?** | *Who?* |
| **¿Cuándo?** | *When?* | **¿Dónde?** | *Where?* |
| **¿Cómo?** | *How?* | **¿Por qué?** | *Why?* |
| **¿Cuánto? ¿Cuánta?** | *How much?* | **¿Cuántos? ¿Cuántas?** | *How many?* |
| **¿De quién?** | *Whose?* | **¿Cuál? ¿Cuáles?** | *What? Which (one)? Which (ones)?* |

These pronouns always have a written accent on the stressed syllable.
When we use interrogative pronouns, the subject (if necessary) always goes after the verb.

## ¿Qué? *(What?)*

| | |
|---|---|
| **¿Qué** es <u>eso</u>? | **What** *is that?* |
| **¿Qué** son <u>los virus</u>? | **What** *are the viruses?* |

To ask about the age of something or somebody we use "**¿Qué edad?**", which is equivalent to "*How old?*". In this case, in Spanish we use the verb "tener" (*to have*) but in English, "*to be*".

| | |
|---|---|
| **¿Qué edad** <u>tienes</u>? | **How old** <u>are</u> *you?* |

## ¿Cuál? ¿Cuáles? *(Which one(s)?)*

The pronoun "**¿Cuál?**" (*Which one?*) has the plural form "**¿Cuáles?**" (*Which ones?*) if we ask about a plural noun. **¿Cuál?** and **¿Cuáles?** can also be equivalent to *What?*

| | |
|---|---|
| **¿Cuál** es la capital de Colombia? | *What is the capital of Colombia?* |
| **¿Cuál** es su nombre? | *What is her name?* |
| **¿Cuáles** son tus libros? | *Which are your books?* |

## ¿Quién? ¿Quiénes? *(Who?)*

To ask about people we use "**¿Quién?**" in singular and "**¿Quiénes?**" in plural.

| | |
|---|---|
| **¿Quién** es tu hermano? | **Who** *is your brother?* |
| **¿Quiénes** son ellos? | **Who** *are they?* |

## ¿Cuándo? *(When?)*

We use "**¿Cuándo?**" when we ask about time, a date, etc.

| | |
|---|---|
| **¿Cuándo** es tu cumpleaños? | **When** *is your birthday?* |
| **¿Cuándo** estás en la escuela? | **When** *are you at school?* |

## ¿Dónde? *(Where?)*

"**¿Dónde?**" is used to ask where people or things are located.

| | |
|---|---|
| **¿Dónde** están tus amigos? | **Where** are your friends? |
| **¿Dónde** está mi diccionario? | **Where** is my dictionary? |

There is a similar pronoun "**¿Adónde?**" (*To where?*) that asks for destinations:

| | |
|---|---|
| **¿Adónde** vas? | **Where** are you going **to**? |

## ¿Cómo? *(How?)*

| | |
|---|---|
| **¿Cómo** estás? | **How** are you? |

Sometimes we use "*what*" instead of "*how*" in English:

| | |
|---|---|
| **¿Cómo** te llamas? | |
| (**¿Cuál** es tu nombre?) | **What**'s your name? |

## ¿Cuánto? ¿Cuánta? *(How much?)* ¿Cuántos? ¿Cuántas? *(How many?)*

These interrogatives will be studied further on.

## ¿Por qué? *(Why?)*

It is used to ask about a reason and is always made up of two words.

| | |
|---|---|
| **¿Por qué** están las llaves en la cocina? | **Why** are the keys in the kitchen? |
| **¿Por qué** está ella en Nueva York? | **Why** is she in New York? |

Try not to confuse "**por qué?**" (*why?*) with "**porque**" (*because*).
"Porque" is the answer to "Por qué?".

| | |
|---|---|
| – **¿Por qué** estás preocupado? | – **Why** are you worried? |
| – **Porque** tengo problemas. | – **Because** I have some problems. |

## ¿De quién? *(Whose?)*

We use "**¿De quién?**" to ask about possession.

| | |
|---|---|
| **¿De quién** es esta casa? | *Whose house is this?* |
| **¿De quién** es el auto azul? | *Whose is the blue car?* |

**¿Por qué?** and **¿De quién?** are interrogatives made up of two words. There are many interrogatives like these ones, formed by a preposition and an interrogative pronoun, which will be studied in unit 12.

---

## TOP VOCABULARY AND EXPRESSIONS

### Rellenar un formulario. Datos personales.
*(Filling out a form. Personal information)*

When we fill out a form, the typical questions that we could be asked would be:

Apellidos: **¿Cuáles son sus apellidos?** *What (Which) are your last names?*

Nombre: **¿Cuál es su nombre? / ¿Cómo se llama?** *What's your name?*

Edad (Age): **¿Qué edad tiene usted? / ¿Cuántos años tiene?** *How old are you?*

Dirección: **¿Cuál es su dirección?** *What's your address?*

Teléfono: **¿Cuál es su número de teléfono?** *What's your telephone number?*

E-mail: **¿Cuál es su dirección electrónica?** *What's your email address?*

To answer we say:

**Mis apellidos son** ....................... *My last names are* .......................

**Mi** ⎡ **nombre es** ...........
**dirección es** ...........
**número de teléfono es** ...........
**dirección electrónica es** ...........

**My** ⎡ *name is* ...............
*address is* ...............
*telephone number is* ...............
*email address is* ...............

**Tengo** ............... **años**   *I am* ............... *years old*

## Unit 12

**Days 23 & 24**

### In this unit we will learn:

. To form questions with prepositions:
Prepositions + interrogative....?
. Vocabulary: Rooms and objects at home.
. Verbs in Spanish.
. Regular and irregular verbs.

**Diálogo /** *Dialog*

Celia y Arturo son compañeros de trabajo y están hablando sobre sus casas.

*Celia and Arturo are colleagues and are talking about their homes.*

| | |
|---|---|
| C: | ¿**Con quién** vives, Arturo? |
| A: | Vivo con mi madre y mi hermana. |
| C: | ¿Es grande tu **casa**? |
| A: | Bueno, sí. Sí es grande. Hay tres **dormitorios**, un gran **salón**, la **cocina**, el **cuarto de baño** y un **aseo**. ¿Y tú? ¿Vives sola? |
| C: | No. Vivo con Daniel en un **apartamento**. No es grande. Tiene dos **dormitorios** y un **salón**, pero la **cocina** y el **baño** son pequeños. |
| A: | ¿**En qué** zona de la ciudad vives? |
| C: | En el centro. |
| A: | Yo vivo en las afueras. Por cierto, ¿**para quién** es ese regalo? |
| C: | Es para Daniel. Hoy es su cumpleaños. |
| A: | ¿Es Daniel tu novio? |
| C: | Bueno, somos buenos amigos. |
| A: | ¿**De dónde** es? |
| C: | Es colombiano. |
| A: | ¿Y **desde cuándo** son "buenos amigos"? |
| C: | Eres muy curioso, Arturo.... |

| | |
|---|---|
| C: | *Who do you live with, Arturo?* |
| A: | *I live with my mother and my sister.* |
| C: | *Is your house big?* |
| A: | *Well, yes. It is big. There are three bedrooms, a big living room, the kitchen, the bathroom and a powder room. And you? Do you live alone?* |
| C: | *No, I live with Daniel in an apartment. It is not big. It has two bedrooms and a living room, but the kitchen and the bathroom are small.* |
| A: | *Whereabouts in the city do you live?* |
| C: | *Downtown.* |
| A: | *I live in the suburbs. By the way, who is that present for?* |
| C: | *It is for Daniel. It is his birthday today.* |
| A: | *Is Daniel your boyfriend?* |
| C: | *Well, we are good friends.* |
| A: | *Where is he from?* |
| C: | *He is Colombian.* |
| A: | *And how long have you been "good friends"?* |
| C: | *You are very curious, Arturo....* |

In unit 11 we learned how to ask questions with interrogative pronouns. Now we will see how these interrogatives are used with prepositions.

## TOP VOCABULARY AND EXPRESSIONS

### Preposiciones + Interrogativos *(Prepositions + interrogatives)*

In English, when we use a preposition that modifies the interrogative, it is placed at the end of the question, but, in Spanish, it goes at the beginning, before the interrogative pronoun.

| | |
|---|---|
| **¿Con** quién estás? | *Who are you **with**?* |
| **¿Para** qué? | *What **for**?* |

Let's review some of the most common prepositions:

| | |
|---|---|
| **a:** | to |
| **con:** | with |
| **de:** | of, from |
| **en:** | in, on, at, about |
| **para:** | for |

| | |
|---|---|
| **¿De** dónde eres? | *Where are you **from**?* |
| **¿En** qué país está (él)? | *Which country is he **in**?* |
| **¿Para** quién es el regalo? | *Who is the gift **for**?* |

These questions can be answered using a long or a short way (preposition + answer):

| | |
|---|---|
| **Soy de** Chile or **De** Chile. | *I'm from Chile or From Chile.* |
| **Está en** Cuba or **En** Cuba. | *He is in Cuba or In Cuba.* |
| (El regalo) **Es para** su padre or | *(The gift) It is for his father or* |
| **Para** su padre. | *For his father.* |

But we have seen that there are some cases in which we use prepositions in Spanish, although they are not used in English:

| | |
|---|---|
| ¿**Por** qué? | *Why?* |
| ¿**De** quién? | *Whose?* |

## VOCABULARIO:

**Habitaciones y objetos de casa** *(Rooms and objects at home)*

| | | | |
|---|---|---|---|
| **cocina:** | kitchen | **recibidor:** | foyer |
| **comedor:** | dining-room | **lámpara(s):** | lamp(s) |
| **salón, sala de estar:** | living-room | **televisor/televisión:** | television set |
| **dormitorio:** | bedroom | **cama:** | bed |
| **baño:** | bathroom | **despertador:** | alarm-clock |
| **aseo:** | toilet / powder room | **planta(s):** | plant(s) |
| **pasillo:** | hallway | **cortina(s):** | curtain(s) |

| | |
|---|---|
| ¿Con quién está Bárbara en el **comedor**? | *Who is Barbara in the dining-room with?* |
| ¿Por qué estás en la **cama**? | *Why are you in bed?* |
| ¿De quién es el **despertador**? | *Whose is the alarm-clock?* |
| ¿Para qué usas la **cama**? | *What do you use the bed for?* |

And now, let's expand our vocabulary and expressions by studying verbs.

## LOS VERBOS EN ESPAÑOL *(VERBS IN SPANISH)*

When we refer to a verb in Spanish we use the infinitive, which is the way we will look it up in a dictionary. These infinitives have three endings ("-ar", "-er", "-ir") and all the verbs are classified according to these endings.

| Verbs ending with: | -ar | | -er | | -ir | |
|---|---|---|---|---|---|---|
| | **cantar** | *to sing* | **comer** | *to eat* | **abrir** | *to open* |
| | **trabajar** | *to work* | **beber** | *to drink* | **salir** | *to go out* |
| | **hablar** | *to speak* | **leer** | *to read* | **escribir** | *to write* |
| | **estudiar** | *to study* | **aprender** | *to learn* | **decidir** | *to decide* |

All the verbs in Spanish are either regular or irregular. A **regular verb** is the one that follows predictable patterns when it is conjugated and an **irregular verb** is the verb that doesn't follow these patterns or has other changes when conjugated.

To conjugate a regular verb, we have to take off the infinitive ending (-ar, -er, -ir) and replace it with the correct ending for each pronoun or subject. The Spanish verbal system has a set of endings that indicate the subject of the sentence, as well as the tense.

The infinitive without the "-ar", "-er", "-ir" ending is called the verb stem.

| cantar | –ar | = | **cant** (stem) | *to sing* |
|---|---|---|---|---|
| comer | –er | = | **com** (stem) | *to eat* |
| abrir | –ir | = | **abr** (stem) | *to open* |

> (yo) **cant<u>o</u>**     *(I sing)*
> (yo) **cant<u>é</u>**     *(I sang)*
> (yo) **cant<u>aré</u>**     *(I will sing)*

## Unit

# 13

**Days 25 & 26**

**In this unit we will learn:**

. The present simple: uses.

. The present tense of regular verbs (ending with "-ar").

## Diálogo / Dialog

Mercedes está consultando unos libros. Enrique está cerca de ella.

*Mercedes is looking through some books. Enrique is near her.*

| | |
|---|---|
| E: | ¡Hola! ¿Qué hace usted? |
| M: | **Estudio** biología. Soy investigadora. |
| E: | ¡Qué interesante! Yo soy profesor. |
| M: | ¿Sí? ¿Y qué **enseña**? |
| E: | **Enseño** español. |
| M: | ¿**Habla** otros idiomas? |
| E: | Sí, **hablo** inglés y un poco de ruso. |
| M: | ¿No **habla** francés? |
| E: | No; sólo unas palabras. |
| M: | Yo también **hablo** inglés. Es muy importante en mi trabajo. |
| E: | ¿Dónde **trabaja**? |
| M: | En un laboratorio. Allí **trabajamos** muchas personas. ¿Y usted? |
| E: | Yo **trabajo** en una escuela de idiomas. |
| M: | Bueno, ustedes **trabajan** con las palabras y nosotros **trabajamos** con los datos. |
| E: | Así es. [Mirando el reloj] Perdone, pero ahora tengo de irme. **Llego** tarde a clase. |
| M: | De acuerdo. ¡Que tenga un buen día! |
| E: | Gracias. Igualmente. ¡Adiós! |

| | |
|---|---|
| E: | *Hello! What are you doing?* |
| M: | *I am studying biology. I am a researcher.* |
| E: | *How interesting! I am a teacher.* |
| M: | *Are you? What do you teach?* |
| E: | *I teach Spanish.* |
| M: | *Do you speak other languages?* |
| E: | *Yes, I speak English and a little Russian.* |
| M: | *Don't you speak French?* |
| E: | *No, just a few words.* |
| M: | *I also speak English. It is very important for my work.* |
| E: | *Where do you work?* |
| M: | *In a lab. There are a lot of us working there. And you?* |
| E: | *I work in a language school.* |
| M: | *Well, you work with words and we work with data.* |
| E: | *That's right! [Looking at his watch] Excuse me but I have to leave. I am late for class.* |
| M: | *Okay, have a nice day!* |
| E: | *Thanks. Same to you. Goodbye!* |

Let's look at how the present tense is formed in Spanish, as well as its uses.

## EL PRESENTE SIMPLE *(THE PRESENT SIMPLE)*

## Uses:

The meaning of this verb tense has several equivalents in English as, in Spanish, the present simple is used:

a) **To express habitual actions at present:**
Ella **va** al trabajo en autobús. — *She **goes** to work by bus.*

b) **To express temporary situations at present:**
Mi madre **está** enferma. — *My mother **is** ill.*

c) **To describe an action that is taking place at the time the word is spoken:**
¿Qué **hacen** los niños ahora? — *What **are** the children **doing** now?\**
(*) The present progressive also exists in Spanish but it is used less frequently than in English.

d) **To express general truths:**
El cielo **es** azul. — *The sky **is** blue.*
Los gatos **comen** ratones. — *Cats **eat** mice.*

e) **To express planned actions in the future. In this case, the moment when the action happens has to be shown:**
El sábado **voy** al cine. — *I'm **going** to the movies on Saturday.*

f) **To make the present action more emphatic:**
**Trabajo** todos los días. — *I **work** everyday.*

In units 13 and 14 we are going to study the present simple of **regular verbs**.
To form the **present simple of regular verbs** we need the verb stem, to which we add the following endings:

## Verbs ending with "-ar".

Ex: **cantar** (*to sing*)    Stem ———▶ **cant**

|  | Ending | Verb form |  |
|---|---|---|---|
| yo | **–o** | cant**o** | *I sing, I am singing, I do sing* |
| tú | **–as** | cant**as** | *you sing, you are singing, you do sing* |
| usted | **–a** | cant**a** | *you sing (formal), "  ,  "* |
| él | **–a** | cant**a** | *he sings, he is singing, he does sing* |
| ella | **–a** | cant**a** | *she sings, she is singing, she does sing* |
| nosotros/as | **–amos** | cant**amos** | *we sing, we are singing, we do sing* |
| ustedes | **–an** | cant**an** | *you (all) sing, you are singing, you do sing* |
| ellos/as | **–an** | cant**an** | *they sing, they are singing, they do sing* |

In Spain, the second person in plural is "vosotros/as" (instead of "ustedes", which is used in Latin American countries). The conjugation of each tense for "vosotros/as" is shown in an appendix.

There are many verbs that follow the same pattern. Some of them are:

**ayudar** (*to help*)          **comprar** (*to buy*)          **enseñar** (*to teach, to show*)
**estudiar** (*to study*)       **hablar** (*to speak*)         **llegar** (*to arrive*)
**preguntar** (*to ask*)        **trabajar** (*to work*)        **visitar** (*to visit*)

| | |
|---|---|
| Ella **estudia** geografía. | *She studies geography.* |
| **Compramos** el periódico todos los días. | *We buy the newspaper everyday.* |
| Ellos **enseñan** inglés. | *They teach English.* |
| Usted **pregunta** muchas cosas. | *You ask about many things.* |

Since the verb forms show us the person and number, it is not necessary to use the subject pronouns "yo" (*I*), "tú" (*you*) and "nosotros/as" (*we*), except for emphatic reasons:

**Hablo** español.          *I speak English.*
<u>Yo</u> **hablo** español.          *I do speak English.*

But the rest of the pronouns are generally used to avoid ambiguity, as "usted" (*you*), "él" (*he*) and "ella" (*she*) have the same verbal form. It also happens with "ustedes" (*you*) and "ellos/as" (*they*).

**Él** <u>canta</u> ópera.          *He sings opera.*
**Usted** <u>canta</u> ópera.          *You sing opera.*

**Ustedes** <u>trabajan</u> duro.          *You work hard.*
**Ellos** <u>trabajan</u> duro.          *They work hard.*

When we refer to animals, things, etc., there is no pronoun to use, as "it" has no equivalent in Spanish. In these cases we use the verb alone conjugated as for "él" or "ella".

El perro salta con la pelota          *The dog jumps with the ball.*
**Salta** con la pelota.          ***It jumps*** *with the ball.*

When we want to structure <u>negative sentences</u> in the present, we simply place "**no**" just before the verb.

|  |  |
|---|---|
| Ella **no** <u>habla</u> ruso. | *She doesn't speak Russian.* |
| **No** <u>estudio</u> en la universidad. | *I'm not studying at university.* |
| Ellos **no** <u>compran</u> leche. | *They don't buy any milk.* |

With questions, we can simply change the intonation (which is the most frequent way) or we can invert the order of the subject (if necessary) and the verb.

|  |  |
|---|---|
| Ustedes estudian español. | *You are studying Spanish.* |
| ¿<u>Ustedes</u> **estudian** español? | *Are you studying Spanish?* |
| ¿**Estudian** <u>ustedes</u> español? | *Are you studying Spanish?* |
|  |  |
| Trabajas en casa. | *You work at home.* |
| ¿**Trabajas** en casa? | *Do you work at home?* |

But if the question starts with an interrogative pronoun, the subject (if necessary) is placed after the verb in most cases.

|  |  |
|---|---|
| ¿Cuándo **estudian** <u>ustedes</u> español? | *When do you study Spanish?* |
| ¿Dónde **trabajas** (<u>tú</u>)? | *Where do you work?* |

## In this unit we will learn:

. Present tense of regular verbs (ending with "-er" and "-ir").

. Vocabulary: Colors.

**Unit**
# 14
**Days 27 & 28**

## Diálogo / *Dialog*

Sara llega a casa y ve a Humberto.

*Sara arrives home and sees Humberto.*

S: Humberto, ¿qué **comes**?
H: Un sándwich de queso. Tengo hambre.
S: ¿**Sabes**? Clara me ha dicho que Enrique **vende** algunas cosas.
H: ¿Qué hace él ahora?
S: **Escribe** cuentos y **aprende** inglés.
H: ¿Y por qué **vende** algunas cosas?
S: Porque él no **vive** en la ciudad y necesita dinero para comprar una casa en el campo. **Vive** allí con sus animales.
H: Sí, recuerdo que tiene un perro **blanco** y dos gatos **marrones** y **negros**. En el campo **ves**, **aprendes** y **descubres** muchas cosas. Es bonito vivir allí. Todo es **verde**.
S: Sí, pero, ¿qué tal si **vemos** nosotros esas cosas?
H: Mmmmm. Ahora **comprendo**. Tú estás interesada en sus cosas.
S: Bueno, creo que **vende** su auto **gris**, una alfombra **roja** y las sillas **verdes** del salón. Clara ha comprado muchas cosas.
H: ¿**Necesitamos** esas cosas?
S: Yo **necesito** un auto y ésta puede ser una oportunidad interesante.
H: Bueno, podemos ir y verlo.

S: *Humberto, what are you eating?*
H: *A cheese sandwich. I am hungry.*
S: *Guess what? Clara has told me that Enrique is selling his house.*
H: *What is he doing now?*
S: *He writes stories and is learning English.*
H: *And why is he selling his house?*
S: *Because he doesn't live in the city and needs the money to buy a house in the country. He lives there with his pets.*
H: *Yes, I remember that he has a white dog and two brown and black cats. In the country you see, learn and discover many things. It is nice to live there. Everything is green.*
S: *Yes, but, how about we go and see those things?*
H: *Mmmm. I understand. You are interested in his things.*
S: *Well, I think he is selling his grey car, a red carpet and the green living room chairs. Clara has bought a lot of things.*
H: *Do we need these things?*
S: *I need a car and this could be a good opportunity.*
H: *Well, we can go and see it.*

Let´s continue reviewing the present simple of regular verbs.

## Verbs ending with "-er".

Ex: **comer** (*to eat*)    Stem ➞ **com**

|  | Ending | Verb form |  |
|---|---|---|---|
| yo | **–o** | com**o** | *I eat, I am eating, I do eat* |
| tú | **–es** | com**es** | *you eat, you are eating, you do eat* |
| usted | **–e** | com**e** | *you eat (formal),  "  ,  "* |
| él | **–e** | com**e** | *he eats, he is eating, he does eat* |
| ella | **–e** | com**e** | *she eats, she is eating, she does eat* |
| nosotros/as | **–emos** | com**emos** | *we eat, we are eating, we do eat* |
| ustedes | **–en** | com**en** | *you (all) eat, you are eating, you do eat* |
| ellos/as | **–en** | com**en** | *they eat, they are eating, they do eat* |

There are also many verbs that follow this pattern. Some of them are:

**beber** (*to drink*)          **aprender** (*to learn*)
**correr** (*to run*)           **ver** (*to see, to watch*)
**vender** (*to sell*)          **comprender, entender\*** (*to understand*)

(\*) "Entender" is a synonym of "comprender" but it is an irregular verb.

**Vendo** autos.            *I sell cars.*
Él **come** carne.          *He eats meat.*
**Vemos** la televisión.    *We watch television.*
Tú **aprendes** español.    *You are learning Spanish.*

For animals and things that we know, we only use the verb (without pronoun).

El gato bebe agua. ➞ **Bebe** agua.
*The cat drinks water.* ➞ ***It drinks** water.*

In negative sentences:

**No comprendo.**              *I don't understand.*
Ellas **no ven** la televisión.   *They don't watch television.*
Los pájaros **no corren.** Vuelan.   *Birds don't run. They fly.*
**No comes** vegetales.        *You don't eat vegetables.*

In questions:

| | |
|---|---|
| ¿**Venden** ustedes su casa? | *Are you selling your house?* |
| ¿**Comprendes?** / ¿**Entiendes?** | *Do you understand?* |
| ¿Qué **bebes**? | *What are you drinking? / What do you drink?* |

And finally:

## Verbs ending with "-ir".

Ex: **abrir** *(to open)*    Stem ➡ **abr**

| | Ending | Verb form | |
|---|---|---|---|
| yo | **-o** | abr**o** | *I open, I am opening, I do open* |
| tú | **-es** | abr**es** | *you open, you are opening, you do open* |
| usted | **-e** | abr**e** | *you open (formal),  "    ,     "* |
| él | **-e** | abr**e** | *he opens, he is opening, he does open* |
| ella | **-e** | abr**e** | *she opens, she is opening, she does open* |
| nosotros/as | **-imos** | abr**imos** | *we open, we are opening, we do open* |
| ustedes | **-en** | abr**en** | *you (all) open, you are opening, you do open* |
| ellos/as | -en | abr**en** | *they open, they are opening, they do open* |

Some verbs that follow this pattern are:

| | | |
|---|---|---|
| **escribir** *(to write)* | **decidir** *(to decide)* | **recibir** *(to receive)* |
| **descubrir** *(to discover)* | **asistir** *(to attend)* | **vivir** *(to live)* |

| | |
|---|---|
| Él **escribe** novelas. | *He writes novels.* |
| Mis padres **no asisten** a la reunión. | *My parents are not attending the meeting.* |
| ¿Dónde **viven** ustedes? | *Where do you live? / Where are you living?* |
| **No recibo** tus mensajes. | *I don't receive your messages.* |
| Los científicos **descubren** medicinas. | *Scientists discover medicines.* |
| Ella **no abre** las ventanas. | *She doesn't open the windows.* |
| ¿**Escribes** cartas a tus amigos? | *Do you write letters to your friends?* |
| **Vive** en mi apartamento (el perro). | *It lives in my apartment.* |

We have already studied the present simple of the three types of verbs in Spanish. All regular verbs follow the same patterns.

To sum up: **PRESENT SIMPLE ENDINGS FOR –AR, –ER, –IR VERBS**

|  | –AR verbs | –ER verbs | –IR verbs |
|---|---|---|---|
| yo | –o | –o | –o |
| tú | –as | –es | –es |
| usted / él / ella | –a | –e | –e |
| nosotros/as | –amos | –emos | –imos |
| ustedes / ellos /as | –an | –en | –en |

## VOCABULARIO:

**Los colores** *(The colors)*

**rojo:** *red*
**anaranjado:** *orange*
**blanco:** *white*
**rosa:** *pink*
**azul marino:** *navy blue*

**azul:** *blue*
**verde:** *green*
**negro:** *black*
**purple:** *morado*
**verde claro\*:** *light green*

**amarillo:** *yellow*
**marrón:** *brown*
**gris:** *gray*
**celeste:** *sky blue*
**verde oscuro\*:** *dark green*

(\*) You can use "claro" (*light*) and "oscuro" (*dark*) to indicate the shades of a color.

El sofá es **gris claro.**        The couch is **light grey**.

## Remember!

The colors are adjectives and have to agree with the noun that they modify in gender and number.

Llevo puesta una camisa **blanca** y **verde**.     *I'm wearing a white and green shirt.*
Ellos todavía tienen el auto **negro**.     *They still have the black car.*
Esas flores son **rojas**, **amarillas** y **blancas**.     *Those flowers are red, yellow and white.*

**In this unit we will learn:**
. Time markers of the present tense.
. The days of the week (I).
. Vocabulary: Jobs and occupations.
. To ask and answer about jobs and occupations.

## Unit
# 15
**Days 29 & 30**

**Diálogo / Dialog**

Santiago se ha mudado a otro barrio y se presenta a Margarita, una vecina.

*Santiago has moved to a new neighborhood and introduces himself to his neighbor Margarita.*

S: ¡Hola! Me llamo Santiago. Soy el nuevo vecino. Vivo en la puerta de al lado.

M: ¡Hola, Santiago! Encantada de conocerle. Yo soy Margarita. Tiene un acento diferente. ¿De dónde es usted?

S: Soy peruano, de Lima.

M: ¿**Quiere** pasar?

S: Gracias, pero sólo **quiero** hacerle una pregunta. La puerta de mi cocina no **cierra** y el **grifo** pierde agua. ¿Podría recomendarme algún **fontanero**? Soy nuevo en este barrio y no conozco a nadie.

M: **Pienso** que otro vecino **puede** ayudarle. Él es **albañil**, pero no está en casa **en este momento**. Hoy es **miércoles** y él no **vuelve** hasta el **viernes** por la noche. No **recuerdo** dónde está ahora, pero tengo su número de teléfono. Es el 332-150-160.

S: Bueno, después **puedo** llamarlo. **Ahora** es hora de comer. Yo siempre **almuerzo** pronto y luego **duermo** la siesta. Más tarde hablaré con él. Muchas gracias.

M: No hay de qué. Recuerde que **puede** verlo el **sábado** o el **domingo**. Por cierto, ¿a qué se dedica usted aquí?

S: Soy **futbolista**. Juego en el equipo local.

M: ¡Oh! ¡Qué interesante!

S: *Hello! My name is Santiago. I am the new neighbor. I live next door.*

M: *Hello, Santiago! Pleased to meet you. I am Margarita. You have a different accent. Where are you from?*

S: *I am Peruvian, from Lima.*

M: *Do you want to come in?*

S: *Thank you but I only want to ask you a question. My kitchen door doesn't close and the faucet leaks water. Could you recommend a plumber? I am new in this neighborhood and I don't know anyone.*

M: *I think that another neighbor can help you. He is a bricklayer, but he is not at home at the moment. Today is Wednesday and he won't be back until Friday evening. I don't remember where he is now but I have his telephone number. It is 332-150-160.*

S: *Well, I can call him later. Now it's time to have lunch. I always have lunch early and then I have a siesta. I'll talk to him later. Thank you very much.*

M: *Don't mention it. Remember that you can see him on Saturday or Sunday. By the way, what do you do?*

S: *I am a soccer player. I play for the local team.*

M: *Oh! How interesting!*

## TIME MARKERS OF THE PRESENT TENSE

Time markers are those words or expressions that are used to show the time when the action takes place (adverbs of time). For the present tense, some of them are:

| | | | |
|---|---|---|---|
| **ahora** | now | **en este momento** | in this moment, at present |
| **hoy** | today | **siempre** | always |
| **esta semana** | this week | **de vez en cuando** | from time to time |
| **este año** | this year | **todos los días** | everyday |
| **este mes** | this month | | |

And the different parts of the day:

| | |
|---|---|
| **por la mañana** | in the morning |
| **por la tarde** | in the afternoon |
| **por la noche** | in the evening, at night |

If these expressions are used with one day, this day is placed just before them:

| | |
|---|---|
| **mañana** | tomorrow |
| **ayer** | yesterday |
| **lunes** | Monday |

**Mañana por la mañana** veo a Luis.  *I'm meeting Luis tomorrow morning.*
**Los lunes por la tarde** estudiamos español.  *We study Spanish on Monday afternoons.*

All these markers are usually placed at the beginning or end of a sentence:

**Ahora** vivo en Monterrey.  *I'm living in Monterrey now.*
**De vez en cuando** comen paella.  *They eat paella from time to time.*
Escribo correos electrónicos **todos los días.**  *I write emails everyday.*
Ella trabaja en un hospital **por la mañana.**  *She works in a hospital in the morning.*
**Esta semana** no trabajas.  *You are not working this week.*

## LOS DÍAS DE LA SEMANA *(THE DAYS OF THE WEEK)*

| | |
|---|---|
| **lunes** | *Monday* |
| **martes** | *Tuesday* |
| **miércoles** | *Wednesday* |
| **jueves** | *Thursday* |
| **viernes** | *Friday* |
| **sábado** | *Saturday* |
| **domingo** | *Sunday* |

Take note that the days of the week are not capitalized in Spanish.

| | |
|---|---|
| Hoy es **martes.** | *Today is Tuesday.* |
| El partido es el **sábado.** | *The match is on Saturday.* |

We will learn more about the forms and uses of the days of the week in unit 36.

## TOP VOCABULARY AND EXPRESSIONS

### Trabajos y ocupaciones *(Jobs and occupations)*

| | | |
|---|---|---|
| **profesor/maestro:** *teacher* | **estudiante:** *student* | **contador:** *accountant* |
| **médico:** *doctor* | **enfermera:** *nurse* | **panadero:** *baker* |
| **arquitecto:** *architect* | **vendedor:** *seller* | **dentista:** *dentist* |
| **albañil:** *bricklayer* | **pintor:** *painter* | **abogado:** *lawyer* |
| **electricista:** *electrician* | **artista:** *artist* | **ama de casa:** *housewife* |
| **conductor de bus:** *bus driver* | **taxista:** *taxi driver* | **futbolista:** *soccer player* |
| **secretario:** *secretary* | **escritor:** *writer* | **periodista:** *journalist* |
| **mecánico:** *mechanic* | **empresario:** *businessman* | **actor/actriz:** *actor/actress* |

Don't forget that these nouns have feminine forms as well (see unit 8).
As we can see, there are many names of jobs that end with "-or/-ora" and "-ista".

To ask about jobs, we can say:

| | |
|---|---|
| **¿Cuál es tu trabajo?** | *What's your job?* |
| **¿Qué haces?** | *What do you do?* |
| **¿A qué te dedicas?** | *What's your job? / What do you do?* |

When we answer, we have to take into account that professions are not preceded by the article "a" when the subject is singular, as it happens in English. We simply use the subject (if necessary), the verb "ser" and the profession.

| | |
|---|---|
| **Soy** empresario. | *I'm a businessman.* |
| **Ellos son** escritores. | *They are writers.* |
| ¿Cuál es su trabajo (de ella)? **Ella es** dentista. | *What's her job? She's a dentist.* |
| ¿A qué se dedica él? **Es** electricista. | *What's his job? He's an electrician .* |

In the last units we have been studying the present simple of regular verbs. Now we will work on irregular verbs and their present simple forms.

## VERBOS IRREGULARES *(IRREGULAR VERBS)*

Irregular verbs also end with "-ar", "-er" or "-ir", but they do not follow the patterns we have studied when they are conjugated. They undergo some changes that may affect either the stem of the verb or the ending (or even both).

### Presente simple de verbos irregulares (I)
*(Present simple of irregular verbs I)*

As the present simple is one of the most irregular tenses, we recommend to study it comparing the conjugation of the three types of verb endings (-ar, -er and –ir), and always remembering the conjugation of regular verbs.

There are some verbs that change a vowel for a diphthong in the verb stem:

**a)** Change of the vowel **"e"** for the diphthong **"ie"**:

Ex: p**e**nsar (*to think*), ent**e**nder (to understand), s**e**ntir (*to feel*).

|  | PENS**AR** | ENTEND**ER** | SENT**IR** |
|---|---|---|---|
| yo | p**ie**nso | ent**ie**ndo | s**ie**nto |
| tú | p**ie**nsas | ent**ie**ndes | s**ie**ntes |
| usted / él / ella | p**ie**nsa | ent**ie**nde | s**ie**nte |
| nosotros/as | pens**amos*** | entend**emos*** | sent**imos*** |
| ustedes / ellos/as | p**ie**nsan | ent**ie**nden | s**ie**nten |

(*) The stem doesn't change when the subject is "nosotros/as".

More examples of verbs that follow this pattern are:

**cerrar** *(to close)*        **comenzar/empezar** *(to start/begin)*        **perder** *(to lose)*

**querer** *(to want/love)*    **recomendar** *(to recommend)*               **preferir** *(to prefer)*

| | |
|---|---|
| ¿Qué p**ie**nsas? | *What do you think?* |
| Ella recom**ie**nda la sopa. | *She recommends the soup.* |
| El curso com**ie**nza en octubre. | *The course begins in October.* |

**b)** Change of the vowel **"o"** for the diphthong **"ue"**:

Ex: rec**o**rdar (*to remember*), v**o**lver (*to come back*), d**o**rmir (*to sleep*).

|  | RECORD**AR** | VOLV**ER** | DORM**IR** |
|---|---|---|---|
| yo | rec**ue**rdo | v**ue**lvo | d**ue**rmo |
| tú | rec**ue**rdas | v**ue**lves | d**ue**rmes |
| usted / él / ella | rec**ue**rda | v**ue**lve | d**ue**rme |
| nosotros/as | record**amos*** | volv**emos*** | dorm**imos*** |
| ustedes / ellos/as | rec**ue**rdan | v**ue**lven | d**ue**rmen |

(*) The stem doesn't change when the subject is "nosotros/as".

More examples are:

**acostar** *(to go to bed)*    **almorzar** *(to have lunch)*    **mostrar** *(to show)*
**costar** *(to cost)*    **contar** *(to count/to tell)*    **soñar** *(to dream)*
**volar** *(to fly)*    **mover** *(to move)*    **doler** *(to hurt/pain)*
**llover** *(to rain)*    **poder** *(can, be able, may)*

Ellos v**ue**lven por la noche.    *They come back in the evening.*
No rec**ue**rdo eso.    *I don't remember that.*
¿Cuánto c**ue**sta este libro?    *How much is this book?*

**c)** Change of the vowel "**u**" for the diphthong "**ue**":

The only example is the verb "jugar" *(to play)*.

|  | JUG**AR** |
|---|---|
| yo | j**ue**go |
| tú | j**ue**gas |
| usted / él / ella | j**ue**gan |
| nosotros/as | jug**amos*** |
| ustedes / ellos/as | j**ue**gan |

(*) The stem doesn't change when the subject is "nosotros/as".

Nosotros j**u**gamos al tenis los fines de semana.    *We play tennis on weekends.*
Él no j**ue**ga al dominó.    *He doesn't play dominoes.*

## In this unit we will learn:
. The present tense of "tener".
. Expressions with the verb "tener".
. The indefinite article.
. Vocabulary: Clothes.
. The verb "llevar puesto".

## Unit
# 16
**Days 31 & 32**

### Diálogo / Dialog

Silvia y Tomás hablan sobre la ropa para una fiesta.

*Silvia and Tomás are talking about clothes for a party.*

| | |
|---|---|
| S: Tengo **una camisa** muy elegante para la fiesta. ¡Mírala! | *S: I have a very elegant shirt for the party. Look at it!.* |
| T: Yo no **tengo ganas de** ir. | *T: I don't feel like going.* |
| S: **Tienes que** ir, Tomás. Es importante para Julia. Ella no tiene muchos amigos en la ciudad. | *S: You have to go, Tomás. It is important for Julia. She doesn't have many friends in the city.* |
| T: Pero ahora **tengo frío** y no me apetece salir. | *T: But I am cold now and I don't feel like going out.* |
| S: ¡Venga, Tomás! | *S: Come on, Tomás!* |
| T: De acuerdo. ¿Qué **ropa** me puedo poner? | *T: Okay, what clothes can I put on?* |
| S: Aquí tienes estos **pantalones** y **un cinturón**. Te puedes poner la **chaqueta** nueva y los **zapatos** negros. | *S: Here are these trousers and a belt. You can put on the new jacket and the black shoes.* |
| T: ¡Uff! Ahora no tengo ganas de cambiarme de **ropa**. [Silvia lo mira desafiante] Está bien, está bien.... ¿Y tú? **¿Qué ropa llevas?** | *T: Uff! I don't feel like changing clothes now. [Silvia looks at him defiantly] Alright, alright.... And you? What clothes are you wearing?* |
| S: Yo llevo **una camisa**, **una falda** azul y **unos zapatos** rojos. | *S: I am wearing a shirt, a blue skirt and red shoes.* |
| T: ¿Quieres tomar algo antes de salir? | *T: Would you like to have something to drink before leaving?* |
| S: No, gracias, no **tengo sed**. Tomás, **tenemos que** darnos prisa. | *S: No, thank you, I am not thirsty. Tomás, we have to hurry up.* |
| T: ¿Vamos en autobús? | *T: Are we going by bus?* |
| S: No, es mejor en taxi. No **tenemos** mucho tiempo. | *S: No, it's better by taxi. We don't have much time.* |
| T: Sí, **tienes razón**. | *T: Yes, you are right.* |

## PRESENTE SIMPLE DEL VERBO "TENER"
### (PRESENT SIMPLE OF THE VERB "TENER")

The verb "tener" (*to have*) is one of the most used verbs in Spanish. It is an irregular verb.

| | |
|---|---|
| yo | ten**go**\* |
| tú | tie**nes** |
| usted / él / ella | tie**ne** |
| nosotros/as | ten**emos**\* |
| ustedes / ellos/as | tie**nen** |

(\*) The stem does not change when the subject is "yo" and "nosotros/as".

It is used to express possession and, in most cases, its equivalent in English is "*to have (got)*".

| | |
|---|---|
| **Tengo** tres amigos en California. | *I have (got) three friends in California.* |
| **¿Tienes** hermanos? | *Do you have any brothers?* |
| Usted no **tiene** auto. | *You don't have a car.* |
| Ella **tiene** dos lámparas en su salón. | *She has two lamps in her living-room.* |
| No **tenemos** trabajo. | *We don't have a job.* |
| ¿Dónde **tienen** ustedes sus boletos? | *Where do you have your tickets?* |
| Ellos **tienen** la nacionalidad americana. | *They have the American nationality.* |

The verb "tener" is also used in the following cases:

### a) To express age:

| | |
|---|---|
| ¿Cuántos años **tienes**? | *How old are you?* |
| **Tengo** diecinueve años. | *I'm nineteen years old.* |

### b) To express sensations:

| | | |
|---|---|---|
| **tener calor** (*to be hot*) | Mi hija tiene calor. | *My daughter is hot.* |
| **tener frío** (*to be cold*) | No tengo frío. | *I am not cold.* |
| **tener hambre** (*to be hungry*) | ¿Tienes hambre? | *Are you hungry?* |
| **tener sed** (*to be thirsty*) | Ellos tienen sed. | *They are thirsty.* |
| **tener suerte** (*to be lucky*) | No tenemos suerte. | *We aren't lucky.* |
| **tener miedo** (*to be afraid*) | ¿Tiene él miedo? | *Is he afraid?* |
| **tener cuidado** (*to be careful*) | No tienes cuidado. | *You aren't careful.* |
| **tener éxito** (*to be successful*) | Madonna tiene éxito. | *Madonna is successful.* |
| **tener prisa** (*to be in a hurry*) | ¿Tienes prisa? | *Are you in a hurry?* |
| **tener razón** (*to be right*) | Ellas tienen razón. | *They are right.* |
| **no tener razón** (*to be wrong*) | Él no tiene razón. | *He is wrong.* |

To express both the age and sensations, we use the verb "tener" in Spanish, whereas in English we use "to be".

### c) To express obligation.
In this case we will have to use "**tener que + infinitive**" (*to have to + infinitive*)

| | |
|---|---|
| **Tenemos que** volver. | *We **have to** come back.* |
| **Tengo que** hablar español. | *I **have to** speak Spanish.* |

### d) When we "feel like" doing something, in Spanish we say "tener ganas de + infinitive".

| | |
|---|---|
| **Tengo ganas de** <u>ver</u> una película. | *I **feel like** <u>watching</u> a film.* |
| Ella no **tiene ganas de** <u>comer</u>. | *She doesn't **feel like** <u>eating</u>.* |

## EL ARTÍCULO INDETERMINADO: UN, UNA, UNOS, UNAS
### [THE INDEFINITE ARTICLE: UN, UNA, UNOS, UNAS, (A, SOME)]

The indefinite article is used when we speak about an object (or a person) that the listener may not identify because we refer to it for the first time or because there are several objects (or people) of the same kind.

The indefinite article has to agree in gender and number with the noun it precedes. Thus, it can be masculine or feminine and singular or plural.

|  | Singular | Plural |
|---|---|---|
| Masculine | **un** (a, an, one) | **unos** (some, a few) |
| Feminine | **una** (a, an, one) | **unas** (some, a few) |

| | |
|---|---|
| Tengo **un** <u>auto</u> rojo. | I have a red car. |
| Necesitamos **una** <u>computadora</u>. | We need a computer. |
| **Unos** <u>amigos</u> vienen de París. | Some friends are coming from Paris. |
| Tienen **unas** <u>casas</u> en Florida. | They have some houses in Florida. |

"Un" has to be used before a feminine singular noun that begins with a stressed "a" or "ha", although it remains feminine in plural:

| | | | | |
|---|---|---|---|---|
| **un** águila | an eagle | **unas** águilas | some eagles |
| **un** hacha | an ax | **unas** hachas | some axes |

These articles can also be used as pronouns, that is, replacing the noun they go with. When the noun is omitted, "un" changes into "uno".

| | |
|---|---|
| Tengo dos libros: **uno** de historia y **uno** de arte. | I have two books: one of history and one of art. |
| (un libro de historia y un libro de arte) | (a history book and an art book) |

The plural forms "unos" and "unas" followed by a number are used to express an approximate quantity. See the difference:

| | |
|---|---|
| Ella tiene **unos vestidos** en el armario. | She has some dresses in the closet. |
| Ella tiene **unos diez vestidos** en el armario. | She has around ten dresses in the closet. |

## TOP VOCABULARY AND EXPRESSIONS

### La ropa *(clothes)*

| | | |
|---|---|---|
| **camisa:** *shirt* | **camiseta:** *T-shirt* | **blusa:** *blouse* |
| **suéter:** *sweater* | **jersey:** *jersey* | **vestido:** *dress* |
| **falda:** *skirt* | **chaqueta:** *jacket* | **traje:** *suit* |
| **abrigo:** *coat* | **sombrero:** *hat* | **gorra:** *cap* |
| **pantalones:** *trousers* | **jeans:** *jeans* | **pantalones cortos:** *shorts* |
| **zapatos:** *shoes* | **botas:** *boots* | **zapatillas deportivas:** *sneakers* |
| **sandalias:** *sandals* | **calcetines:** *socks* | **ropa interior:** *underwear* |
| **pijama:** *pajamas* | **cinturón:** *belt* | **corbata:** *tie* |
| **guantes:** *gloves* | **bufanda:** *scarf* | **llevar puesto:** *to wear* |

**¿Qué llevas puesto?** Llevo (**puestos**)* <u>unos</u> **pantalones,** <u>una</u> **camiseta** y <u>una</u> **camisa.**
*What are you wearing? I'm wearing a pair of trousers, a T-shirt and a shirt.*

**¿Qué lleva puesto** tu madre? Ella **lleva (puesto)*** <u>un</u> **vestido** y <u>una</u> **chaqueta.**
*What is your mother wearing? She's wearing a dress and a jacket.*

(*) Sometimes there is no need to say "puesto", as it is understood.

The word "puesto" agrees in gender and number with the noun it precedes:

| | |
|---|---|
| ¿Quién lleva **puesto** <u>un suéter</u>? | *Who is wearing a sweater?* |
| Él lleva **puesta** <u>una gorra</u>. | *He is wearing a cap.* |
| Yo no llevo **puestos** <u>unos calcetines</u> rojos. | *I am not wearing red socks.* |

The verb "llevar puesto" is not used in the continuous form in Spanish.

## Unit
# 17
**Days 33 & 34**

### In this unit we will learn:
. The present simple of irregular verbs (II).
. Spelling changes to maintain the pronunciation of some verbs.

**Diálogo /** *Dialog*

Ana y Bernardo se encuentran en la calle.

*Ana and Bernardo run into each other in the street.*

A: ¿Dónde **vas**, Bernardo?

B: **Voy** al supermercado. Hoy **vienen** unos amigos a cenar y necesito algunas cosas.

A: ¿Quiénes **van**?

B: Lourdes, Manuel y Santos.

A: ¿Lourdes? ¿La arquitecta?

B: Sí, bueno, ahora ella **dirige** una empresa. **Construyen** puentes.

A: Lo **sé**. La **conozco**. ¿Y qué harás de cena?

B: Ellos siempre me **piden** tortilla de papas y eso es lo que yo les hago.

A: Suena muy bien pero, ¿no es mucho trabajo? ¿No prefieres cenar fuera?

B: No, no es mucho trabajo. A veces **salgo** a cenar, pero prefiero cenar en casa con los amigos.

A: ¿Y **vas** al supermercado a pie?

B: Sí. No **traigo** muchas cosas y nunca **manejo** cuando **voy** allí. Está muy cerca.

A: ¿Cómo? Perdona pero no **oigo** nada con este viento.

B: **Digo** que el supermercado está muy cerca de casa y **voy** andando.

A: Bueno, pues te acompaño. Yo también **voy** en esa dirección.

A: *Where are you going, Bernardo?*

B: *I am going to the supermarket. Today some friends are coming for dinner and I need some things.*

A: *Who is going?*

B: *Lourdes, Manuel and Santos.*

A: *Lourdes? The architect?*

B: *Yes, well, she runs a firm now. They build bridges.*

A: *I know. I know her. And what will you make for dinner?*

B: *They always ask me for a potato omelette and that is what I make for them.*

A: *It sounds very good but, isn't it too much work? Don't you prefer to have dinner out?*

B: *No, it isn't much work. I sometimes have dinner out, but I prefer to have dinner with my friends at home.*

A: *And are you going to the supermarket on foot?*

B: *Yes. I don't bring many things and I never drive when I go there. It is very near.*

A: *What? Sorry but I can't hear anything with this wind.*

B: *I said that the supermarket is very near my house and I go walking.*

A: *Well, I'll go with you. I am also going that way.*

## PRESENTE SIMPLE DE VERBOS IRREGULARES (II)
### (PRESENT SIMPLE OF IRREGULAR VERBS II)

There are some <u>verbs that change the ending of the first person in singular (yo)</u>:

**a)** Ending with "**-oy**".

For the other subjects the verbs are conjugated as regular verbs ending with "-ar".
Ex: dar (*to give*), ir (*to go*).

|                    | DAR   | IR*   |
|--------------------|-------|-------|
| yo                 | doy   | voy   |
| tú                 | das   | vas   |
| usted / él / ella  | da    | va    |
| nosotros/as        | damos | vamos |
| ustedes / ellos/as | dan   | van   |

(*) The verb "ir" is very irregular, and, in present, we will have to use the letter "v" for each person.

Another example that follows this pattern is the verb "estar" (see unit 2).

**Voy** al trabajo en auto.    *I go to work by car.*
No **estoy** contento.    *I am not happy.*

**b)** Ending with "**-go**".

The first person changes, but, for the other subjects, the verbs are conjugated as regular ones ending with "-er" or "-ir".

|                    | HACER    | OÍR*  |
|--------------------|----------|-------|
| yo                 | hago     | oigo  |
| tú                 | haces    | oyes  |
| usted / él / ella  | hace     | oye   |
| nosotros/as        | hacemos  | oímos |
| ustedes / ellos/as | hacen    | oyen  |

(*) The ver "oír" follows the rule for the endings but it undergoes other changes: the use of an "i" in the first person in singular (yo) and a "y" for the second and third persons in singular and plural.

Some other verbs that follow this pattern are:

- **obtener** *(to get)*
- **suponer** *(to suppose)*
- **decir** *(to say/tell)*
- **tener** *(to have)*
- **traer** *(to bring)*
- **salir** *(to go out)*
- **venir** *(to come)*

In some of these verbs we could see other changes, such as a vowel for a diphthong or "e" for "i" in the verb stem.

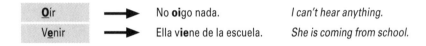

| **O**ír | ➝ | No **oi**go nada. | *I can't hear anything.* |
| **Ve**nir | ➝ | Ella **vie**ne de la escuela. | *She is coming from school.* |

**c)** Ending with "**-zco**".

1) There are many verbs ending with "-acer", "-ecer" and "-ocer", whose first person in singular (yo) ends with "-zco". The others are conjugated with the endings of regular "-er" verbs. Ex: ofrecer *(to offer)*, parecer *(to seem/look/look like)*, conocer *(to know)*.

|  | OFREC**ER** | PAREC**ER** | CONOC**ER** |
|---|---|---|---|
| yo | ofrez**co** | parez**co** | conoz**co** |
| tú | ofrec**es** | parec**es** | conoc**es** |
| usted / él / ella | ofrec**e** | parec**e** | conoc**e** |
| nosotros/as | ofrec**emos** | parec**emos** | conoc**emos** |
| ustedes / ellos/as | ofrec**en** | parec**en** | cono-cen |

Other verbs that follow this pattern are:

- **crecer** *(to grow)*
- **nacer** *(to be born)*
- **obedecer** *(to obey)*
- **desaparecer** *(to disappear)*
- **reconocer** *(to recognize)*

No **conozco** a esa persona.      *I don't know that person.*
Yo **ofrezco** lo que tengo.      *I offer what I have.*

2) If the verb ends with "-ucir", the first person in singular ends with "-zco", but the rest of them are conjugated as a regular "-ir" verb. Ex: producir (*to produce/make*).

| | PRODUCIR |
|---|---|
| yo | produ**zco** |
| tú | produc**es** |
| usted / él / ella | produc**e** |
| nosotros/as | produc**imos** |
| ustedes / ellos/as | produc**en** |

Some more examples of this type of verbs are:

**conducir** *(to drive)*　　**traducir** *(to translate)*　　**reducir** *(to reduce)*

No **traduzco** documentos. **Traduzco** libros.
*I don't translate documents. I translate books.*

## Apart from these verbs, whose main change takes place for the first person in singular, there are some more irregular verbs:

**a)** Verbs ending with "**-uir**".

These verbs are conjugated as regular "-ir" verbs but they add "y" just before the ending, except for "nosotros/as". Ex: construir (*to build*).

| | CONSTRUIR |
|---|---|
| yo | construy**o** |
| tú | construy**es** |
| usted / él / ella | construy**e** |
| nosotros/as | constru**imos** |
| ustedes / ellos/as | construy**en** |

Some more examples of this type of verbs are:

**incluir** *(to include)*　　　　**destruir** *(to destroy)*
**distribuir** *(to distribute)*　　**contribuir** *(to contribute)*

Soy albañil y **construyo** casas.　　*I am a bricklayer and I build houses.*

**b)** Change of the vowel "**e**" for "**i**" in the verb stem.

There are verbs that change an "e" for an "i" in the verb stem, except for the first person in plural (nosotros/as). Ex: pedir (*to ask for*).

|  | PED**IR** |
|---|---|
| yo | pi**d**o |
| tú | pi**des** |
| usted / él / ella | pi**d**e |
| nosotros/as | ped**imos** |
| ustedes / ellos/as | pi**den** |

This also happens with:

| | | |
|---|---|---|
| **decir** (*to say/tell*) | **corregir** (*to correct*) | **elegir** (*to choose*) |
| **reír** (*to laugh*) | **sonreír** (*to smile*) | **repetir** (*to repeat*) |
| **conseguir** (*to get*) | **servir** (*to serve*) | **vestir[se]** (*to get dressed*) |

| | |
|---|---|
| Yo siempre **pido** la factura. | *I always ask for the bill.* |
| Ellos **corrigen** sus errores. | *They correct their mistakes.* |

**c)** Very irregular verbs.

There are some verbs that are very irregular, and, when they are conjugated, there are changes in the verb stem and endings. Clear examples are the verb "ser" (see unit 4), or the verb "ir" (*to go*) (see at the beginning of this unit). Another one is the verb "haber" (*to have*), which is the auxiliary verb to make the perfect tenses.

|  | HAB**ER** |
|---|---|
| yo | he |
| tú | has |
| usted / él / ella | ha |
| nosotros/as | hemos |
| ustedes / ellos/as | han |

In addition to these irregular verbs, there are some others that undergo some **spelling changes to maintain the pronunciation of the verb**. In most cases, these changes affect the first person in singular (yo). The most common changes are:

**a) g ⟶ j**

There are some verbs that change the "g" into "j".
Ex: **dirigir** (*to lead/direct*).

| yo **dirijo** | ~~yo dirigo~~ |
|---|---|

The "g" is maintained for the rest of the subjects: diriges, dirige, dirigimos, dirigen.
More examples: **elegir/escoger** (*to choose*), **proteger** (*to protect*), **recoger** (*to pick up*), **coger** (*to take/catch*).

**b) c ⟶ z**

Other verbs change the "c" into "z".
Ex: **vencer** (*to win*).

| yo **venzo** | ~~yo venco~~ |
|---|---|

Another example: **convencer** (*to convince/persuade*).

**c) gu ⟶ g**

To preserve the original pronunciation of the verb, some verbs change "gu" into "g" in the first person (yo).
Ex: **seguir** (*to go on/continue*).

| yo **sigo** | ~~yo siguo~~ |
|---|---|

Other verbs that follow this pattern are: **perseguir** [*to pursue/chase (after)*], **distinguir** (*to distinguish/discern*).

**Remember!**

This little guide of irregular verbs will help you notice the changes that many verbs undergo in the present tense....but there are many others that are regular, so don't get discouraged and have fun with verbs in Spanish!

## Unit
# 18
**Days 35 & 36**

**In this unit we will learn:**
. The present simple of "poder".
. "Poder" versus "can".
. The verbs "saber" and "conocer".
. También (*also/too*) and tampoco (*neither/not...either*)
. Cardinal numbers (20-99).

**Diálogo / Dialog**

Mario e Isabel hablan sobre un viaje a Madrid.

*Mario and Isabel are talking about a trip to Madrid.*

M: Pronto voy a Madrid. Quiero ver muchas cosas allí.
I: ¿**Conoces** la ciudad?
M: No, no la **conozco**.
I: ¿Y tienes alguna guía?
M: No, no tengo, pero **puedo** conseguir información en internet.
I: ¿Vas solo?
M: No, mis hijos vienen conmigo. Bueno, Luisa viene y Víctor, **también**, pero María no **puede** venir.
I: ¿Y tu esposa?
M: Ella no **puede** venir **tampoco**. No toma vacaciones. Y tú, Isabel, ¿**conoces** Madrid?
I: Sí, es una ciudad bonita, con muchos museos y una interesante vida nocturna. ¿Cuánto tiempo van a estar allí?
M: **Podemos** ir **veinticinco** o **treinta** días. Así veo **también** a mis hermanos y primos, que viven en España.
I: ¿Y cuándo van ustedes para allá?
M: No lo **sé**. En verano, pero no **sé** exactamente la fecha. ¿Quieres venir con nosotros **también**?
I: Muchas gracias. **Sé** que disfrutarán mucho, pero **tampoco puedo** ir. Yo me voy a Argentina en verano.

M: *I am going to Madrid soon. There are a lot of things I want to see there.*
I: *Do you know the city?*
M: *No, I don't know it.*
I: *And do you have a guide?*
M: *No, I don't have one, but I can get some information off the internet.*
I: *Are you going alone?*
M: *No, my children are coming with me. Well, Luisa is coming and so is Víctor, but María cannot come.*
I: *And your wife?*
M: *She can't come, either. She doesn't take vacation. And you, Isabel, do you know Madrid?*
I: *Yes, it is a nice city, with many museums and an interesting nightlife. How long are you going to be there?*
M: *We can go for twenty-five or thirty days. Then I can also see my brothers and cousins, who live in Spain.*
I: *And when are you going there?*
M: *I don't know. In summer, but I don't know the date exactly. Would you also like to come with us?*
I: *Thank you very much. I know you will enjoy it a lot, but I can't go either. I am going to Argentina in the summer.*

In this unit we will deal with some verbs that are very common in Spanish. One of them is "poder" (*can, be able, may*).

## PRESENTE SIMPLE DEL VERBO "PODER"
### *(PRESENT SIMPLE OF THE VERB "PODER")*

|  | PODER |
|---|---|
| yo | **puedo** |
| tú | **puedes** |
| usted / él / ella | **puede** |
| nosotros/as | **podemos** |
| ustedes / ellos/as | **pueden** |

## The verb "poder" is almost always followed by an infinitive and is used:

**a) To express ability:**
**Puedo** resolver este problema. — *I can solve this problem.*

**b) To show options:**
Mañana **puedes** ir al teatro o al cine. — *Tomorrow you can go to the theater or to the movies.*

**c) To express permission and prohibition:**
Ella **puede** llegar tarde. — *She can be late.*
Ellos no **pueden** fumar aquí. — *They can't smoke here.*

**d) To express future possibility:**
**Puede** que llueva mañana. — *It may rain tomorrow.*

**e) To ask for information or a favor:**
¿**Puede** usted decirme la hora? — *Can you tell me the time?*
¿**Pueden** ayudarme? — *Can you help me?*

**f) In questions, to know if we can do something or not:**
¿**Puedo** pasar? — *May I come in?*
¿**Podemos** venir mañana? — *Can we come tomorrow?*

The verb "poder" is, in some cases, equivalent to "*can*", but "*can*" is also used to mean "*to know how to*". In this situation we use "**saber**" in Spanish.

## EL VERBO "SABER" EN PRESENTE *(THE VERB "SABER" IN PRESENT)*.

|  | SABER |
|---|---|
| yo | **sé** |
| tú | **sabes** |
| usted / él / ella | **sabe** |
| nosotros/as | **sabemos** |
| ustedes / ellos/as | **saben** |

"Saber" is used when we mean "to know" (*to have knowledge*):

| No **sé** la respuesta. | *I don't know the answer.* |
|---|---|
| ¿**Sabe** él mi dirección? | *Does he know my address?* |
| ¿Qué **sabes** de mi país? | *What do you know about my country?* |

And "to know how to do something" (*can*). In this latter case, the verb "saber" precedes an infinitive.

| Ellos **saben** hablar inglés. | *They can speak English.* |
|---|---|
| No **sabemos** nadar. | *We can't swim.* |
| Él **sabe** jugar al tenis. | *He can play tennis.* |

The verbs **"saber"** and **"conocer"** are synonyms, although there are some differences between them.

Both mean "to have knowledge", but, "conocer" is also used to mean "to know", or "to be acquainted with". When it is followed by a person we have to use the preposition "a" in between.

| **Conozco** <u>a</u> tu padre. | *I know your father.* |
|---|---|
| El taxista **conoce** la ciudad. | *The taxi driver knows the city.* |

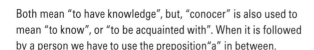

## TAMBIÉN Y TAMPOCO *("ALSO/TOO" AND "NEITHER/NOT...EITHER")*

Both adverbs are used to show agreement with something just said. If the sentence is affirmative, we show agreement with "**también**" *(also/too)* and, if it is negative, with "**tampoco**" *(neither/not...either)*.

| | |
|---|---|
| - Vivo en Los Ángeles. | – *I live in Los Angeles.* |
| - Yo **también** (vivo en Los Ángeles). | – *Me, too. (I also live in Los Angeles).* |
| | |
| - Ella no tiene hambre. | – *She isn't hungry.* |
| - Yo **tampoco** (tengo hambre). | – *Neither am I. (I am not hungry, either).* |

As we have just seen, both expressions can be part of a small structure (Yo también) or a longer one (Yo también vivo en Los Ángeles).

The Spanish language is very flexible and, sometimes, the position of an element is not relevant to the meaning of the sentence. This also happens with "también" and "tampoco". Keep in mind:

**a) "También" can go before the verb or at the end of the sentence:**

| | |
|---|---|
| **También** tengo un auto azul. | *I also have a blue car.* |
| Tengo un auto azul, **también**. | *I have a blue car, too.* |

In short sentences, we only use the subject and "también".

| | |
|---|---|
| Ella sabe la respuesta. **Yo, también**. | *She knows the answer. Me, too.* |

**b) "Tampoco" can precede the verb, but the sentence has to be affirmative:**

| | |
|---|---|
| **Tampoco** estudiamos italiano. | *We don't study Italian, either.* |

It can also be placed at the end of the sentence, but, in this case, the verb has to be negative:

| | |
|---|---|
| No estudiamos italiano **tampoco**. | *We don't study Italian, either.* |

In short sentences, we only use the subject and "tampoco".

| | |
|---|---|
| Usted no sabe manejar camiones. **Yo, tampoco**. | *You can't drive trucks. Me, neither.* |

# SPANISH IN 100 DAYS

## NÚMEROS CARDINALES 20-99 *(CARDINAL NUMBERS 20-99)*

Up to number 30, all numbers are made up of one word.
To say these numbers, the final **"e"** of **"veinte"** changes into **"i"** and we add the numbers from **"uno"** to **"nueve"**.

| | |
|---|---|
| 20 – veinte | 26 – veintiséis |
| 21 – veintiuno/a | 27 – veintisiete |
| 22 – veintidós | 28 – veintiocho |
| 23 – veintitrés | 29 – veintinueve |
| 24 – veinticuatro | 30 – treinta |
| 25 – veinticinco | |

From 31 to 99, all numbers are written in two words (except for the tens), linked by "y".

| | | | |
|---|---|---|---|
| | | | uno/a |
| **30** | treinta | | dos |
| **40** | cuarenta | | tres |
| **50** | cincuenta | | cuatro |
| **60** | sesenta | y | cinco |
| **70** | setenta | | seis |
| **80** | ochenta | | siete |
| **90** | noventa | | ocho |
| | | | nueve |

| | | |
|---|---|---|
| **48: cuarenta y ocho** | **29: veintinueve** | **66: sesenta y seis** |
| **39: treinta y nueve** | **87: ochenta y siete** | **51: cincuenta y uno/a** |

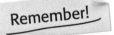
Remember!

When numbers end with "uno/una", they have to agree in gender with the noun they go with. "Uno" becomes "un" before the noun.

Tengo **treinta y un** <u>años</u>.          *I am thirty-one years old.*
Hay **veintiuna** <u>niñas</u> en la clase.          *There are twenty-one girls in the classroom.*

## In this unit we will learn:
. The verb "hacer".

. Expressions with "hacer".

. Vocabulary: The weather.

. Differences among "bueno", "malo", "bien" and "mal".

## Unit
# 19
**Days 37 & 38**

**Diálogo** / *Dialog*

Emilio vuelve a casa y ve a Raquel en la cocina.

*Emilio returns home and sees Raquel in the kitchen.*

E: ¿Qué **haces**?

R: **Hago** la comida: sopa de cebolla y pollo frito. Espero que estén **buenos**.

E: ¡Estupendo! Tengo mucha hambre. **Hace** mucho tiempo que no como sopa de cebolla. Es un buen menú para hoy porque **hace frío**. ¡Brrr!

R: ¿Sí? ¿**Qué tiempo hace**?

E: **Está nublado** y **hace viento**. Es un **mal** día para estar en la calle.

R: ¿Y cuál es el **pronóstico del tiempo** para mañana?

E: Mañana **hará sol** y **buen tiempo**.

R: Eso espero. Quiero ir a ver a mi madre. Por cierto, ¿has visto a Ricardo?

E: Sí.

R: ¿Cómo está? **Hace** semanas que no lo veo.

E: **Está bien**, pero un poco enojado hoy.

R: ¿Qué **hace** ahora? ¿Por qué está enojado?

E: Es conductor de camiones y trabaja mucho. Hoy está enojado porque se le ha averiado el camión y ha perdido el celular.

R: Bueno, todos tenemos días **buenos** y días **malos**.

---

E: *What are you doing?*

R: *I am cooking dinner: onion soup and fried chicken. I hope they are good.*

E: *Great! I am very hungry. I haven't had onion soup for a long time. It's a good menu for today because it is cold. Brrr!*

R: *Is it? What's the weather like?*

E: *It is cloudy and windy. It is a bad day to be in the street.*

R: *And what is the weather forecast for tomorrow?*

E: *It'll be sunny and nice weather tomorrow.*

R: *I hope so. I want to see my mother. By the way, have you seen Ricardo?*

E: *Yes.*

R: *How is he? I haven't seen him for weeks.*

E: *He is fine, but a bit annoyed today.*

R: *What does he do now? Why is he annoyed?*

E: *He is a truck driver and works a lot. Today he is annoyed because his truck is broken-down and he has lost his cell phone.*

R: *Well, we all have good days and bad days.*

## EL VERBO "HACER" *(THE VERB "HACER")*

The verb "hacer" is also widely used in Spanish. It is equivalent to the verbs "to do" and "to make" (as well as some others) in English.

As we learned in unit 17, it is an irregular verb. In present, it is conjugated with a change in the first person in singular (yo).

|  | HACER |
|---|---|
| yo | ha**go** |
| tú | hac**es** |
| usted / él / ella | hac**e** |
| nosotros/as | hac**emos** |
| ustedes / ellos/as | hac**en** |

| Yo **hago** mi cama. | *I make my bed.* |
|---|---|
| ¿Qué **haces**? | *What are you doing? What are you making?* |

"**Hacer**"is used in a wide range of expressions that are used in daily conversations. In context, it can refer to almost any activity.

The verb "hacer" seldom stands alone. It is almost always followed by a noun: **hacer** <u>la comida</u> (*to make the meal*), **hacer** <u>la limpieza</u> (*to do the cleaning*), **hacer** <u>un favor</u> (*to do a favor*), **hacer** <u>una película</u> (*to make a film*), etc.

| Nosotros **hacemos** páginas web. | *We make web pages.* |
|---|---|
| Ellos **hacen** preguntas y yo contesto. | *They ask questions and I answer.* |
| ¿Dónde **hacen** ustedes la fiesta? | *Where will you have the party?* |

## EXPRESIONES CON EL VERBO "HACER"
### (EXPRESSIONS WITH THE VERB "HACER")

a) **In weather terminology. Typically, weather terms use the third person in singular (hace) followed by a noun:**

| | |
|---|---|
| **Hace** <u>calor</u>. | *It is hot.* |
| **Hace** <u>frío</u>. | *It is cold.* |
| **Hace** <u>viento</u>. | *It is windy.* |
| **Hace** <u>sol</u>. | *It is sunny.* |

b) **In time expressions. "Hace" is followed by a period of time:**

- to indicate how long ago something happened:

Ella vivió en EEUU **hace** <u>dos años</u>.      *She lived in the USA two years ago.*

- to indicate how long ago an action or situation began. In this case we use the present tense (the present perfect continuous in English), the expression "**desde hace**" and a period of time.

Estudio español **desde hace** <u>un mes</u>.      *I've been studying Spanish for a month.*
Él juega al béisbol **desde hace** <u>dos años</u>.      *He has been playing baseball for two years.*

We can also say:
**Hace** <u>un mes</u> **que** estudio español.      *I've been studying Spanish for a month.*
**Hace** <u>dos años</u> **que** él juega al béisbol.      *He has been playing baseball for two years.*

So we see that if we invert the order of the elements, "desde" is omitted and the relative "que" is placed after the period of time.

The verb "hacer" is also used in many other cases and idiomatic expressions, some of which will be studied further on.

## TOP VOCABULARY AND EXPRESSIONS

### El tiempo *(the weather)*

**sol:** *sun*
**soleado:** *sunny*
**lluvia:** *rain*
**lluvioso:** *rainy*
**llover:** *to rain*
**niebla:** *fog*

**nieve:** *snow*
**nevar:** *to snow*
**tormenta:** *storm*
**relámpago:** *lightning*
**trueno:** *thunder*

**nube:** *cloud*
**nublado:** *cloudy*
**viento:** *wind*
**brisa:** *breeze*
**huracán:** *hurricane*

**pronóstico (previsión) del tiempo:** *weather forecast*

**Está soleado = Hace sol:** *It is sunny*
**Está nublado:** *It is cloudy*
**Está lluvioso:** *It is rainy*
**Hay niebla:** *It is foggy*
**Hay tormenta:** *It is stormy*
**Hace buen tiempo:** *It's good weather*

**Hace calor:** *It is hot*
**Hace frío:** *It is cold*
**Está templado:** *It is warm*
**Hace fresco:** *It is cool*
**Hace viento:** *It is windy*
**Hace mal tiempo:** *It's bad weather*

We can see that some idioms are expressed with "está....", "hay....." or "hace.....".
There are no rules to form these expressions, so we'll have to memorize them.

> Hoy **hace calor** y **está nublado.**   *Today it is hot and cloudy.*
> **Hace frío** y **hay tormenta.**   *It is cold and stormy.*
> El **pronóstico del tiempo** es terrible.   *The weather forecast is terrible.*

In some of the latter expressions we find the adjectives "buen" and "mal". Let's look at them together now, as they can be confusing.

## USO DE "BUENO", "BUEN", "BIEN", "MALO" Y "MAL"
### (USE OF "GOOD", "WELL", "BAD" AND "BADLY")

**Bueno** (*good*) and **malo** (*bad*) are adjectives. It means that they modify the nouns they go with.

In Spanish, the usual position of adjectives is after the noun, but sometimes they can go before it. "Bueno" and "malo" always follow the noun. If they precede it, they have to change into "buen" and "mal", respectively. This only happens with singular masculine nouns.

| | |
|---|---|
| El <u>tiempo</u> es **bueno.** | *The weather is fine.* |
| Hace **buen** <u>tiempo.</u> | *It's good weather.* |
| | |
| Es un <u>auto</u> **bueno.** | *It's a good car.* |
| Es un **buen** <u>auto.</u> | *It's a good car.* |
| | |
| Tengo un <u>día</u> **malo.** | *I have a bad day.* |
| Tengo un **mal** <u>día.</u> | *I have a bad day.* |

Adjectives have to agree with the noun in gender and number. Thus we have "bueno", "buena", "malo" and "mala" in singular and "buenos", "buenas", "malos" and "malas" in plural.

| | |
|---|---|
| Es una <u>oportunidad</u> **buena.** | *It's a good oportunity.* |
| Es una **buena** <u>oportunidad.</u> | *It's a good oportunity.* |
| | |
| Los <u>niños</u> son **buenos.** | *The children behave well.* |
| Son **buenos** <u>niños.</u> | *They are good children.* |
| | |
| Ella es una <u>persona</u> **mala.** | *She is a bad person.* |
| Ella es una **mala** <u>persona.</u> | *She is a bad person.* |

The meaning of each pair of sentences (with the adjective before and after the noun) is similar, but, with other adjectives, the meaning of the sentences may be different.

In unit 22 we will study adjectives in depth and review this further.

Another important point to take into account is that the meaning of the sentence changes if these adjectives follow the verb "ser" or "estar":

| | |
|---|---|
| **Él es bueno.** | *He is a good person.* |
| **Él está bueno.** | *He is healthy (he has gotten over an illness).* |
| **Ellos son malos.** | *They are bad people.* |
| **Ellos están malos.** | *They are sick./ They are unpleasant. (things)* |

The adjectives "**bueno**" (*good*) and "**malo**" (*bad*) can be mistaken for the adverbs "**bien**" (*well*) and "**mal**" (*badly*).

"**Bien**" is equivalent to: *fine, okay, alright, excellently, appropriately, in a good manner....*

These adverbs may be the answer to the question "*How...?*" and have no masculine, feminine, singular or plural forms. They are invariable.

## DIFFERENCES BETWEEN "BUENO" AND "BIEN", "MALO" AND "MAL"

**a)** Adverbs ("bien", "mal") do not have a noun close to them.

**b)** "Bueno" and "malo" can be placed after the verbs "ser" and "estar", but "bien" and "mal" can't follow the verb "ser".

| | |
|---|---|
| Mi madre **está bien**. | *My mother is fine.* |
| ~~Mi madre es bien.~~ | |

<table>
<tr><td>

**In this unit we will learn:**
. Reflexive verbs.
. Adverbs of frequency. How often?
. The verb "soler".
. Vocabulary: Routines.
. How to express habitual actions.

</td><td>

**Unit**

# 20

**Days 39 & 40**

</td></tr>
</table>

### Diálogo / Dialog

Juan y Dolores hablan sobre sus hábitos.

*Juan and Dolores are talking about their routines.*

D: ¿Qué **sueles** hacer por la mañana, Juan?
J: **Suelo despertarme** temprano, **me levanto, me ducho, desayuno,** **me visto** y **me voy** al trabajo. ¿Y tú? ¿Qué **sueles** hacer?
D: Yo **siempre me levanto** tarde porque trabajo por las noches. **Me lavo** la cara y **desayuno. Suelo desayunar** café con leche y tostadas.
J: Yo **nunca** tomo café. **Me pongo** nervioso.
D: Y cuando terminas de trabajar, ¿qué haces?
J: **Me voy** al gimnasio con un amigo y hacemos ejercicio. **Nos cansamos** un poco pero luego **nos sentimos** mejor.
D: Yo voy al gimnasio **dos o tres veces a la semana,** pero **normalmente** voy por la mañana o después de **almorzar.**
J: Después **suelo irme** a casa, **me quito** la ropa, **me pongo** el pijama, **ceno, veo la televisión** y **me voy a la cama.** Ese es un día típico en mi vida.
D: Por la tarde yo ordeno el apartamento, voy al supermercado, paseo durante un rato o voy a ver a los amigos. Y **siempre me voy** al hospital antes de las 8. Empiezo a trabajar a las 8:30.
J: ¿Y cómo vas al hospital?
D: **A veces** voy en autobús, pero, si tengo prisa, **manejo** mi auto.
J: Yo **nunca manejo.** No me gusta.
D: Bueno, Juan, ahora **me voy** a ver a Luisa. ¿**Te acuerdas** de ella?

D: *What do you usually do in the morning, Juan?*
J: *I usually wake up early, I get up, take a shower, have breakfast, get dressed and go to work. And you? What do you usually do?*
D: *I always get up late because I work at night. Then I wash my face and have breakfast. I usually have coffee with milk and toast for breakfast.*
J: *I never have coffee. I get nervous.*
D: *And when you finish work, what do you do?*
J: *I go to the gym with a friend and we exercise. We get a little tired but we feel better later.*
D: *I go to the gym two or three times a week, but I usually go in the morning or after lunch.*
J: *Then I usually go home, take off my clothes, put on my pajamas, have supper, watch television and go to bed. That is a typical day in my life.*
D: *In the afternoon I straighten up the apartment, go to the supermarket, walk for a while or see my friends. And I always go to the hospital before 8:00. I start work at 8:30.*
J: *And how do you get to the hospital?*
D: *I sometimes go by bus but, if I am in a hurry, I drive my car.*
J: *I never drive. I don't like it.*
D: *Well, Juan, I am seeing Luisa now. Do you remember her?*

## VERBOS REFLEXIVOS *(REFLEXIVE VERBS)*

Reflexive verbs are those that indicate an action in which the subject (*doer*) and object (*receiver*) are the same person.

| | |
|---|---|
| Yo **me lavo.** | *I wash myself.* |

A reflexive verb needs reflexive pronouns to be expressed.

## Reflexive pronouns:

| | | |
|---|---|---|
| yo | **me** | myself |
| tú | **te** | yourself |
| usted / él / ella | **se** | yourself (usted), himself, herself, itself |
| nosotros/as | **nos** | ourselves |
| ustedes / ellos/as | **se** | yourselves (ustedes), themselves |

In Spain, the reflexive pronoun for the second person in plural (vosotros/as) is "**os**".

Take note that, unlike in English, reflexive pronouns are placed just before the conjugated verb in Spanish.

| | |
|---|---|
| **Me** <u>levanto</u> temprano. | *I get up early.* |
| Ella **se** <u>ducha</u> por la mañana. | *She takes a shower in the morning.* |

A reflexive verb can be identified by the ending "**-se**" (*oneself*) attached to the infinitive: **callar<u>se</u>** (*to shut up*), **poner<u>se</u>** (*to put on clothes*), **vestir<u>se</u>** (*to get dressed*).

Reflexive verbs are conjugated in the same manner as non-reflexive verbs and they can be regular o irregular, but we can't forget to add the reflexive pronoun immediately before the conjugated verb. When we drop the reflexive ending (-se), we will know if the infinitive form ends with "-ar", "-er" or "-ir", and so we will conjugate it.

| | CALL**AR(SE)** | PON**ER(SE)***  | VEST**IR(SE)**** |
|---|---|---|---|
| yo | **me** call**o** | **me** pong**o** | **me** vist**o** |
| tú | **te** call**as** | **te** pon**es** | **te** vist**es** |
| usted / él / ella | **se** call**a** | **se** pon**e** | **se** vist**e** |
| nosotros/as | **nos** call**amos** | **nos** pon**emos** | **nos** vest**imos** |
| ustedes / ellos/as | **se** call**an** | **se** pon**en** | **se** vist**en** |

(*) We already know that the verb "poner" has an irregular form for the first person in singular (yo).

(**) The verb "vestir" changes the "e" into an "i" in the verb stem, except for "nosotros/as".

More examples of reflexive verbs are:

**acordarse:** *to remember*     **quedarse:** *to stay/remain*
**levantarse:** *to get up*     **dormirse:** *to fall asleep*
**cansarse:** *to get tired*     **irse:** *to go away*
**llamarse:** *to be named*     **ducharse:** *to take a shower*
**casarse:** *to get married*     **sentarse:** *to sit down*
**mirarse:** *to look at oneself*     **enojarse:** *to get angry*
**cortarse:** *to cut oneself*     **sentirse:** *to feel*
**preocuparse:** *to worry*     **lavarse:** *to wash oneself*
**despertarse:** *to wake up*     **quitarse (ropa):** *to take off (clothes)*

| | |
|---|---|
| Ella **se mira** en el espejo. | *She looks (is looking) at herself in the mirror.* |
| No **te preocupes**. | *Don't worry.* |
| Ellos no **se enojan**. | *They don't get angry.* |
| ¿Cómo **se llama** tu padre? | *What's your father's name?* |
| **Nos casamos** en marzo. | *We are getting married in March.* |
| **Me quedo** en un hotel. | *I'm staying at a hotel.* |
| Ustedes **se cansan**. | *You get tired.* |

If the reflexive verb is not conjugated (it appears in infinitive or gerund), the reflexive pronoun is usually attached to the infinitive or the gerund.

| | |
|---|---|
| Es un champú para <u>lavar</u>**me** el pelo. | *It's a shampoo to wash my hair.* |
| Ella está <u>vistiéndo</u>**se**. | *She is getting dressed.* |

## ADVERBIOS DE FRECUENCIA *(ADVERBS OF FREQUENCY)*

The adverbs of frequency indicate how often an action or a situation takes place. Obviously they are the answer to the questions "**¿Con qué frecuencia....?**" (*How often...?*) or "**¿Cuántas veces.....?**" (*How many times....?/How often...?*)

The most common ones are:

**siempre:** *always*
**normalmente:** *usually*
**a menudo:** *often*
**a veces, algunas veces:** *sometimes*

**pocas veces, raras veces:** *seldom, rarely*
**de vez en cuando:** *from time to time*
**casi nunca:** *hardly ever*
**nunca, jamás:** *never*

### Remember!

As we know, Spanish is a very flexible language and certain elements can change position with no change in meaning. This happens with the adverbs of frequency. They can be placed in initial, middle and final positions, but, in most cases, they go either at the beginning or the end of the sentence.

| | |
|---|---|
| **¿Con qué frecuencia** vas al cine? | *How often do you go to the movies?* |
| Voy al cine **a menudo**. | *I often go to the movies.* |
| **¿Con qué frecuencia** se levanta él temprano? | *How often does he get up early?* |
| **A veces** se levanta temprano. | *He sometimes get up early.* |
| Su padre (de ella) se enoja **de vez en cuando**. | *Her father gets angry from time to time.* |
| **Siempre** tenemos hambre. | *We are always hungry.* |

We have to pay special attention to "**nunca**" and "**casi nunca**":

**a) If the sentence starts with "nunca" or "casi nunca", the verb is affirmative:**

**Nunca** <u>como</u> carne porque soy vegetariano.  *I never eat meat because I am a vegetarian.*

**b) If "nunca" or "casi nunca" are placed at the end, the verb has to be negative:**

<u>No como</u> carne **casi nunca**.  *I hardly ever eat meat.*

When we use "normalmente" (*usually*) , we can almost always replace it for the verb "**soler**" in Spanish. (See unit 15, present of irregular verbs, section b).

The verb "**soler**" (already conjugated) precedes the main verb in infinitive.

**Ella normalmente va** al trabajo en bus.
**Ella suele ir** al trabajo en bus.  *She usually goes to work by bus.*

Pay attention to the position of the reflexive pronoun if we use a reflexive verb.

**Normalmente (yo) <u>me</u> levanto** a las 7.
**(Yo) Suelo levantar<u>me</u>** a las 7.

*I usually get up at 7.*

Another way to express how often we do things is:

**una vez** *(once)*
**dos veces** *(twice)*
**muchas veces** *(many times)*

**al día / al mes / al año** *(a day / a month / a year)*
**a la semana** *(a week)*

Voy al gimnasio **tres veces a la semana.**
Él se afeita **una vez al día.**
Navegamos por internet **muchas veces al mes.**

*I go to the gym three times a week.*
*He shaves himself once a day.*
*We surf the internet many times a month.*

## TOP VOCABULARY AND EXPRESSIONS

### Hábitos y rutinas *(habits and routines)*

**despertarse:** to wake up
**levantarse:** to get up
**lavarse:** to wash oneself
**desayunar:** to have breakfast
**vestirse:** to get dressed
**ir al trabajo:** to go to work
**manejar, conducir:** to drive
**navegar por internet:** to surf the internet

**almorzar:** to have lunch
**dormir una siesta:** to have a nap/siesta
**ir al cine:** to go to the movies
**hacer ejercicio:** to do exercise
**ver la televisión:** to watch television
**cenar:** to have dinner/supper
**irse a la cama:** to go to bed

Suelo **desayunar** café y tostadas.

*I usually have some coffee and toast for breakfast.*

¿Con qué frecuencia **vas al trabajo** a pie?
Nunca **manejo** mi auto.
¿Cuántas veces **haces ejercicio** a la semana?

*How often do you go to work on foot?*
*I never drive my car.*
*How many times a week do you do exercise?*

## In this unit we will learn:
. Demonstrative adjectives and pronouns.
. The indirect object.
. To express likes or dislikes: the verb "gustar".

# Unit
# 21
**Days 41 & 42**

### Diálogo / Dialog

Cristóbal y Alba están en una floristería.

*Cristóbal and Alba are at the florist's.*

C: **¿Te gustan** esas flores?
A: **¿Éstas** o **aquéllas?**
C: **Ésas** de ahí.
A: Sí, son bonitas, ¿por qué?
C: Hoy es el cumpleaños de Brenda y quiero hacer**le** un regalo.
A: ¡Es verdad! Hoy es 30 de junio. No me acordaba. Bueno, **esas** flores son lindas, pero **le** puedes comprar **esto**, también.
C: **¿Este** jarrón? Mmmm. Prefiero **ése**. ¿No **te gusta?**
A: ¡Oh, sí! **Ése me encanta.** Es muy colorido. Es un buen regalo para Brenda. A ella **le gustan** mucho los colores.
C: **¿Te apetece** acompañarme a su casa? **Le** llevamos el regalo, **le** damos un beso, tomamos algo con ella y nos vamos. Ella tiene que trabajar.
A: Sí, **me gusta** el plan. Bueno, entonces, tú **le** puedes comprar esas flores y yo **le** compro el jarrón. También **le** podemos escribir una nota.
C: Buena idea.
A: [A la florista] ¿Nos envuelve este jarrón y esas flores, por favor? Son un regalo.
C: ¿Y puede darnos también una tarjeta, por favor?

C: *Do you like those flowers?*
A: *These ones or those ones?*
C: *Those ones over there.*
A: *Yes, they are nice, why?*
C: *Today is Brenda's birthday and I want to give her a gift.*
A: *It's true! Today is June 30th. I didn't remember. Well, those flowers are beautiful, but you can also buy this for her.*
C: *This vase? Mmmm. I prefer that one. Don't you like it?*
A: *Oh, yes! I love that one. It's colorful. It's a good present for Brenda. She likes colors a lot.*
C: *Do you feel like going to her house with me? We'll take her the present, give her a kiss, eat something with her and leave. She has to work.*
A: *Yes, I like the plan. Well, then, you can buy those flowers and I'll buy the vase for her. We can also write a note to her.*
C: *It's a good idea.*
A: *[To the florist] Could you wrap up this vase and those flowers, please? They are a gift.*
C: *And could you also give us a card, please?*

## ADJETIVOS Y PRONOMBRES DEMOSTRATIVOS
### (DEMONSTRATIVE ADJECTIVES AND PRONOUNS)

**Demonstrative adjectives** are used to indicate the distance between the speaker(s) and the object(s) they refer to. They are always placed before a noun with which they have to agree in gender and number.

**a) If the distance is short, we will use:**

**Este** + singular masculine noun.
**Esta** + singular feminine noun.
**Estos** + plural masculine noun.
**Estas** + plural feminine noun.

| | |
|---|---|
| **Este** libro. | *This book.* |
| **Esta** casa. | *This house.* |
| **Estos** hombres. | *These men.* |
| **Estas** flores. | *These flowers.* |

**b) If the object is relatively near the speaker:**

**Ese** + singular masculine noun.
**Esa** + singular feminine noun.
**Esos** + plural masculine noun.
**Esas** + plural feminine noun.

| | |
|---|---|
| **Ese** libro. | *That book.* |
| **Esa** casa. | *That house.* |
| **Esos** hombres. | *Those men.* |
| **Esas** flores. | *Those flowers.* |

**c) If the object is far from the speaker (and the listener):**

**Aquel** + singular masculine noun.
**Aquella** + singular feminine noun.
**Aquellos** + plural masculine noun.
**Aquellas** + plural feminine noun.

| | |
|---|---|
| **Aquel** libro. | *That book.* |
| **Aquella** casa. | *That house.* |
| **Aquellos** hombres. | *Those men.* |
| **Aquellas** flores. | *Those flowers.* |

So we can see that *"that"* is equivalent to the singular "ese/esa", "aquel/aquella", and *"those"* is equivalent to the plural "esos/esas", "aquellos/aquellas".

| | |
|---|---|
| **Este** profesor es español. | *This teacher is Spanish.* |
| **Estas** muchachas estudian inglés. | *These girls are studying English.* |
| Vivo en **esa** casa. | *I live in that house.* |
| Tú necesitas **esos** documentos. | *You need those documents.* |
| **Aquel** niño se llama Miguel. | *That boy's name is Miguel.* |
| **Aquellas** naranjas son deliciosas. | *Those oranges are delicious.* |

We can also omit the noun after the demonstrative adjective, but we will have to use demonstrative pronouns instead.

**Demonstrative pronouns** replace both the demonstrative adjective and the noun. Their masculine, feminine, singular and plural forms are exactly the same as those for demonstrative adjectives, but they need a graphic accent to show this difference.

Thus:

| | | | | | |
|---|---|---|---|---|---|
| este libro ➡ **éste** | ese libro ➡ **ése** | aquel libro ➡ **aquél** |
| esta casa ➡ **ésta** | esa casa ➡ **ésa** | aquella casa ➡ **aquélla** |
| estos hombres ➡ **éstos** | esos hombres ➡ **ésos** | aquellos hombres ➡ **aquéllos** |
| estas flores ➡ **éstas** | esas flores ➡ **ésas** | aquellas flores ➡ **aquéllas** |

Esta casa es grande pero **ésa** es pequeña.
*This house is big but that (one) is small.*

Ese diccionario es caro. **Éste** es barato.
*That dictionary is expensive. This one is cheap.*

No quiero esos zapatos. Quiero **aquéllos.**
*I don't want those shoes. I want those ones over there.*

There are also neuter forms that do not change for gender or number: **esto**, **eso** and **aquello**. They are used when we refer to abstract ideas, an unknown object or something non-specific. These pronouns do not have a graphic accent as they can't be mistaken.

| **esto** | (this matter, this thing) |
|---|---|

| ¿Qué es **esto**? | What is this? |
|---|---|

| **eso** | (that matter, that thing) |
|---|---|

| No entiendo **eso**. | I don't understand that. |
|---|---|

| **aquello** | (that matter, that thing) |
|---|---|

| ¿Recuerdas **aquello**? | Do you remember that? |
|---|---|

## EL OBJETO INDIRECTO (THE INDIRECT OBJECT)

The indirect object tells us "to whom" or "for whom" the action is directed.
The indirect objects are:

| SUBJECT PRONOUNS | INDIRECT OBJECT PRONOUNS | |
|---|---|---|
| yo | **me** | me |
| tú | **te** | you |
| usted | **le** | you |
| él | **le** | him, it |
| ella | **le** | her, it |
| nosotros/as | **nos** | us |
| ustedes | **les** | you |
| ellos/as | **les** | them |

These pronouns either precede a conjugated verb or
follow an infinitive or gerund, being attached to them:

Mi hija **me** <u>da</u> su amor.   *My daughter gives me her love.*
Quiero <u>dar</u>**le** un regalo.   *I want to give him a present.*

To emphasize who the receiver of the action is, we sometimes add the preposition "a" and the receiver to the sentence (at the beginning or at the end). The receiver, in this case, can be a name, a noun or a pronoun. If it is a pronoun, we have to use subject pronouns, except for "yo" and "tú", that change into "mí" and "ti", respectively.

> Mi hija **me** da su amor **a mí**.
> Quiero dar**le** un regalo **a él**. (**a Juan, a mi padre**)

Another verb that needs these pronouns is "gustar".

## EL VERBO "GUSTAR" *[THE VERB "GUSTAR"(TO LIKE)]*

The verb "**gustar**" (*to like, to be pleasant to*) is unique in Spanish, as the subject of this verb is not placed before it but after it. What we use before the verb "gustar" is an indirect object, that is, to whom the action is directed.

> **Me** gusta <u>el baloncesto</u>.   *<u>Basketball</u> is pleasant to **me**. (I like basketball).*
> **Nos** gusta <u>la paella</u>.   *<u>The paella</u> is pleasant to **us**. (We like paella).*

| | | |
|---|---|---|
| (a mí) | **me** | el arte |
| (a ti) | **te** | Bárbara |
| (a usted / él / ella) | **le** | gusta → cantar |
| (a nosotros/as) | **nos** | ellos |
| (a ustedes / ellos/as) | **les** | gustan → los perros |

The verb "gustar" is conjugated in singular (gusta) or in plural (gustan) depending on the subject that follows it. The preposition "a" + a noun or pronoun may also be used to clarify or emphasize.

| | |
|---|---|
| (A mí) **Me gusta** el arte. | *I like art.* |
| A ustedes no **les gusta** cantar*. | *You don't like singing.* |
| A mi amiga **le gustan** los perros. | *My friend likes dogs.* |
| (A ti) No **te gustan** ellos. | *You don't like them.* |
| A Juan **le gusta** tocar el piano. | *Juan likes playing the piano.* |

(*) When the verb "gustar" is followed by another verb, this latter one has to be infinitive. (Be careful because in English you generally use a gerund).

If the verb "gustar" is negated, "no" is placed just before the pronoun (me, te, le.....)

| | |
|---|---|
| **No** me gustan los caracoles. | *I don't like snails.* |

Other verbs that follow this pattern are:

**apetecer** *(to feel like)*
**encantar** *(to love/like very much)*

| | |
|---|---|
| ¿**Te apetece** un helado? | *Do you feel like an ice-cream?* |
| **A Luisa le encanta** jugar al tenis. | *Luisa loves playing tennis.* |

<table>
<tr><td>

**In this unit we will learn:**
. To describe people. Adjectives: position and agreement with the noun.
. "Ser" and "estar" + adjective.
. "Parecer" + adjective
. Vocabulary: Adjectives (physical appearance).

</td><td>

Unit

**22**

**Days 43 & 44**

</td></tr>
</table>

### Diálogo / Dialog

Milton y Carmen tienen una charla.

*Milton and Carmen are having a talk.*

| | |
|---|---|
| C: | Milton, y tu hermano...¿Cómo se llama? |
| M: | Andrés. |
| C: | ¿Y cómo es? |
| M: | Es **delgado** y **de estatura media**. Tiene los ojos **marrones** y una **gran** nariz. ¡Ah! Y es **calvo**. |
| C: | Entonces no **te pareces** a él. |
| M: | No no **nos parecemos**. Además, él lleva gafas. |
| C: | ¿Dónde vive? |
| M: | Vive en España. Tiene una novia **española** y, aunque las cosas son **caras** allí, le gusta vivir en ese país. |
| C: | A mí me gusta México. Los mejicanos son muy **simpáticos**. Este verano voy a Cancún en mi auto **nuevo**. |
| M: | ¿Tienes un auto **nuevo**? |
| C: | Sí. Ahora tengo un auto **cómodo** y **rápido**, pero no es muy **grande**. Es **rojo**. |
| M: | Y **caro**, supongo. |
| C: | Bueno, no es **barato**, pero no me compro un auto todos los días. |
| M: | Mi auto es **viejo** pero no tengo dinero para comprar uno **nuevo**. En realidad, no lo uso. |
| C: | Pues puedes vender ese auto y alquilar uno cuando quieras. |
| M: | Mmmm. Esa idea **parece interesante**. |

| | |
|---|---|
| C: | *Milton, and your brother.... What's his name?* |
| M: | *Andrés.* |
| C: | *And what does he look like?* |
| M: | *He is thin and average height. He has brown eyes and a big nose. Ah! And he is bald.* |
| C: | *Then you don't look like him.* |
| M: | *No, we don't look like each other. Furthermore, he wears glasses.* |
| C: | *Where does he live?* |
| M: | *He lives in Spain. He has a Spanish girlfriend and, although things are expensive there, he likes living in that country.* |
| C: | *I like Mexico. Mexican people are very friendly. This summer I am going to Cancun with my new car.* |
| M: | *Do you have a new car?* |
| C: | *Yes. Now I have a comfortable and fast car, but it isn't very big. It's red.* |
| M: | *And expensive, I suppose.* |
| C: | *Well, it is not cheap, but I don't buy a car everyday.* |
| M: | *My car is old but I don't have money to buy a new one. In fact, I don't use it.* |
| C: | *Then you can sell that car and rent one when you want.* |
| M: | *Mmmm. That idea seems interesting.* |

## LOS ADJETIVOS *(ADJECTIVES)*

We use adjectives to describe or identify objects, people, situations, etc.

| | |
|---|---|
| Tengo un auto **rojo**. | *I have a red car.* |
| Ella vive en una casa **grande**. | *She lives in a big house.* |

They are usually placed after the noun they modify and have to agree with it in gender and number.

---

**Adjectives ending in "o" change it for "a" and those ending with "-án", "-ón" or "-dor" add "-a" to show feminine agreement:**

| | |
|---|---|
| Quiero una corbata **roja**. | *I want a red tie.* |
| Rosa es una muchacha **habladora**. | *Rosa is a talkative girl.* |

---

**Most adjectives that end with a consonant or a vowel other than "o" have the same form for masculine and feminine.**

| | |
|---|---|
| Es un hombre **elegante**. | *He is an elegant man.* |
| Es una mujer **elegante**. | *She is an elegant woman.* |
| El ejercicio es **difícil**. | *The exercise is difficult.* |
| Es una situación **difícil**. | *It's a hard (difficult) situation.* |

---

**In plural, adjectives ending with a vowel add "-s" and adjectives ending with a consonant add "-es". Ex: caro/a (*expensive*), azul (*blue*).**

| | |
|---|---|
| Esos libros son **caros**. | *These books are expensive.* |
| Aquellas botas son **caras**. | *Those boots are expensive.* |
| Tenemos los ojos **azules**. | *We have blue eyes.* |

---

**As we already know, feminine adjectives of nationality or origin must agree with the noun, although the masculine form ends with a consonant.**

| | |
|---|---|
| Conozco a unas actrices **españolas**. | *I know some Spanish actresses.* |

When an adjective ending in "z" is made plural, the "z" changes into "c" before the "-es" plural ending.

| | |
|---|---|
| Soy muy **feliz**. | I am very happy. |
| Ellos son muy **felices**. | They are very happy. |

An adjective that describes two or more nouns of different gender is masculine plural.

El muchacho y la muchacha son **altos**.   The boy and the girl are tall.

The usual **position of adjectives in Spanish** is <u>after the noun</u> they modify.

| | |
|---|---|
| Tengo una <u>computadora</u> **japonesa**. | I have a Japanese computer. |
| Mi madre trabaja en | My mother works for an important firm. |
| una <u>empresa</u> **importante**. | |

However, in certain cases adjectives go before the noun. We have to be very careful because this order may affect the meaning.

| | |
|---|---|
| Ella es <u>una cantante</u> **famosa**. | She is a famous singer. |
| Ella es una **famosa** <u>cantante</u>. | |

But:

| | |
|---|---|
| Es <u>un hombre</u> **pobre**. | He is a poor man. |
| Es <u>un</u> **pobre** <u>hombre</u>. | He is an unfortunate man. |

| | |
|---|---|
| Tomás es <u>un amigo</u> **viejo**. | Tomás is an old (elderly) friend. |
| Tomás es <u>un</u> **viejo** <u>amigo</u>. | Tomás is an old (long-time) friend. |

The adjective "grande" (big/large) always follows the noun. When it is placed before a singular noun, it changes into "gran" (but the meaning is also different). In plural, it is always "grandes".

| | |
|---|---|
| Ellos tienen <u>un auto</u> **grande**. | They have a big car. |
| Ellos tienen <u>un</u> **gran** <u>auto</u>. | They have a great car. |
| Ellos tienen <u>autos</u> **grandes**. | They have big cars. |
| Ellos tienen **grandes** <u>autos</u>. | They have great cars. |

## SER / ESTAR + ADJETIVO *(SER / ESTAR + ADJECTIVE)*

In previous units we learned that adjectives that are combined with the verbs "ser" and "estar" can change their meaning.

**The verb "ser" indicates a permanent feature:**

Miguel **es** <u>alegre</u>.      *Miguel is cheerful.*

**The verb "estar" indicates a temporary state:**

Miguel **está** <u>alegre</u>.      *Miguel is happy (now).*

But apart from these cases, there are many adjectives with a different meaning depending on the verb they follow ("ser" or "estar", see unit 10):

**Ser despierto:** *to be wide-awake / sharp*  ≠  **Estar despierto:** *not to be sleeping*
**Ser listo:** *to be clever*  ≠  **Estar listo:** *to be ready*
**Ser nuevo:** *to be brand new*  ≠  **Estar nuevo:** *to look new*
**Ser bueno**  ≠  **Estar bueno** *(see unit 19)*

## PARECER + ADJETIVO *(PARECER + ADJECTIVE)*

The verb "**parecer**" (*to look, to seem*) is often used before adjectives.

**Parece** difícil.      *It seems difficult.*
**Parece** caro.      *It looks expensive.*

When the subject of the verb "parecer" is a person, we are referring to the physical appearance:

**Pareces** cansado.      *You look tired.*
Ella **parece** deprimida.      *She looks depressed.*
Ustedes **parecen** aburridos.      *You look bored.*

**OTROS USOS DEL VERBO "PARECER"** (Other uses of the verb "parecer")

**a)** The verb **"parecer"** can also be conjugated as a reflexive verb **(parecerse)**.
In this case, it means "to look like somebody", "to resemble". In these sentences, you always need the preposition "a" after this verb.

> **Te pareces <u>a</u> tu padre.**          *You look like your father.*

**b)** In the expression **"Parece que...."** (*It seems that....*).

> **Parece que** hace frío.          *It seems that it is cold.*

**c)** When somebody gives their opinion.
In this case it is conjugated as a verb with an indirect object (see unit 21).

> **Me parece que** tienes un problema.          *I think (that) you have a problem.*
> **Nos parece que** es tarde.          *We think (that) it is late.*

---

## TOP VOCABULARY AND EXPRESSIONS

### Adjetivos sobre el aspecto físico *(Adjectives of physical appearance)*

| | | |
|---|---|---|
| **alto:** *tall* | **bajo:** *short* | **de estatura media:** *medium/average height* |
| **delgado:** *thin* | **gordo:** *fat, plump* | **regordete:** *chubby* |
| **moreno:** *dark-haired* | **rubio:** *fair-haired* | **pelirrojo:** *red-haired* |
| **calvo:** *bald* | **esbelto:** *slim* | **fuerte:** *strong* |
| **débil:** *weak* | **hermosa:** *beautiful* | **bonita, linda:** *pretty, good-looking* |
| **joven:** *young* | **viejo:** *old* | **bonito, lindo:** *handsome, good-looking* |

**Other adjectives related to how someone looks are:**

| | | |
|---|---|---|
| **asustado:** *frightened* | **cansado:** *tired* | **aburrido:** *bored* |
| **deprimido:** *depressed* | **triste:** *sad* | |
| **sorprendido:** *surprised* | **contento:** *happy* | |

¿Cómo es ella? Ella es **alta** y **delgada**.
*What does she look like? She is tall and thin.*

Pareces **asustado** y **sorprendido**.
*You look frightened and surprised.*

## Unit

# 23

**Days 45 & 46**

### In this unit we will learn:
. The time: Asking and telling the time.
. "¿Qué hora es?" versus "¿A qué hora es?".
. The verb "venir".
. Vocabulary: Banking.

**Diálogo** / *Dialog*

Lucas se encuentra con Minerva en el banco.

*Lucas runs into Minerva at the bank.*

| | |
|---|---|
| M: | ¡Hola, Lucas! ¿De dónde **vienes**? |
| L: | **Vengo** de mi casa. Ya es tarde. **¿Qué hora es?** |
| M: | Son las dos menos cuarto. |
| L: | ¿Y **a qué hora** cierra este banco? |
| M: | **A las dos en punto.** |
| L: | Sólo quiero **sacar dinero** y recoger una **tarjeta de crédito** nueva. |
| M: | Pero puedes **sacar dinero** en el **cajero automático.** |
| L: | No, no funciona. |
| M: | Yo **vengo** siempre a esta hora porque hay poca gente. |
| L: | Por cierto, esta noche tocas con la orquesta. |
| M: | Sí. |
| L: | **¿A qué hora** es el concierto? |
| M: | **A las ocho y media.** Es aquí mismo. En el auditorio que está junto al banco. |
| L: | Perfecto. Yo acabo de trabajar **a las siete.** Tengo tiempo de llegar a casa, ducharme, vestirme y **venir** aquí. |
| M: | Bueno, yo ya he terminado. **Es hora d**e irme. |
| L: | Muy bien. Pues nos vemos esta noche, entonces. |
| M: | ¡Hasta luego, Lucas! |
| L: | ¡Hasta luego! |

| | |
|---|---|
| M: | *Hello, Lucas! Where are you coming from?* |
| C: | *I'm coming from my house. It is late. What time is it?* |
| M: | *It's a quarter to two.* |
| L: | *And what time does this bank close?* |
| M: | *At two o'clock.* |
| L: | *I only want to withdraw some money and collect a new credit card.* |
| M: | *But you can take out money from the ATM.* |
| L: | *No, it doesn't work.* |
| M: | *I always come at this time because there are few people.* |
| L: | *By the way, tonight you are playing with the orchestra.* |
| M: | *Yes.* |
| L: | *What time is the concert?* |
| M: | *At half past eight. It's just here. At the auditorium that is close to the bank.* |
| L: | *Perfect! I finish work at seven. I have some time to get home, take a shower, get dressed and come here.* |
| M: | *Well, I have already finished. It's time to go.* |
| L: | *Okay, so we'll meet tonight, then.* |
| M: | *See you later, Lucas!* |
| L: | *See you later!* |

## LA HORA: PREGUNTAR Y DECIR LA HORA
### (THE TIME: ASKING AND TELLING THE TIME)

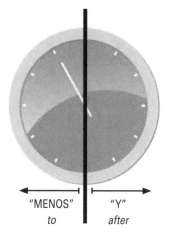

Unlike in English, to tell the time in Spanish we always say the hours first and then the minutes.

The hours are preceded by **"Son las......"*** *(It's.....).*

(*) "Es la ......" *(t's.....)* is used when the hour is "one".

"MENOS"
*to*

"Y"
*after*

After the hour we say "**y**" (*after*) or "**menos**" (*to*), followed by the minutes.

| | | |
|---|---|---|
| **10:05** | Son las diez **y** cinco. | *It's five after ten.* |
| **08:20** | Son las ocho **y** veinte. | *It's twenty after eight.* |
| **01:10** | Es la una **y** diez. | *It's ten after one.* |
| **06:35** | Son las siete **menos** veinticinco. | *It's twenty-five to seven.* |
| **11:50** | Son las doce **menos** diez. | *It's ten to twelve.* |
| **01:40** | Son las dos **menos** veinte. | *It's twenty to two.* |

To say "*o'clock*" we use "**en punto**":

| | | |
|---|---|---|
| **04:00** | Son las cuatro **en punto**. | *It's four o'clock.* |
| **12:00** | Son las doce **en punto**. | *It's twelve o'clock.* |
| **01:00** | Es la una **en punto**. | *It's one o'clock.* |

"**Y media**" is the equivalent to "*half past*" and "**cuarto**" means "*a quarter*":

| | | |
|---|---|---|
| **07:30** | Son las siete **y media**. | *It's half past seven.* |
| **05:45** | Son las seis **menos cuarto**. | *It's a quarter to six.* |
| **03:15** | Son las tres **y cuarto**. | *It's a quarter after three.* |

In order to avoid ambiguity, after telling the time we can add:

**de la mañana**     *in the morning*
**de la tarde**     *in the afternoon*
**de la noche**     *in the evening*

Or simply:

**a.m. :** *am*      **p.m. :** *pm*

Son las diez **de la noche**
Son las diez **p.m.**      *It's ten p.m.*

Son las cinco **de la mañana**
Son las cinco **a.m.**      *It's five a.m.*

To ask the time we say:

**¿Qué hora es?**     *What time is it?*

Colloquially we can also ask:

**¿Qué hora tiene(s)?**     *What time is it? (Literally: What time do you have?)*

– **¿Qué hora es?**     – *What time is it?*
– Son las nueve menos cuarto.     – *It's a quarter to nine.*

And to ask at what time something happens, we say: **¿A qué hora...?** *(At) What time...?*

    **¿A qué hora** es el concierto? *What time is the concert?*

To answer we have to say "**a la(s)**" (*at*) and then the time.

    – ¿A qué hora es la clase de español?     *– What time is the Spanish lesson?*
    – Es **a las** siete y media.     *– It's at half past seven.*

    El programa acaba **a la** una.     *The program ends at one.*

**Mediodía** (*noon*) and **medianoche** (*midnight*) are also words we can use when telling the time, but then the article "la(s)" is omitted.

    – ¿A qué hora almuerzan ustedes?     *– What time do you have lunch?*
    – **A mediodía**.     *– At noon.*

    Vuelvo a casa **a medianoche**.     *I come back home at midnight.*

The word "**hora**" is found in expressions such as:

| | |
|---|---|
| Es **hora** de + infinitive | *It's time to + infinitive* |
| ¡Es la **hora**! | *Time's up!* |
| ¡Ya era **hora**! | *And about time too!* |
| **hora** punta | *rush hour* |

## EL VERBO "VENIR" *(THE VERB "VENIR")*

The verb "**venir**" means "*to come*".

It is an irregular verb that is conjugated the same as the verb "sentir" (see unit 15), but, in present, the first person in singular (yo) is "vengo" (like "tener" – yo tengo).

**"Venir"** is commonly used with some prepositions:

**a) Venir a + noun (*to come to + noun*):**
    **Vengo a** la <u>ciudad</u> todas las semanas.  *I come to the city every week.*
    Ellos nunca **vienen a** mi <u>casa</u>.     *They never come to my house.*

**b) Venir a + infinitive (*to come to + infinitive*):**

¿**Vienes a** <u>comprar</u> el periódico?     *Are you coming to buy the newspaper?*

**c) Venir de + noun (*to come from + noun*):**

¿**Vienen** ustedes **del** <u>cine</u>?     *Are you coming from the movies?*

Mi hermana **viene del** supermercado.     *My sister is coming from the supermarket.*

**d) Venir de + infinitive (*to come from + gerund*):**

Él **viene de** <u>pasear</u> al perro.     *He is coming from walking the dog.*

## TOP VOCABULARY AND EXPRESSIONS

### Los bancos *(Banking)*

**banco:** *bank*
**cheque:** *check*
**saldo:** *balance*
**cheque de viaje:** *traveler's check*
**préstamo:** *loan*
**deuda:** *debt*
**abrir/cerrar una cuenta:** *to open/close an account*
**pagar en efectivo:** *to pay (in) cash*
**ingresar (dinero):** *to pay in, to deposit*

**tarjeta de crédito:** *credit card*
**cambiar dinero:** *to exchange money*
**depósito:** *deposit*
**hipoteca:** *mortgage*
**cuenta corriente:** *checking account*
**cajero automático:** *ATM*
**(en) efectivo:** *(in) cash*
**pagar con cheque:** *to pay by check*
**sacar (dinero):** *to take out, to withdraw*

Tengo una **deuda** por una **hipoteca**.
*I have a debt for a mortgage.*

¿**Paga** usted **en efectivo** o **con cheque**?
*Do you pay in cash or by check?*

Vengo del **banco**.
*I'm coming from the bank.*

¿Quiere ella **abrir una cuenta**?
*Does she want to open an account?*

No usamos nuestra **tarjeta de crédito**.
*We don't use our credit card.*

**In this unit we will learn:**

. The present participle (gerund).

. Uses of the gerund.

. The present progressive. Form and uses.

. "Todavía", "aún" and "ya" ("*still*", "*yet*" and "*already*").

**Diálogo / Dialog**

Matías y Blanca, su esposa, están hablando por teléfono.

*Matías and Blanca, his wife, are talking on the phone.*

| | |
|---|---|
| M: | Son las 7 de la tarde, Blanca. ¿Todavía **estás trabajando**? |
| B: | Sí, **aún estoy trabajando**. ¿Qué haces tú? |
| M: | **Estoy leyendo** el periódico. |
| B: | ¿Hay alguna noticia interesante hoy? ¿Qué **está pasando** en el mundo? Últimamente **estamos viendo** cosas terribles. |
| M: | Pues... Muchas personas **están perdiendo** sus trabajos por la crisis, la temperatura de los mares **está aumentando** y mi equipo de fútbol favorito **sigue ganando**. |
| B: | ¿Y qué hay del puente? ¿**Siguen construyendo** el puente sobre el río? |
| M: | No. **Ya no** lo **están construyendo**. Las obras están detenidas. También **estoy leyendo** que la ballena azul **está desapareciendo**. Y hay un artículo interesante sobre la relajación. |
| B: | ¿La relajación? |
| M: | Sí. Los científicos **están investigando** por qué hay gente que no puede dormir por la noche. |
| B: | Bueno, ¿y los niños? ¿**Están haciendo** sus deberes? |
| M: | Sí, **todavía están estudiando**. |
| B: | Muy bien. Yo acabo pronto y voy para casa. |
| M: | De acuerdo. Yo **sigo leyendo** un rato. En realidad, **ya estoy descansando**. |

*M: It is 7:00 in the evening, Blanca. Are you still working?*

*B: Yes, I am still working. What are you doing?*

*M: I am reading the newspaper.*

*B: Is there any interesting news today? What is happening in the world? We are seeing terrible things lately.*

*M: Err... A lot of people are losing their jobs because of the crisis, the temperature of the oceans is going up and my favorite soccer team keeps on winning.*

*B: And what about the bridge? Are they still building the bridge over the river?*

*M: No. They have stopped building it. The projects have been put on hold. I am also reading that the blue whales are disappearing. And there is an interesting article about relaxation.*

*B: Relaxation?*

*M: Yes. Scientists are investigating why there are some people who can't sleep at night.*

*B: Well, and the children? Are they doing their homework?*

*M: Yes, they are still studying.*

*B: Okay, I'll finish soon and head home.*

*M: Alright. I'll keep reading for a while. In fact, I am relaxing already.*

## EL GERUNDIO *[THE PRESENT PARTICIPLE (GERUND)]*

The Spanish present participle is formed by adding "**-ando**" to the stem of "**-ar**" verbs and "**-iendo**" to the stems of "**-er**" and "**-ir**" verbs.

| hablar ➡ hablando | comer ➡ comiendo | partir ➡ partiendo |
|---|---|---|
| *speak* *speaking* | *eat* *eating* | *split* *splitting* |

## This verb form is invariable.

As we see, the way the gerund is formed in regular verbs is simple, but when the verb is irregular, although the endings are the same as for regular verbs, there are some more changes:

**a) Verbs that change "e" into "i" in the verb stem keep this change in the gerund.**

| decir ➡ diciendo | pedir ➡ pidiendo | repetir ➡ repitiendo |
|---|---|---|
| *say* *saying* | *ask for* *asking for* | *repeat* *repeating* |

**b) Verbs ending in "-ir" with a stem change "e-ie" or "o-ue" in present, show "i" and "u" in the gerund.**

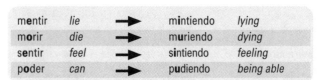

| mentir | *lie* | ➡ | mintiendo | *lying* |
|---|---|---|---|---|
| morir | *die* | ➡ | muriendo | *dying* |
| sentir | *feel* | ➡ | sintiendo | *feeling* |
| poder | *can* | ➡ | pudiendo | *being able* |

**c) If the "i" in the ending "-iendo" is preceded by a vowel, it changes for "y".**

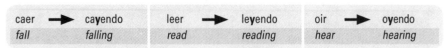

| caer ➡ cayendo | leer ➡ leyendo | oír ➡ oyendo |
|---|---|---|
| *fall* *falling* | *read* *reading* | *hear* *hearing* |

The present participle of the verb "ir" is "**yendo**" (*going*).

**d) Reflexive verbs add the pronoun (me, te, se,...) after the gerund (attached to it), and make necessary a graphic accent upon the "a" or the "e" of the gerund ending.**

| | | | | |
|---|---|---|---|---|
| mirarse | *look at oneself* | ➤ | mirán**dose** | *looking at oneself* |
| levantarse | *get up* | ➤ | levantán**dose** | *getting up* |
| sentirse | *feel* | ➤ | sintién**dose** | *feeling* |

## USOS DEL GERUNDIO
### [USES OF THE PRESENT PARTICIPLE (GERUND)]

**a) The most common use of the present participle is to combine with the verb "estar" (never "ser") to form progressive tenses:**

| | |
|---|---|
| Luis **está comiendo**. | *Luis is eating.* |
| **Estoy repitiendo** el ejercicio. | *I am repeating the exercise.* |
| ¿Qué **estás leyendo**? | *What are you reading?* |

**b) It is also used in the progressive sense with the verbs "ir" (*to go*), "venir" (*to come*), "seguir" (*to keep on*) and "continuar" (*to go on/continue*).**

| | |
|---|---|
| María **viene cantando** una canción. | *María is coming, singing a song.* |
| Ellos **siguen hablando**. | *They keep on talking.* |

**c) The gerund in Spanish cannot be used as a noun or adjective, as it is in English, nor can it be the subject or object of a sentence. In these cases we use the infinitive in Spanish.**

| | |
|---|---|
| Me gusta **cantar**. | *I like **singing**.* |
| **Fumar** es un mal hábito. | ***Smoking** is a bad habit.* |

## PRESENTE PROGRESIVO O CONTINUO
### *(THE PRESENT PROGRESSIVE OR CONTINUOUS)*

The present progressive or continuous is formed by the present of "estar" and the gerund of the main verb, and expresses an ongoing action.

> **Subject + present of "estar" + gerund + (complements)**

**(Yo) Estoy estudiando** español.   *I am studying Spanish.*

Thus, this is the tense that we use when we refer to an action that is taking place at the moment of speaking or near that moment.

Ella **está escribiendo** un correo electrónico.
*She is writing an email.*

**Estoy leyendo** un libro interesante.
*I am reading an interesting book.*

We have to take into account that sometimes we can also use the present simple to mean an action that is happening when we are referring to it.

¿Qué **estás haciendo** ahora?
¿Qué **haces** ahora?   *What are you doing now?*

We don't use the present progressive to express habits or repeated actions, except when you use the adverb "siempre" (*always*).

Juan **siempre** está sonriendo.   *Juan is always smiling.*

With reflexive verbs, the pronoun can be placed either before the verb "estar" or after the gerund (attached to it).

Ella **se** está lavando la cara.
Ella está lavándo**se** la cara.   *She is washing her face.*

This tense is also used when we refer to an action happening recently or lately.

**Últimamente** está lloviendo mucho.   *It has been raining a lot lately.*

## TOP VOCABULARY AND EXPRESSIONS

### "Todavía", "Aún" y "Ya" *(Still, yet and already)*

The adverbs "**todavía**" and "**aún**" both mean "*still/yet*".
They can be placed before or after the verb.

| | |
|---|---|
| **Todavía (aún)** tengo esos documentos. | *I still have those documents.* |
| Está nevando **todavía (aún)**. | *It's still snowing.* |
| Ella no vive **todavía (aún)** en su casa nueva. | *She isn't living in her new house yet.* |
| ¿**Todavía (aún)** sales con él? | *Are you still going out with him?* |

"**Ya**" has several uses, but its most common meanings are "*already*" and "*now*" for affirmative sentences, and "*not anymore/no more*" in negative sentences ("**ya no**"). It is usually placed before the verb.

| | |
|---|---|
| **Ya** tengo el celular nuevo. | *I already have the new cell phone.* |
| **Ya** vuelve la lluvia. | *The rain is back now.* |
| **Ya no** voy al gimnasio. | *I'm not going to the gym anymore.* |
| **Ya no** les gusta bailar. | *They don't like dancing anymore.* |

## Unit
# 25
**Days 49 & 50**

**In this unit we will learn:**
. The impersonal form "hay".
. Indefinite pronouns.
. Prepositions and adverbs of place.
. Vocabulary: Personal items.

**Diálogo / Dialog**

Paula va a la ciudad donde vive su amigo Leonardo.

*Paula has gone to the city where her friend Leonardo lives.*

| | | | |
|---|---|---|---|
| L: | Esta noche **hay** fiestas en algunos bares. | *L:* | *There are parties in a few bars tonight* |
| P: | Sí, lo sé. Es el día del patrón de la ciudad. | *P:* | *Yes, I know. It is the local patron's day.* |
| L: | Como ves, no hay mucha gente en la calle. | *L:* | *As you can see, there aren't many people in the street.* |
| P: | ¿Dónde están **todos**? | *P:* | *Where is everybody?* |
| L: | Ya están en la fiesta del bar que está **entre** el ayuntamiento y la escuela, **enfrente de** la estación, o en el **otro** bar, **cerca del** banco. Son muy famosas. ¿Te apetece ir a **alguna**? | *L:* | *They are already at the party in the bar that is between the town hall and the school, across from the station, or at the other bar, near the bank. They are very famous. Do you feel like going to any of them?* |
| P: | Sí, pero no por mucho tiempo. Estoy un poco cansada. | *P:* | *Yes, but not for long. I am a little tired.* |
| L: | Muy bien. | *L:* | *Okay.* |
| P: | Me llevo la **cámara de fotos**. [No la encuentra] ¿Dónde está mi **cámara**? ¿Y mis **lentes**? ¿Y el **celular**? | *P:* | *I'll take my camera. [She can't find it] Where is my camera? And my glasses? And my cell phone?* |
| L: | **Todo** está **en tu bolso**. ¿No te acuerdas? **Hay** otro **celular en** la mesa. Ése es mío. | *L:* | *Everything is in your purse. Don't you remember? There is another cell phone on the table. That one is mine.* |
| P: | **En** la mesa no hay **nada**. | *P:* | *There is nothing on the table.* |
| L: | Entonces está **en** el dormitorio. Ahora lo busco. Bueno, ¿a qué fiesta prefieres ir? | *L:* | *Then, it is in the bedroom. I'll look for it now. Well, which party do you prefer to go to?* |
| P: | No sé. No conozco ninguna. ¿Cuál recomiendas? | *P:* | *I don't know. I don't know any of them. Which one do you recommend?* |
| L: | Vamos a la calle y lo decidimos allí. | *L:* | *Let's go to the street and we'll decide there.* |
| P: | ¡Perfecto! | *P:* | *Perfect!* |

## LA FORMA IMPERSONAL "HAY" (*THE IMPERSONAL FORM "HAY"*)

"**Hay**" (*there is / there are*) is an impersonal form of the verb "haber". That is why this verb has no subject.
We use it to refer to the existence of something, when we know or suppose that the listener doesn't have this information.
This form is invariable in Spanish, unlike in English, where we find two forms (*there is / there are*).

| | |
|---|---|
| **Hay** <u>un libro</u> en la mesa. | ***There is*** *a book on the table.* |
| **Hay** <u>tres libros</u> en la mesa. | ***There are*** *three books on the table.* |
| ¿Qué **hay** en la caja? | *What is there in the box?* |
| No **hay** estudiantes en la clase. | *There aren't any students in the classroom.* |
| No **hay** leche en el refrigerador. | *There isn't any milk in the fridge.* |

It is very common to find "hay" with indefinite pronouns, which we are now going to study.

## PRONOMBRES INDEFINIDOS (*INDEFINITE PRONOUNS*)

Indefinite pronouns are those pronouns that refer to no particular person or thing.
In Spanish, as in English, most of the words used as indefinite pronouns sometimes function as adjectives or adverbs.
Some of the indefinite pronouns have masculine, feminine, singular and plural forms, so <u>they must agree with the noun they refer to</u>.

The most usual ones are:

| | |
|---|---|
| **alguien** | somebody, anybody |
| **algo** | something, anything |
| **alguno, alguna, algunos, algunas** | one, some (things or people) |

> Hay **alguien** en la puerta. — *There is someone at the door.*
> ¿Tienes **algo** para mí? — *Have you got something for me?*
> **Algunos** (de ellos) van al cine esta tarde. — *Some (of them) are going to the movies this afternoon.*

| | |
|---|---|
| **mucho, mucha** | much |
| **muchos, muchas** | many |

> Hay **mucho** por hacer. — *There is much to do.*
> – ¿Hay galletas en la caja? — *Are there any cookies in the box?*
> – Sí, hay **muchas**. — *Yes, there are many.*

| | |
|---|---|
| **(un) poco, (una) poca** | (a) little |
| **(unos) pocos, (unas) pocas** | (a) few |

They all refer to a small quantity, but when we use "un, una, unos, unas" before these pronouns, we mean that there is a small but sufficient quantity.

> Hay **poco** (pan). — *There is little (bread).*
> Hay **unas pocas** (fotos). — *There are a few (photos).*
> ¿Te gusta el tenis? **Un poco**. — *Do you like tennis? A little.*

| | |
|---|---|
| **nadie** | nobody, anybody |
| **nada** | nothing, anything |
| **ninguno, ninguna, ningunos, ningunas** | none, neither, nobody, no one |

If these pronouns are placed before the verb, it has to be affirmative. If they go after it, the verb has to be negative.

> **Nadie** <u>es</u> perfecto. — *Nobody is perfect.*
> <u>No hay</u> **nadie** en la puerta. — *There is nobody at the door.*

No tengo **nada** en los bolsillos.  
**Ninguna** (de ellas) va al parque.  
No conozco a **ninguno** de ellos.

*I have got nothing in my p[...]*  
*None of them are going to [...]*  
*I know none/neither of them.*

| | |
|---|---|
| **todo** | *everything* |
| **todos, todas** | *everybody, all* |

Me gusta **todo**.  
**Todos** (ellos) saben tocar el violín.  
Vienen **todos** a mi fiesta.

*I like everything.*  
*All (of them) can play the violin.*  
*They are all coming to my party*  
*(everybody is coming).*

| | |
|---|---|
| **otro, otra** | *another (one)* |
| **otros, otras** | *others* |

Ésta no me gusta. Quiero **otra**.  
Algunos están aquí. Los **otros**  
están fuera.

*I don't like this one. I want another one.*  
*Some (of them) are here. The others*  
*are out.*

## TOP VOCABULARY AND EXPRESSIONS

### Preposiciones y adverbios de lugar *(Prepositions and adverbs of place)*

Prepositions and adverbs of place or position are the elements that will show us where something or somebody is or where the action occurs.

Apart from those that we have already learned (aquí, allí,....), some of the most common ones are:

| | | | |
|---|---|---|---|
| **en** | *in, on, at* | **entre** | *between, among* |
| **encima (de)** | *on, on top (of)* | **debajo (de)** | *under* |
| **arriba** | *above, upstairs* | **abajo** | *below, downstairs* |
| **por encima de** | *over, above* | **por debajo de** | *below* |
| **dentro (de)** | *in, inside* | **fuera (de)** | *out (of), outside* |
| **lejos (de)** | *far (from), away (from)* | **cerca (de)** | *near, nearby* |
| **delante (de)** | *in front of* | **detrás (de)** | *behind* |
| **enfrente (de)** | *across from* | **delante (de)** | *in front (of)* |
| **a la derecha** | *on/to the right* | **a la izquierda** | *on/to the left* |

| | |
|---|---|
| La estación está **entre** el banco y la tienda. | *The station is between the bank and the shop.* |
| Hay carne **en** el refrigerador. | *There is some meat in the fridge.* |
| Hay alguien **en** la puerta. | *There is someone at the door.* |
| Nueva York está lejos **de** Buenos Aires. | *New York is far from Buenos Aires.* |
| No hay nada **detrás de** la puerta. | *There is nothing behind the door.* |
| El perro está **debajo de** la mesa. | *The dog is under the table.* |
| El supermercado está allí, **a la izquierda**. | *The supermarket is there, on the left.* |
| Hay un buzón **delante de** mi casa. | *There is a mail box in front of my house.* |

## VOCABULARIO:

**Objetos personales** *(Personal items)*

**lentes, gafas:** *glasses*
**celular:** *cell phone*
**lápiz de labios:** *lipstick*
**agenda:** *notebook*
**cámara de fotos:** *camera*
**collar:** necklace

**bolso:** *purse*
**ropa:** *clothes*
**maquillaje:** *make-up*
**reloj:** *watch*
**joya:** *jewel*
**pulsera/brazalete:** *bracelet*

**billetera, cartera:** *wallet*
**llavero:** *key ring*
**llave:** *key*
**maletín:** *briefcase*
**pendientes:** *earrings*
**anillo:** *ring*

| | |
|---|---|
| Tus **lentes** están encima de los libros. | *Your glasses are on (top of) the books.* |
| Ella tiene su **lápiz de labios** en su **bolso**. | *She has her lipstick in her purse.* |
| El **llavero** está cerca de la **cámara**. | *The key ring is near the camera.* |
| ¿Tienes algo en la **billetera**? | *Do you have anything in your wallet?* |
| Tengo algunas **joyas**: un **collar**, unos **pendientes** y tres **anillos**. | *I have some jewels: a necklace, some earrings and three rings.* |

<table>
<tr><td>

**In this unit we will learn:**

. To describe people physically.

. To describe someone's personality.

. Adjectives for descriptions.

. Cardinal numbers (100- 999).

. Vocabulary: The face.

</td><td>

**Unit**

# 26

**Days 51 & 52**

</td></tr>
</table>

## Diálogo / *Dialog*

Pablo y Luisa se ven en la calle.

*Pablo and Luisa meet in the street.*

| | |
|---|---|
| P: | ¡Luisa! ¡Qué **linda** estás! |
| L: | Bueno, hoy me he maquillado un poco. |
| P: | No necesitas maquillaje. Eres una mujer muy **hermosa**. |
| L: | Gracias. |
| P: | ¿**A quién te pareces**? ¿A tu padre o a tu madre? |
| L: | **Me parezco** a los dos. Tengo los **ojos grandes** y el **pelo moreno**, como mi padre, y la **nariz pequeña**, como mi madre. |
| P: | ¿**Cómo son tus padres**? |
| L: | Como te digo, mi padre es **alto, moreno, delgado**, tiene los **ojos grandes** y las **orejas grandes**, también. Mi madre es **de estatura media**, tiene el **cabello rubio, largo** y **liso**, los **ojos verdes** y una **nariz pequeña**. |
| P: | ¿**Y cómo son de carácter**? |
| L: | Mi padre no es muy **hablador**. Es **tímido, generoso** y muy **trabajador**. Mi madre es muy **simpática, alegre**, y un poco **presumida**. Tú eres **pelirrojo**. ¿**A quién te pareces**? |
| P: | No lo sé. No **me parezco** mucho a mis padres. Ellos son **morenos** y **bajos** y yo soy **pelirrojo** y **alto**. Trabajo en una fábrica con **doscientos quince** compañeros y soy el único **pelirrojo**. |
| L: | [Risas] Por eso eres especial. |
| P: | Sí... y porque soy un tipo **encantador** [risas]. |

| | |
|---|---|
| P: | *Luisa! How pretty you are!* |
| L: | *Well, I put on a little makeup today.* |
| P: | *You don't need any makeup. You are a very beautiful woman.* |
| L: | *Thank you.* |
| P: | *Who do you look like? Your father or your mother?* |
| L: | *I look like both of them. I have big eyes and dark hair, like my father, and a small nose, like my mother.* |
| P: | *What do your parents look like?* |
| L: | *As I have told you, my father is tall, dark-haired, thin, he has big eyes and his ears are big, too. My mother is average height, she has long straight fair hair, green eyes and a small nose.* |
| P: | *And what are they like?* |
| L: | *My father is not very talkative. He is shy, generous and very hardworking. My mother is very friendly, cheerful, and a little snobbish. You are red-haired. Who do you look like?* |
| P: | *I don't know. I don't look like my parents very much. They are dark-haired and short and I am red-haired and tall. I work in a factory with two hundred fifteen colleagues and I am the only red-haired person.* |
| L: | *[Laughs] That's why you are special.* |
| P: | *Yes... and because I am a charming guy [laughs].* |

When we want somebody to describe themselves or other people, in Spanish we ask:

> **¿Cómo + verb "ser" + subject?**

| | |
|---|---|
| **¿Cómo eres (tú)?** | *What are you like? / What do you look like?* |
| **¿Cómo es usted?** | *What are you like? / What do you look like?* |
| **¿Cómo es tu hermana?** | *What is your sister like? / What does your sister look like?* |
| **¿Cómo son ellos?** | *What are they like? / What do they look like?* |

But we can see that these questions are a little ambiguous, as they ask about physical and personality features. In English these questions are different, depending on what the speaker is interested in.

## DESCRIPCIONES FÍSICAS *(PHYSICAL DESCRIPTIONS)*

As we have just seen, to ask about a physical description we say:

| | |
|---|---|
| **¿Cómo eres (tú)?** | *What do you look like?* |
| **¿Cómo es ella?** | *What does she look like?* |

In English it is very clear that we are asking about physical features, but in Spanish, if we want to state clearly that we are asking about somebody's appearance, we can simply add "<u>físicamente</u>" (*physically*).

| | |
|---|---|
| **¿Cómo eres** <u>físicamente</u>**?** | *What do you look like?* |
| **¿Cómo es** tu madre <u>físicamente</u>**?** | *What does your mother look like?* |

And to answer we can use those adjectives that we studied in unit 22, as well as the ones we will study in this unit.

Soy **de estatura media**, **delgado** y **moreno**.
*I am medium height, thin and dark-haired.*

Mi madre es **baja**, **rubia** y **bonita**.
*My mother is short, fair-haired and pretty.*

Another question related to how someone looks is:

**¿A quién te pareces?**      *Who do you look like?*

In this case we are referring to a person we may look like and the answer could be:

**Me parezco a** mi madre.      *I look like my mother.*

The verb "**parecerse**" needs the preposition "**a**" before introducing the person, but in a question it is also necessary.

– ¿**A** quién <u>se parece</u> Ricardo?      – *Who does Ricardo look like?*
– Él <u>se parece</u> **a** su hermano.      – *He looks like his brother.*

## TOP VOCABULARY AND EXPRESSIONS

### La cara *(The face)*

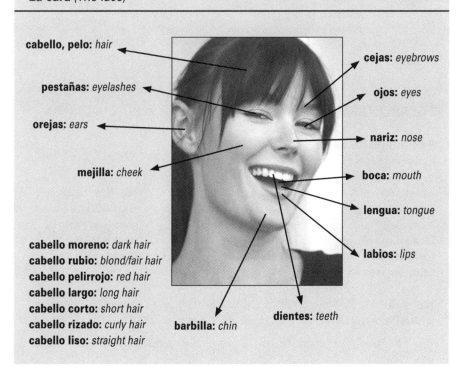

**cabello, pelo:** *hair*

**cejas:** *eyebrows*

**pestañas:** *eyelashes*

**ojos:** *eyes*

**orejas:** *ears*

**nariz:** *nose*

**mejilla:** *cheek*

**boca:** *mouth*

**lengua:** *tongue*

**cabello moreno:** *dark hair*
**cabello rubio:** *blond/fair hair*
**cabello pelirrojo:** *red hair*
**cabello largo:** *long hair*
**cabello corto:** *short hair*
**cabello rizado:** *curly hair*
**cabello liso:** *straight hair*

**labios:** *lips*

**barbilla:** *chin*

**dientes:** *teeth*

## DESCRIPCIONES DE PERSONALIDAD *(DESCRIPTIONS OF PERSONALITY)*

In order to ask about someone's personality, we use the same sentence used for physical descriptions:

**¿Cómo eres? - ¿Cómo es Pedro?**

But, if we want to stress that we are asking about somebody's character, we can add "<u>de carácter</u>" to the question.

| | |
|---|---|
| **¿Cómo eres** <u>de carácter</u>**?** | *What are you like?* |
| **¿Cómo es** Pedro <u>de carácter</u>**?** | *What is Pedro like?* |

And to answer these questions we can use the following adjectives:

---

## VOCABULARIO:

**Adjetivos para describir la personalidad o el carácter**
*(Adjectives to describe the personality or character)*

| | | |
|---|---|---|
| **ambicioso:** *ambitious* | **pesado:** *annoying* | **engreído:** *big-headed* |
| **encantador:** *charming* | **alegre:** *cheerful* | **presumido:** *conceited* |
| **loco:** *crazy, nuts* | **simpático:** *friendly, nice* | **generoso:** *generous* |
| **tacaño:** *mean* | **trabajador:** *hard-working* | **amable:** *kind* |
| **haragán, vago:** *lazy* | **educado:** *polite* | **tímido:** *shy* |
| **hablador:** *talkative* | | |

**¿Cómo es Pedro (de carácter)?** Es un muchacho **encantador**. Es muy **amable** y **simpático**.
*What is Pedro like? He is a charming boy. He is very kind and friendly.*

Tu prima es **haragana** y **engreída**. *Your cousin is lazy and big-headed.*

---

## NÚMEROS CARDINALES (100-999) *[CARDINAL NUMBERS (100-999)]*

**100 – cien**

Between 101 and 199, we have to use **"ciento"** instead of **"cien"**:

**101 – ciento uno**
**102 – ciento dos**
**116 – ciento dieciséis**
**145 – ciento cuarenta y cinco**
**199 – ciento noventa y nueve**

The rest of the "hundreds" follow a fairly regular pattern:

| | |
|---|---|
| **200 – doscientos** | **205 – doscientos cinco** |
| **300 – trescientos** | **389 – trescientos ochenta y nueve** |
| **400 – cuatrocientos** | **412 – cuatrocientos doce** |
| **500 – quinientos** | **595 – quinientos noventa y cinco** |
| **600 – seiscientos** | **633 – seiscientos treinta y tres** |
| **700 – setecientos** | **721 – setecientos veintiuno** |
| **800 – ochocientos** | **868 – ochocientos sesenta y ocho** |
| **900 – novecientos** | **999 – novecientos noventa y nueve** |

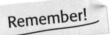

## Remember!

When the things that you are counting are feminine, there is a feminine form for some numbers:

Up to number 199, the only figure with a feminine form is "uno" ("una"), so:

| (31) Treinta y **una** muchachas. | *Thirty-one girls.* |
|---|---|
| (101) Ciento **una** flores. | *One hundred one flowers.* |
| (191) Ciento noventa y **una** páginas. | *One hundred ninety-one pages.* |

From 200 on, the ending "-cientos" does also have a feminine form: "-cientas":

| (200) **Doscientas** botellas. | *Two hundred bottles.* |
|---|---|
| (301) **Trescientas** una mesas. | *Three hundred one tables.* |
| (745) **Setecientas** cuarenta y cinco mujeres. | *Seven hundred forty-five women.* |

## Unit 27

**Days 53 & 54**

### In this unit we will learn:

. Direct objects pronouns.

. The use of no quantifiers for uncountable and plural nouns.

. Vocabulary: The shopping list.

### Diálogo / Dialog

Maya va al mercado a comprar vegetales y habla con el dependiente.

*Maya has gone to the market to buy some vegetables and is talking to the greengrocer.*

| | |
|---|---|
| M: | ¡Hola! ¡Buenos días! |
| D: | ¡Buenos días! ¿Qué le pongo? |
| M: | Quiero **un kilo de naranjas** y **medio kilo de fresas.** |
| D: | Las fresas hacen 550 gramos. ¿Está bien? |
| M: | Sí, está bien. |
| D: | Aquí tiene. ¿Algo más? |
| M: | Sí. ¿Tiene **pepinos**? |
| D: | Sí. Son muy buenos y están baratos. **¿Los** quiere grandes? |
| M: | No, **los** prefiero pequeños. Póngame algunos. ¡Ah! Y quiero **una bolsa de papas**, también. |
| D: | Aquí **la** tiene ¿Algo más? |
| M: | No sé..... |
| D: | ¿**Lechugas, tomates, zanahorias**,......? |
| M: | ¿Están frescas las **zanahorias**? |
| D: | Sí, **las** tengo muy frescas. |
| M: | ¿Puedo ver**las**? |
| D: | Aquí **las** tiene. |
| M: | Pues me llevo unas pocas. ¿Cuánto es todo? |
| D: | Son 325 pesos. |
| M: | Aquí tiene. Gracias. |
| D: | Gracias a usted. |
| M: | ¡Adiós! |
| D: | ¡Adiós! |

| | |
|---|---|
| M: | *Hello! Good morning!* |
| D: | *Good morning! What will it be?* |
| M: | *I'd like a kilo of oranges and half a kilo of strawberries.* |
| D: | *The strawberries come out to a little more than half a kilo. Is that okay?* |
| M: | *Yes, it's fine.* |
| D: | *Here you are. Anything else?* |
| M: | *Yes. Do you have cucumbers?* |
| D: | *Yes. They are very good and cheap. Do you want them big?* |
| M: | *No, I prefer them small. Give me some. Ah! And I also want a bag of potatoes.* |
| D: | *Here you are. Anything else?* |
| M: | *I don't know...* |
| D: | *Lettuce, tomatoes, carrots...?* |
| M: | *Are the carrots fresh?* |
| D: | *Yes, I have them very fresh.* |
| M: | *Can I see them?* |
| D: | *Here you are.* |
| M: | *I'll take a few. How much is everything?* |
| D: | *It's 325 pesos.* |
| M: | *Here you are. Thank you.* |
| D: | *Thanks to you.* |
| M: | *Goodbye!* |
| D: | *Goodbye!* |

## PRONOMBRES DE OBJETO DIRECTO *(DIRECT OBJECT PRONOUNS)*

Direct objects are the answer to the questions "¿a quién?" or "¿qué?" (*whom? or what?*).

| | |
|---|---|
| – **¿A quién** ves? | – *Whom do you see?* |
| – Veo <u>a Luis</u>. | – *I see Luis.* |
| – **¿Qué** quieren ellos? | – *What do they want?* |
| – Ellos quieren <u>unas botas</u>. | – *They want some boots.* |

In these examples, "Luis" and "unas botas" are direct objects. We may substitute these direct objects for direct object pronouns.

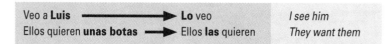

| | | |
|---|---|---|
| Veo a **Luis** ➝ | **Lo** veo | *I see him* |
| Ellos quieren **unas botas** ➝ | Ellos **las** quieren | *They want them* |

Here are the direct object pronouns:

| SUBJECT PRONOUNS | DIRECT OBJECT PRONOUNS | |
|---|---|---|
| yo | **me** | *me* |
| tú | **te** | *you* |
| usted | **lo, la** | *you* |
| él | **lo** | *him, it\** |
| ella | **la** | *her, it\** |
| nosotros/as | **nos** | *us* |
| ustedes | **los, las** | *you* |
| ellos/as | **los, las** | *them\** |

(*) The direct pronoun "it" (or plural "them") has masculine and feminine forms. In Spanish we have to choose the pronoun according to the gender and number of the noun that is replaced.

| | |
|---|---|
| Antonio compra **el periódico.** ➝ | Antonio **lo** compra. |
| *Antonio buys the newspaper.* | *Antonio buys it.* |
| Mi padre come **carne.** ➝ | Mi padre **la** come. |
| *My father eats meat.* | *My father eats it.* |
| Tenemos **tres cuadros.** ➝ | **Los** tenemos. |
| *We have three pictures.* | *We have them.* |
| ¿Vendes **estas** camisas? ➝ | ¿**Las** vendes? |
| *Do you sell these shirts?* | *Do you sell them?* |

We have to pay attention to the position of the direct object in Spanish, as it is placed immediately before the conjugated verb, and not after the verb, as in English.

But when the pronoun is used with an infinitive or present participle (gerund), it may be placed in two positions: either just before the conjugated verb that precedes the infinitive or gerund, or following the infinitive or gerund, being attached to them:

| | |
|---|---|
| Quiero comprar un <u>auto</u>. | *I want to buy a car.* |
| **Lo** quiero comprar. | *I want to buy it.* |
| Quiero comprar**lo**. | *I want to buy it.* |
| Ellos están visitando a <u>su madre</u>. | *They are visiting their mother.* |
| Ellos **la** están visitando. | *They are visiting her.* |
| Ellos están visitándo**la**. | *They are visiting her.* |

In case the sentence is negative, "no" precedes the verb, but, if we place the pronoun before the verb, "no" goes before the pronoun:

| | |
|---|---|
| Ellos **no** quieren ver<u>me</u> (a mí). | *They don't want to see me.* |
| Ellos **no** <u>me</u> quieren ver (a mí). | *They don't want to see me.* |
| No **te** necesito (a ti). | *I don't need you.* |
| Él está cantándo**la** (la canción). | *He is singing it (the song).* |
| No estamos estudiándo**lo** (inglés). | *We are not studying it (English).* |
| Paco **lo** lee todos los días (el periódico). | *Paco reads it every day (the newspaper).* |

## NOMBRES PLURALES E INCONTABLES SIN CUANTIFICADORES
### *(PLURAL AND UNCOUNTABLE NOUNS WITH NO QUANTIFIERS)*

When we use a plural noun or an uncountable noun in a sentence, not specifying its quantity, it is very common to use the noun alone without any quantifier in Spanish.

| | |
|---|---|
| Hay **niños** en la clase. | *There are <u>some</u> children in the classroom.* |
| ¿Venden ustedes **libros**? | *Do you sell books?* |
| Quiero **pan**. | *I want <u>some</u> bread.* |
| No tienes **dinero**. | *You don't have <u>any</u> money.* |

## TOP VOCABULARY AND EXPRESSIONS

### La lista de la compra *(The shopping list)*

#### PRODUCTOS ALIMENTICIOS: *GROCERIES*

**Fruta:** *fruit*

| | |
|---|---|
| **manzana:** *apple* | **plátano, banana:** *banana* |
| **coco:** *coconut* | **piña, ananás:** *pineapple* |
| **limón:** *lemon* | **mango:** *mango* |
| **melocotón:** *peach* | **pera:** *pear* |
| **fresa:** *strawberry* | **sandía:** *watermelon* |
| **naranja:** *orange* | **uva:** *grape* |
| **melón:** *melon* | **ciruela:** *plum* |

## Verdura, vegetales: *vegetables*

| | | |
|---|---|---|
| **tomate:** *tomato* | **espinacas:** *spinach* | **calabaza:** *pumpkin* |
| **papa:** *potato* | **pepino:** *cucumber* | **ají, pimiento:** *pepper* |
| **cebolla:** *onion* | **arvejas, guisantes:** *peas* | **lechuga:** *lettuce* |
| **ajo:** *garlic* | **coliflor:** *cauliflower* | **zanahoria:** *carrot* |
| **col, repollo:** *cabbage* | | |

## Carne: *meat*

| | | |
|---|---|---|
| **pollo:** *chicken* | **cordero:** *lamb* | **res:** *beef* |
| **cerdo:** *pork* | **filete:** *steak* | **chuleta:** *chop* |
| **salchicha:** *sausage* | **hamburguesa:** *hamburguer* | **costillas:** *ribs* |
| **jamón:** *ham* | **tocineta, bacon:** *bacon* | |

## Pescado y mariscos: *fish and seafood*

| | | |
|---|---|---|
| **sardina:** *sardine* | **salmón:** *salmon* | **lenguado:** *sole* |
| **trucha:** *trout* | **atún:** *tuna* | **cangrejo:** *crab* |
| **langosta:** *lobster* | **mejillones:** *mussels* | **calamar:** *squid* |

## Productos lácteos: *dairy products*

| | |
|---|---|
| **leche:** *milk* | **mantequilla:** *butter* |
| **queso:** *cheese* | **nata, crema:** *cream* |
| **yogurt:** *yoghurt* | |

## Otros: *others*

| | | |
|---|---|---|
| **huevo:** *egg* | **arroz:** *rice* | **pan:** *bread* |
| **pasta:** *pasta* | **mermelada:** *jam* | **cereales:** *cereal* |
| **azúcar:** *sugar* | **harina:** *flour* | |

## RECIPIENTES: *CONTAINERS*

**una bolsa de limones:** *a bag of lemons*
**una lata de cola:** *a can of coke*
**una botella de vino:** *a bottle of wine*
**una lata de sardinas:** *a tin of sardines*
**un saco de papas:** *a sack of potatoes*
**un cartón de leche:** *a carton of milk*
**un bote de mermelada:** *a jar of jam*
**una caja de cereales:** *a box of cereal*

But you can also ask for:

**una docena de huevos:** *a dozen eggs*
**un racimo de uvas:** *a bunch of grapes*
**una barra de pan:** *a loaf of bread*
**un trozo de queso:** *a piece of cheese*
**un kilo de tomates:** *a kilo of tomatoes*
**medio kilo de carne:** *half a kilo of meat*
**una libra de arroz:** *a pound of rice*
**un litro de jugo:** *a litre of juice*

Necesito **una lata de sardinas, dos kilos de tomates** y **un trozo de queso**.
*I need a tin of sardines, two kilos of tomatoes and a piece of cheese.*

Ella quiere **un cartón de leche** y **una docena de huevos**.
*She wants a carton of milk and a dozen eggs.*

## Unit
# 28
**Days 55 & 56**

### In this unit we will learn:
. Adverbs of quantity.
. "¿Cuánto?" "¿Cuántos?".
. To ask for prices, quantities, weights and measures.
. "Muy" and "mucho".
. Expressions of quantity.

**Diálogo / Dialog**

Lorena y Francisco están tomando un café y charlando.

*Lorena and Francisco are having coffee and talking.*

| | |
|---|---|
| F: | ¿Quieres leche? |
| L: | Sí, **un poco** de leche, por favor. |
| F: | ¿Azúcar? |
| L: | Sí, gracias. |
| F: | ¿**Cuánto**? |
| L: | Le pongo **bastante** azúcar al café. Oye, ayer vi a tu hermano. Es **muy** alto. ¿**Cuánto mide**? |
| F: | Mide dos metros. |
| L: | ¿Y **cuánto pesa**? |
| F: | Pesa **mucho**. Doscientas veinte libras, **más** o **menos**. |
| L: | Eso no es **demasiado**. Está **muy** fuerte. |
| F: | Sí, come **mucho**, y **varias** veces al día. |
| L: | ¿Tiene hijos? |
| F: | Sí. |
| L: | ¿**Cuántos** hijos tiene? |
| F: | Dos. Y son **muy** fuertes, como él. |
| L: | No conozco a **mucha** gente así. |
| F: | **Nosotros dos** somos delgados y **ambos** comemos, pero no comemos **tanto**. |
| L: | Bueno, hay **algo de** tarta. Hay **suficiente** tarta para los dos. ¿Quieres? |
| F: | Sí, me encantan **todos** los pasteles. |
| L: | Aquí tienes. |
| F: | Gracias. |

| | |
|---|---|
| F: | *Would you like some milk?* |
| L: | *Yes, a little milk, please.* |
| F: | *Sugar?* |
| L: | *Yes, thank you.* |
| F: | *How much?* |
| L: | *I put a lot of sugar in my coffee. Listen, I saw your brother yesterday. He is very tall. How tall is he?* |
| F: | *He is two meters tall.* |
| L: | *And how much does he weigh?* |
| F: | *He weighs a lot. Two hundred twenty pounds, more or less.* |
| L. | *That is not too much. He is very strong.* |
| F: | *Yes, he eats a lot, and several times a day.* |
| L: | *Does he have any children?* |
| F: | *Yes.* |
| L: | *How many children does he have?* |
| F: | *Two. And they are very strong, like him.* |
| L: | *I don't know many people like that.* |
| F: | *We two are thin and both of us eat, but we don't eat so much.* |
| L: | *Well, there is some cake. There is enough cake for us both. Do you want some?* |
| F: | *Yes, I love all kinds of cake.* |
| L: | *Here you are.* |
| F: | *Thank you.* |

## ADVERBIOS DE CANTIDAD *(ADVERBS OF QUANTITY)*

These adverbs express how much there is of something.

| | |
|---|---|
| **demasiado/a*** | *too much* |
| **demasiados/as*** | *too many* |
| **bastante/s*** | *quite, enough* |
| **suficiente** | *enough* |
| **mucho/a*** | *much, a lot (of)* |
| **muchos/as*** | *many, a lot (of)* |
| **(un/a) poco/a* (de)** | *(a) little* |
| **(unos/as) pocos/as*** | *(a) few* |
| **tanto/a*** | *as / so much* |
| **tantos/as*** | *as / so many* |
| **muy** | *very* |
| **más** | *more* |
| **menos** | *less, fewer* |
| **nada de**** | *no* |
| **ningún/a**** | *no* |

(*) The singular forms refer to uncountable nouns and the plural forms refer to countable nouns (in plural).

(**) "Nada de" is used before uncountable nouns and "ningún, ninguna" before countable nouns.

| | |
|---|---|
| Tenemos **demasiado** pan. | *We have too much bread.* |
| Hay **demasiadas** naranjas en el árbol. | *There are too many oranges in the tree.* |
| ¿Tienes **bastante** leche? | *Do you have enough milk?* |
| Sí, tengo **suficiente**. | *Yes, I have enough.* |
| Hay **mucha** nieve en la calle. | *There is a lot of snow on the street.* |
| ¿Tiene ella **muchos** amigos? | *Does she have many friends?* |
| Necesitamos **un poco de** nata para el pastel. | *We need a little cream for the cake.* |
| No necesito **tanto** azúcar. | *I don't need so much sugar.* |
| El auto es **muy** caro. | *The car is very expensive.* |
| ¿Quieres **más** vino? | *Would you like some more wine?* |
| Tenemos **menos** dinero. | *We have less money.* |
| No hay **nada de** café. | *There is no coffee.* |
| No tienen **ninguna** foto. | *They have no photos.* |

## USO DE "¿CUÁNTO?", "¿CUÁNTA?", "¿CUÁNTOS?", "¿CUÁNTAS?"
### (USE OF HOW MUCH AND HOW MANY)

To ask about quantities we have to use **¿Cuánto?**, **¿Cuánta?**, **¿Cuántos?** and **¿Cuántas?**

a) **¿Cuánto?** (*how much?*) is used before uncountable masculine nouns:
¿Cuánto vino tienes en casa? — *How much wine do you have at home?*

b) **¿Cuánta?** (*how much?*) is used before uncountable feminine nouns:
¿Cuánta mantequilla necesitas? — *How much butter do you need?*

c) **¿Cuántos?** (*how many?*) is used before countable masculine nouns in plural:
¿Cuántos niños hay en el parque? — *How many children are there in the park?*

d) **¿Cuántas?** (*how many?*) is used before countable feminine nouns in plural:
¿Cuántas naranjas hay? — *How many oranges are there?*

But, in all these cases, we can omit the noun if we know what we are talking about.

| | |
|---|---|
| Tengo poco vino. **¿Cuánto** (vino) tienes? | *I have little wine. How much (wine) do you have?* |
| Necesito mantequilla. **¿Cuánta** necesitas? | *I need some butter. How much do you need?* |
| Hay muchas naranjas. **¿Cuántas** hay? | *There are a lot of oranges. How many are there?* |

**¿Cuánto?** is also used when we ask about prices. In this case the word "dinero" *(money)* is often left out as everybody knows that we refer to it.
In Spanish we use the verbs "costar" or "valer" *(to cost)* when talking about prices.

| | |
|---|---|
| **¿Cuánto cuesta** esa chaqueta? | *How much is that jacket?* |
| **¿Cuánto valen** los tomates? | *How much are the tomatoes?* |

When asking for a total price:

| | |
|---|---|
| **¿Cuánto es (todo)**? | *How much is it (all)?* |

But **¿cuánto?** can also appear together with the verbs "medir" (*to measure*) or "pesar" (*to weigh*) when we ask about measures or weights.

| | |
|---|---|
| **¿Cuánto mide** tu hermano? | *How tall is your brother?* |
| **¿Cuánto pesas** (tú)? | *How much do you weigh?* |

## "MUY" Y "MUCHO" ("VERY" AND "MUCH/A LOT")

These words are sometimes confused, but we will see that their use is not so confusing.

**"Muy"** (*very*) is used before adjectives or adverbs, and never stands alone:

| | |
|---|---|
| Ella es **muy** <u>linda</u>. | *She is very pretty.* |
| Es **muy** <u>tarde</u>. | *It's very late.* |

When a sentence calls for the simple word "muy", it becomes **"mucho"** (*much, a lot*):

| | |
|---|---|
| ¿Es ella linda? Sí, **mucho**. | *Is she pretty? Yes, very.* |

**"Mucho"** is used before uncountable nouns or alone.

| | |
|---|---|
| Él compra **mucho** pescado. | *He buys a lot of fish.* |
| Ellos no corren **mucho**. | *They don't run much.* |
| ¿Te gustan los vegetales? No, no **mucho**. | *Do you like vegetables? No, not much.* |

More expressions of quantity (pay attention to those that have both genders):

**Demasiado** + adjective

*too + adjective*

Esta maleta es **demasiado** pesada.

*This suitcase is too heavy.*

**Suficiente** + noun

*enough + noun*

Hay **suficiente** combustible en el tanque.

*There is enough fuel in the tank.*

**Suficientemente** + adjetive

*adjective + enough*

La casa no está **suficientemente** limpia.

*The house isn't clean enough.*

**Ambos, ambas (los/las dos)**

*both*

**Ambos/Los dos** viven en San Francisco.

*Both of them live in San Francisco.*

**Nosotros/as, ustedes and ellos/as** + number

*we, you, they + number*

**Nosotras** tres somos españolas.

*We three are Spanish.*

**Varios, varias** + <u>countable noun in plural</u>   *several + countable noun in plural*

Hay **varios** <u>diccionarios</u> en la biblioteca.   *There are several dictionaries in the library.*

**Cada**   + <u>countable noun</u>   *each /every + countable noun*

**"Cada"** has an invariable form regardless of what follows:

**Cada** <u>libro</u> cuesta veinte dólares.   *Each book is twenty dollars.*

In a plural situation, "**cada**" is usually followed by a number:

Voy al gimnasio **cada** <u>tres días</u>.   *I go to the gym every three days.*

**Todo, toda** + <u>determiner</u>   *the whole + singular noun / all + (det)*
+ <u>singular or uncountable noun</u>   *+ uncountable noun*

Ella no lee **todo** <u>el periódico</u>.   *She doesn't read the whole newspaper.*
**Toda** <u>la leche</u> está en el refrigerador.   *All (the) milk is in the fridge.*

| **Todos, todas** + <u>determiner + plural noun</u> | *all (of) + det. + plural noun / every + singular noun* |
|---|---|
| Él se levanta temprano **todos** los días. | *He gets up early every day.* |
| **Todas** esas computadoras son japonesas. | *All these computers are Japanese.* |

**"Todos, todas"** can also go before **"nosotros/as"**, **"ustedes"** or **"ellos/as"** *(all of us/you/them).*

| **Todos** <u>ellos</u> hablan inglés y español. | *All of them speak English and Spanish.* |
|---|---|

| **Algo de** + <u>uncountable noun</u> | *some + noun* |
|---|---|
| Tenemos **algo de** <u>dinero</u> en el banco. | *We have some money in the bank.* |

| **Nada de** + <u>uncountable noun</u> | *no + noun* |
|---|---|
| No hay **nada de** <u>agua</u> en la botella. | *There is no water in the bottle.* |

| **Los demás / las demás** + <u>noun in plural</u> | *the rest of (the) + noun in plural* |
|---|---|
| **Los demás** <u>abrigos</u> son para mujer. | *The rest of the coats are for women.* |
| Tengo **las demás** <u>fotos</u> en casa. | *I have the rest ot the pictures at home.* |

## In this unit we will learn:
. To ask for and to borrow things.
. To ask for a favor.
. Expressions to confirm and excuse.
. Cardinal numbers (1000-millions)

## Unit
# 29
**Days 57 & 58**

**Diálogo / Dialog**

Pedro y su esposa, Mercedes, están en casa.

*Pedro and his wife, Mercedes, are at home.*

M: ¡Eh! Pareces preocupado. ¿Qué te pasa?

P: Quiero recoger un paquete en la oficina de correos pero no puedo ir. No tengo tiempo. Tú tienes tiempo libre ahora. **¿Puedes ayudarme?**

M: ¡Claro que sí! Pero hay un problema. Mi auto está averiado y la oficina de correos está lejos. **¿Puedes prestarme** tu auto?

P: ¡Por supuesto! Pero no tiene combustible. **¿Puedes ir** antes a la bomba, por favor?

M: ¡Claro!

P: Aquí tienes **2.500** pesos para el combustible y para pagar el paquete. Bueno, **¿puedes hacerme** otro favor?

M: ¿Qué quieres ahora?

P: Ese paquete es para mi tía Sara. **¿Puedes llevarlo** a su casa?

M: Mmmm... **Me temo que no**. Sabes que estoy muy enfadada con tu tía Sara. ¿Por qué no vas tú? [Mirando el reloj] ¡Ah! Ahora comprendo. Es hora de tu programa favorito.

M: *Eh! You look worried. What's the matter with you?*

P: *I want to pick up a package from the post office but I can't go. I have no time. You have some free time now. Can you help me?*

M: *Yes, of course! But there is a problem. My car is broken down and the post office is far away. Can I borrow your car?*

P: *Of course! But it has no gas. Can you go to the gas station before, please?*

M: *Sure!*

P: *Here are 2,500 pesos for the gas and to pay for the package. Well, can you do me another favor?*

M: *What do you want now?*

P: *That package is for my aunt Sara. Can you take it to her house?*

M: *Mmmm...I'm afraid not. You know that I am mad at your aunt Sara. Why don't you go yourself? [Looking at her watch] Ah! I understand now. It's time for your favorite show.*

## VERBOS Y EXPRESIONES PARA PEDIR COSAS (VERBS AND EXPRESSIONS WHEN ASKING FOR AND BORROWING THINGS)

The most common structures that we use when we ask someone for something start like these:

**¿Puedes + infinitive ........?**
**¿Puede usted + infinitive...?**     *Can you + infinitive.........?*
**¿Pueden ustedes + infinitive...?**

**¿Puedes pasar**me la sal?          *Can you pass me the salt?*
**¿Puede usted decir**me la hora?    *Can you tell me the time?*
**¿Pueden ustedes cerrar** la puerta? *Can you close the door?*

As we can see, we use questions with the verb "poder" conjugated and another verb in infinitive.

Besides these structures, we can also say:

**¿Me das**  + (determinant) + noun?

**¿Me das** un pastel?          *Can you give (pass) me a pastry?*

And we use the verbs "prestar" and "dejar" (to lend) instead of "pedir prestado" (to borrow).

**¿Me prestas**  + (determinant) + noun? or

**¿Me dejas**  + (determinant) + noun?

**¿Me prestas** tu bicicleta?   *May I borrow your bicycle?*
**¿Me dejas** tu diccionario?   *Can I borrow your dictionary?*

When we ask for a favor we can use several questions:

**Remember!**

In some Latin American countries, the verb "**prestar**" means "*to give*", instead of "*to lend*".

## PEDIR UN FAVOR (ASKING FOR A FAVOR)

| | |
|---|---|
| **¿Puedes hacerme un favor?** | *Can you do me a favor?* |
| **¿Me haces un favor?*** | *Can you do me a favor?* |
| **¿Puedes hacer algo por mí?** | *Can you do something for me?* |
| **¿Puedes ayudarme?** | *Can you help me?* |
| **¿Puedes echarme/darme una mano?** | *Can you lend me a hand?* |

(*) This common sentence is expressed in present simple, but the meaning is exactly the same as the others.

In all these cases we can see that the verbs "hacer(me)" "dar(me)", "prestar(me)", "dejar(me)", "ayudar(me)" and "echar(me)" need an indirect object pronoun (me, te, le.....).
If we use a noun or a name instead of these pronouns*, we have to use the preposition "a" introducing the noun, the name or even a subject pronoun (but "a yo" and "a tú" change for "a mí" and "a ti").
(*) In many cases, these pronouns also appear in the sentence.

| | |
|---|---|
| ¿Puedes prestarle la bicicleta **a** <u>Ana</u>? | *Can Ana borrow your bicycle?* |
| ¿Puedes hacerles un favor **a** <u>mis padres</u>? | *Can you do my parents a favor?* |
| ¿Puedes ayudarle **a** <u>él</u>? | *Can you help him?* |

When asking for something or for a favor, we can also use a more formal structure than those just seen, but we will learn this when we study the conditional tense "podría" (*could*).
**1.000** – mil

## TOP VOCABULARY AND EXPRESSIONS

### Expresiones de confirmación y disculpa
*(Expressions to confirm and excuse)*

In order to answer all the questions quoted above affirmatively we can use any of these expressions:

| | |
|---|---|
| **¡Claro!** | *Sure!* |
| **¡Claro que sí!** | *Yes of course!* |
| **¡Por supuesto!** | *Of course!* |

| | |
|---|---|
| – ¿Puede usted hacerme un favor? | *– Can you do me a favor?* |
| – **¡Claro que sí!** | *– Yes of course!* |

But, on the contrary, if the answer is negative or we want to give an excuse we will use:

| | |
|---|---|
| **¡Claro que no!** | *Of course not!* |
| **¡Por supuesto que no!** | *Of course not!* |
| **Lo siento pero...** | *I am sorry but.....* |
| **Me temo que.....** | *I am afraid that.....* |

¿Puedes dejarme el coche? **Lo siento pero** lo necesito yo.
*May I borrow your car? I am sorry but I need it myself.*

¿Puedes prestarme algo de dinero? **Me temo que** no puedo.
*Can you lend me some money? I'm afraid I can't.*

¿No quieres otro whisky? **¡Por supuesto que no!**
*Wouldn't you like another whisky? Of course not!*

All these expressions can also be used in any situation when we need to emphasize an affimation or negation, or give an excuse politely.

¿Tienen ellos hijos? **¡Claro que sí!**
*Do they have children? Yes of course!*

¿Te apetece comer cordero? **Lo siento, pero** no me gusta la carne.
*Do you feel like eating lamb? I am sorry but I don't like meat.*

## NÚMEROS CARDINALES 1000-MILLONES
### (CARDINAL NUMBERS 1000-MILLIONS)

**1.001** – mil uno/una
**1.348** – mil trescientos/as cuarenta y ocho
**2.000** – dos mil
**3.000** – tres mil
**15.000** – quince mil
**275.000** – doscientos/as setenta y cinco mil
**497.000** – cuatrocientos/as noventa y siete mil
**995.876** – novecientos/as noventa y cinco mil, ocho cientos/as setenta y seis

**1.000.000** – un millón
**2.000.000** – dos millones
**33.000.000** – treinta y tres millones

## Remember!

The words "cien/ciento" and "millón" have plural forms ("cientos/as" and "millones")
when there is a number higher than one before them, but "mil" does not have a plural
form in this case.

400 – cuatro<u>cientos/as</u>
5.000.000 – cinco <u>millones</u>
3.000 – tres <u>mil</u>

But "cientos/as", "miles" and "millones" are used when we can't determine an exact figure:

Hay **cientos** de hormigas.  *There are hundreds of ants.*
Hay **miles** de personas en el parque.  *There are thousands of people at the park.*
Ella tiene algunos **millones** de pesos.  *She has millions of pesos.*

Note that a dot, not a comma, is used to separate the thousands and millions in
Spanish. The comma is used to express decimals.

| 5,3 | cinco coma tres | *5.3* | *five point three* |
|---|---|---|---|
| 0,7 | cero coma siete | *0.7* | *zero point seven* |

## Unit
# 30
**Days 59 & 60**

### In this unit we will learn:
. Expressions on the telephone.
. To leave and take messages on the phone.
. Vocabulary: The telephone.
. The past simple in Spanish.
. The preterite. Preterite of regular verbs.
. Time markers in the past.

## Diálogo / Dialog

Julio, el hermano de Bernardo, y Lucrecia hablan por teléfono.

*Julio, Bernardo's brother, and Lucrecia are talking on the phone.*

J: **¿Aló?**

L: ¡Buenos días! **¿Se puede poner** Bernardo, por favor?

J: ¡Buenos días! No, Bernardo no está en casa. **Soy** Julio, su hermano. **¿Quién le llama?**

L: **Soy** Lucrecia Pérez.

J: **¿Quiere dejarle un mensaje?**

L: Sí. Dígale que **ayer llamé** al director de la empresa donde trabaja Bernardo. No lo **encontré**, pero **me devolvió la llamada** y hablé con él. Me **dijo** que Bernardo no estaba en el trabajo y **me preocupé**. **Llamé** a Bernardo a su celular, pero nadie **contestó**. ¿Está todo bien?

J: Sí, todo está bien, gracias. **Ayer** Bernardo tuvo el día libre y no **trabajó** porque **viajó** a Santiago. Allí **pasó** todo el día y **regresó** por la noche.

L: Pero anoche también lo **llamé**.

J: Pues no sé....

L: Bueno, dígale que **el otro día** me **visitaron** unos amigos franceses. Él los **conoció** el año pasado.
[Se cae la llamada]

J: ¿Lucrecia? **¿Aló? ¿Aló?**

L: **¿Sí?** ¿Julio? Parece que **se cayó la llamada**.

---

J: *Hello?*

L: *Good morning! May I speak to Bernardo, please?*

J: *Good morning! No, Bernardo is not in. This is Julio, his brother. Who's calling?*

L: *This is Lucrecia Pérez.*

J: *Would you like to leave a message for him?*

L: *Yes. Tell him that yesterday I phoned the director of the company where Bernardo works. I didn't find him, but he called me back and I talked to him. He told me that Bernardo wasn't at work and I got worried. I called Bernardo on his cell phone but nobody answered. Is everything alright?*

J: *Yes, everything is fine, thank you. Yesterday Bernardo had a free day and didn't work because he traveled to Santiago. There he spent the whole day and came back at night.*

L: *But last night I also called him.*

J: *I don't know....*

L: *Well, tell him that the other day some French friends visited me. He met them last year. [The call is cut off]*

J: *Lucrecia? Hello? Hello?*

L: *Hello? Julio? It seems that the call was cut off.*

## TOP VOCABULARY AND EXPRESSIONS

### Expresiones al teléfono *(Telephone expressions)*

In this unit we will review the expressions that we use when we make or receive a phone call. When the phone is ringing and we pick up the receiver we can say:

| | |
|---|---|
| **¿Hola?** | |
| **¿Aló?** | |
| **¿Sí?** | *Hello?* |
| **¿Dígame?** | |
| **¿Buenas?** | |

Or, more politely:

| | |
|---|---|
| **¡Buenos días!** | *Good morning* |
| **¡Buenas tardes/noches!** | *Good afternoon/evening* |

Then we may hear:

**Soy** Antonio Pérez. **¿Puedo hablar con** Luis Martín, por favor?
*This is Antonio Pérez. May I speak to Luis Martín, please?*

**¿Se puede poner** Luis Martín?   *May I speak to Luis Martín?*

And we can answer:

**No está en casa (en la oficina)** en este momento.
*He/She is not in at the moment.*

**Soy yo.**   *(Your name) Speaking.*
**Un momento, por favor.**   *Hang on / hold on / wait a second.*

Let's review some different scenarios, and learn some common expressions used when speaking on the phone:

| | |
|---|---|
| **¿Quién (le) llama?** | *Who's calling?* |
| **¿De parte de quién?** | *Who's calling?* |
| **¿Con quién desea hablar?** | *Who would you like to speak to?* |
| **Se cortó la llamada.** | *The call was cut off.* |
| **Se cayó la llamada.** | *The call was cut off.* |
| **Le paso (con)....** | *I'll put you through (to) .....* |
| **Le llamo después/más tarde.** | *I'll call back later.* |
| **Espere en línea, por favor.** | *Hold the line, please.* |
| **No se oye nada.** | *The line is dead.* |

**Esto es un contestador automático. Por favor, deje su mensaje después de la señal.**
*This is an answering machine. Please, leave your message after the beep.*

With regard to messages, we can say:

| | |
|---|---|
| **¿Quiere dejar algún mensaje?** | *Would you like to leave a message?* |
| **¿Puedo tomar un mensaje?** | *Can I take a message?* |
| **Quiero dejar(le) un mensaje.** | *I would like to leave (him, her) a message.* |

## VOCABULARIO:

**El teléfono** *(The telephone)*

**teléfono:** *telephone, phone*
**tarjeta telefónica:** *telephone card / calling card*
**celular:** *cellular, cell phone*
**número de teléfono:** *telephone number*
**marcar un número:** *to dial a number*
**sonar (el teléfono):** *to ring*
**devolver la llamada:** *to call back*
**llamar (por teléfono):** *to phone, to ring*
**esperar en línea:** *to hold the line*
**hacer una llamada:** *to make a call*
**colgar:** *to hang up*
**llamada telefónica:** *telephone call*

**cabina telefónica:** *telephone booth*

---

## EL PASADO SIMPLE *(THE PAST SIMPLE)*

Unlike in English, in Spanish there are two simple past tenses, known as the preterite and the imperfect. They are simple tenses as they are formed by a word. Although the English simple past can be conveyed in Spanish using the preterite or the imperfect, these two tenses are very different and not interchangeable.

## EL PRETÉRITO INDEFINIDO *(THE PRETERITE)*

The preterite is used when we refer to completed actions, that is, when the verb shows an action that has a clear end. It describes a single action or several actions that occurred at a fixed time in the past. That is why the time when the action takes place usually appears in the sentence.

Ayer **fui** al cine.     *Yesterday I went to the movies.*
Ella **compró** miel la semana pasada.     *She bought some honey last week.*
**Me levanté**, **me duché** y **salí** de mi casa.     *I got up, took a shower and went out of my house.*

## EL PRETÉRITO INDEFINIDO DE VERBOS REGULARES
### (PRETERITE OF REGULAR VERBS)

The preterite forms are made by removing the infinitive ending of the verb (-ar, -er or -ir) and replacing it with an ending that indicates who is performing the action.

We will learn these endings with practical examples: **hablar** (*to speak*), **aprender** (*to learn*) and **escribir** (*to write*). The preterite is equivalent to "*spoke*", "*learned*" and "*wrote*", respectively.

|  | **-AR** HABL**AR** | **-ER** APREND**ER** | **-IR** ESCRIB**IR** |
|---|---|---|---|
| yo | habl**é** | aprend**í** | escrib**í** |
| tú | habl**aste** | aprend**iste** | escrib**iste** |
| usted / él / ella | habl**ó** | aprend**ió** | escrib**ió** |
| nosotros/as | habl**amos** | aprend**imos** | escrib**imos** |
| ustedes / ellos/as | habl**aron** | aprend**ieron** | escrib**ieron** |

Nosotros **aprendimos** muchas cosas el año pasado.
*We learned a lot of things last year.*

Cervantes **escribió** "Don Quijote".  *Cervantes wrote "Don Quixote".*
¿Con quién **hablaste**?  *Who did you speak to?*
Ellos no la **llamaron** la semana pasada.  *They didn't phone her last week.*
**Viví** dos años en Santo Domingo.  *I was living in Santo Domingo for two years.*

You may notice that "-er" and "-ir" verbs follow the same pattern in the preterite. You might also have noticed that in the first person in plural (nosotros/as) the same conjugation is used for both the present simple and the preterite for "-ar" and "-ir" verbs. Thus "hablamos" can mean either "*we speak*" or "*we spoke*", and "escribimos" can mean either "*we write*" or "*we wrote*". The context will make clear what is meant.

Reflexive verbs conjugate the same way:

Ayer **me levanté** tarde. *I got up late yesterday.*

## MARCADORES DE TIEMPO EN PASADO (ADVERBIOS)
### ([TIME MARKERS IN THE PAST (ADVERBS)])

They are words and expressions that show the time when the action occurred in the past. They are mainly used with the preterite, the imperfect indicative and the past continuous. Although Spanish is a very flexible language, the common position of these expressions is either at the beginning or end of the sentence.

| | |
|---|---|
| **ayer** | *yesterday* |
| **ayer por la mañana** | *yesterday morning* |
| **ayer por la tarde** | *yesterday afternoon* |
| **ayer por la noche** | *yesterday evening* |
| **anoche** | *last night* |
| **anteayer** | *the day before yesterday* |
| **la semana pasada** | *last week* |
| **el mes pasado** | *last month* |
| **el año pasado** | *last year* |
| **el domingo pasado** | *last Sunday* |
| **el otro día** | *the other day* |
| **hace tres días** | *three days ago* |

**El otro día** <u>compré</u> un reloj.
*I bought a watch the other day.*

**Anoche** no <u>vi</u> la película de la televisión.
*I didn't watch the film on television last night.*

Ellos <u>me visitaron</u> **la semana pasada**.
*They visited me last week.*

## Unit
# 31
**Days 61 & 62**

**In this unit we will learn:**
. The preterite of irregular verbs.
. "Desde", "hasta" and "durante".
. Question tags in Spanish (¿no?, ¿verdad?)

**Diálogo /** *Dialog*

María ve a Ramón un poco cansado y le pregunta si todo va bien.

*María sees Ramón a little tired and asks him if everything is alright.*

M: Ramón, pareces cansado. ¿Estás bien?
R: Sí, estoy bien, gracias. Muy cansado, pero bien.
M: ¿Por qué estás cansado? ¿Qué **hiciste** ayer?
R: Ayer me levanté temprano y **fui** de excursión con Laura, Esmeralda y Joaquín.
M: ¿Dónde **estuvieron**?
R: La semana pasada **leí** un artículo sobre una aldea en la montaña. Yo **estuve** allí hace mucho tiempo. Se lo **dije** a mis amigos y **quisimos** ir allí a pasar un día.
M: ¿Cómo **fueron** hasta allá?
R: **Fuimos** en auto desde aquí hasta la aldea y luego caminamos todo el día. **Conocimos** allí a un muchacho y él **fue** nuestro guía durante unas horas. **Estuvimos** allí desde las 10 de la mañana hasta las 6 de la tarde.
M: **Almorzaron** allí, ¿verdad?

M: *Ramón, you look tired. Are you okay?*
R: *Yes, I am fine, thank you. Very tired, but fine.*
M: *Why are you tired? What did you do yesterday?*
R: *Yesterday I got up early and went on a hike with Laura, Esmeralda and Joaquín.*
M: *Where were you?*
R: *Last week I read an article about a village in the mountains. I was there long ago. I told my friends and we wanted to go there and spend a day.*
M: *How did you get there?*
R: *We went by car from here up to the village and then we were walking the whole day. We met a boy and he was our guide for a few hours. We were there from 10 in the morning until 6 in the afternoon.*
M: *You had lunch there, didn't you?*

R: Sí, **pudimos** comer algo en un pequeño "restaurante". Luego Laura **quiso** ir al río y **tuvo** un accidente. **Se cayó** y **se cortó** en una pierna. No **fue** nada serio pero no **supimos** qué hacer. No **teníamos** botiquín.

M: ¿No **pidieron** ayuda?

R: Bueno, sí, **buscamos** a alguien en la aldea y ellos la **curaron**. Después, como ya se hizo un poco tarde, **volvimos** a la ciudad.

M: **Hicieron** fotos, ¿verdad?

R: Sí, **hicimos** muchas fotos. Te las enseñaré algún día.

R: *Yes, we could eat something in a small "restaurant". Afterwards Laura wanted to go to the river and she had an accident. She fell down and cut her leg. It wasn't serious but we didn't know what to do. We didn't have a first-aid kit.*

M: *Didn't you ask for help?*

R: *Well, yes, we looked for somebody in the village and they took care of her. Then, as it was getting late, we came back to the city.*

M: *You took some pictures, didn't you?*

R: *Yes, we took a lot of pictures. I'll show you some day.*

## EL PRETÉRITO INDEFINIDO DE LOS VERBOS IRREGULARES
### (THE PRETERITE OF IRREGULAR VERBS)

**a)** In preterite there are some verbs that change the vowel in the stem ("e" for "i" or "o" for "u") for the third person in singular (él, ella) and plural (ellos, ellas). Ex: **pedir** [*to ask (for)*, to order], **dormir** (*to sleep*).

|                      | PEDIR           | DORMIR          |
|----------------------|-----------------|-----------------|
| yo                   | ped**í**        | dorm**í**       |
| tú                   | ped**iste**     | dorm**iste**    |
| usted / él / ella    | p**i**d**ió**   | d**u**rm**ió**  |
| nosotros/as          | ped**imos**     | dorm**imos**    |
| ustedes / ellos/as   | p**i**d**ieron**| d**u**rm**ieron**|

Ellos **pidieron** champán y caviar.
El niño **durmió** tranquilamente.

*They ordered champagne and caviar.*
*The boy slept quietly.*

**b)** Some verbs have an orthographical change in the verb stem.
Ex: **buscar** (*to look for*), **pagar** (*to pay*).

|  | BUSCAR | PAGAR |
|---|---|---|
| yo | bus**qué** | pa**gué** |
| tú | buscaste | pagaste |
| usted / él / ella | buscó | pagó |
| nosotros/as | buscamos | pagamos |
| ustedes / ellos/as | buscaron | pagaron |

Ya **pagué** mis deudas.  *I already paid my debts.*

**c)** If there is an unstressed "i" between vowels, it changes into "y". Ex: **leer** (*to read*).

|  | LEER |
|---|---|
| yo | leí |
| tú | leíste |
| usted / él / ella | le**yó** |
| nosotros/as | leímos |
| ustedes / ellos/as | le**yeron** |

¿Qué libro **leyó** Francisco?  *What book did Francisco read?*

**d)** Some common verbs are irregular in the preterite. In these cases, the stress is upon the stem in the first and third persons in singular (yo, usted-él-ella). Ex: **saber** (*to know*), **poder** (*can*), **decir** (*to say*).

|  | SABER | PODER | DECIR |
|---|---|---|---|
| yo | **su**pe | **pu**de | **di**je |
| tú | supiste | pudiste | dijiste |
| usted / él / ella | **su**po | **pu**do | **di**jo |
| nosotros/as | supimos | pudimos | dijimos |
| ustedes / ellos/as | supieron | pudieron | dijeron |

We can see that these verbs are highly irregular.

**e)** The verbs "ser" (*to be*) and "ir" (*to go*) have the same irregular form in the preterite.

|  | SER - IR |
|---|---|
| yo | fui |
| tú | fuiste |
| usted / él / ella | fue |
| nosotros/as | fuimos |
| ustedes / ellos/as | fueron |

Él **fue** piloto durante cinco años.     *He was a pilot for five years.*
Él **fue** al teatro anoche.     *He went to the theater last night.*

**f)** Other important verbs with several irregularities are "estar" (*to be*) and "hacer" (*to do/make*).

|  | ESTAR | HACER |
|---|---|---|
| yo | estuve | hice |
| tú | estuviste | hiciste |
| usted / él / ella | estuvo | hizo |
| nosotros/as | estuvimos | hicimos |
| ustedes / ellos/as | estuvieron | hicieron |

La semana pasada **estuve** en California.     *I was in California last week.*
¿**Hiciste** los deberes ayer?     *Did you do your homework yesterday?*

**g)** The preterite of the impersonal form "hay" (*there is, there are*) is "**hubo**".

**Hubo** muchos accidentes de tráfico el año pasado.
*There were a lot of traffic accidents last year.*

## TOP VOCABULARY AND EXPRESSIONS

### "DESDE", "HASTA" Y "DURANTE"
*("Since/from", "until/to" and "during/for")*

We know that "desde" (*from*) and "hasta" [*(up) to*] can be prepositions of place:

> **Desde** aquí no te puedo ver.     *I can't see you from here.*
> Caminé **hasta** la estación.     *I walked up to the station.*

But now we will study them as prepositions of time and conjunctions.

"**Desde**" means "***from***":

> Nosotros trabajamos **desde** las 9 de la mañana.
> *We work from 9:00 a.m.*

And it also means "***since***":

> Ese puente está ahí **desde** 1900.
> *That bridge has been there since 1900.*

But it is also a conjunction. In this case it is followed by "**que**" and a sentence, that is, by a (subject and a) verb.

> Ella vive en esta ciudad **desde que** (ella) <u>se mudó</u> hace tres años.
> *She lives in this city since she moved three years ago.*

> Tengo pesadillas **desde que** (yo) <u>vi</u> esa película.
> *I've had nightmares since I watched that film.*

"**Hasta**", as a preposition of time, is equivalent to "***until***" and "***to***".

> Estuve en el hospital **hasta** las 3.
> *I was in the hospital until/till 3:00.*

> Ellos trabajaron desde enero **hasta** julio.
> *They were working from January to July.*

It also functions as a conjuction, followed by **"que"** and a subject or a verb.

Él lo estudió **hasta que** lo aprendió.     *He studied it until he learned it.*

**"Durante"** is a preposition that means *"during"* and *"for"*.
It can go before a determiner and a noun that indicates an activity (*during*).

Se durmió **durante** la cena.     *He fell asleep during the dinner.*
No lo escuché **durante** la conferencia.     *I didn't listen to him during the lecture.*

Or before a period of time (*for*).

Habló **durante** dos horas.     *He was speaking for two hours.*

Ellos estuvieron en Argentina **durante** seis meses.
*They were in Argentina for six months.*

## ¿NO?, ¿VERDAD? *(QUESTION TAGS IN SPANISH)*

In Spanish-speaking countries you will often hear "**¿no?**" or "**¿verdad?**" at the end of a sentence. It doesn't matter the type of verb in the sentence, the question tag is always the same. These two expressions are only used to confirm what has been said. They correspond to English question endings such as *"isn't it?"*, *"do they?"*, *"aren't you?"*, etc.

Ese auto es caro, **¿verdad?**     *That car is expensive, isn't it?*
Ustedes no fueron a la fiesta, **¿verdad?**     *You didn't go to the party, did you?*
Él habla español, **¿no?**     *He speaks Spanish, doesn't he?*
Compraste jugo de naranja, **¿no?**     *You bought orange juice, didn't you?*

## Unit 32

**Days 63 & 64**

**In this unit we will learn:**
. To express actions that started and finished in the past: verbs "ser" and "estar".
. The verb "dar".
. The verb "tener".
. Use of "¿Cuándo fue la primera/última vez que...?"
. Vocabulary: Crimes.

**Diálogo / Dialog**

A Cristina le robaron el bolso la semana pasada y le cuenta su experiencia a Miguel.

*Cristinas's purse was stolen last week and she is telling Miguel about her experience.*

M: Alguien me dijo que **tuviste** una mala experiencia la semana pasada.
C: Sí, me **robaron** el bolso.
M: ¿Cómo ocurrió?
C: No lo sé. Fui a un bar con una amiga y puse el bolso en una silla, junto a nosotras. Cuando quise pagar, el bolso ya no estaba allí.
M: **¿Cuándo fue la última vez que lo viste?**
C: No lo recuerdo bien. **Estuvimos** en el bar durante un rato.
M: ¿Y qué hiciste entonces?
C: Fui a la comisaría. **Estuve** allí dos horas. **Fue** una experiencia horrible. Pero dos días después la **policía** me llamó y me dijeron que tenían el bolso. Fui de nuevo a la comisaría y me lo **dieron.** Me dijeron que **arrestaron** al **ladrón.** Les **di** las gracias y me fui a casa aliviada. El **ladrón** no se llevó nada del bolso.

M: ¿Quién **fue**?
C: Me dijeron que **fue** un chico bajo y rubio. Pero no recuerdo a ningún chico bajo y rubio en el bar.
M: Después de todo, **tuviste** mucha suerte. A mí me han **robado** varias veces.
C: ¿Sí? **¿Cuándo fue la primera vez que** te robaron?
M: **Fue** hace mucho tiempo. Ya te contaré.

M: *Someone told me that you had a bad experience last week.*
C: *Yes, my purse was stolen.*
M: *How did it happen?*
C: *I don't know. I went to a bar with a friend and I put my purse on a chair, next to us. When I wanted to pay, the purse was gone.*
M: *When did you last see it?*
C: *I don't remember very well. We were at the bar for a while.*
M: *And what did you do then?*
C: *I went to the police station. I was there for two hours. It was a terrible experience. But two days later the police called me and told me that they had the purse. I went back to the police station and they gave it to me. They told me that they had arrested the thief. I thanked them for it and went home relieved. The thief didn't take anything from my purse.*
M: *Who was the thief?*
C: *They told me it was a short and blond boy. But I don't remember a short and blond boy at the bar.*
M: *You were very lucky, after all. I have been robbed several times.*
C: *Have you? When were you robbed for the first time?*
M: *It was a long time ago. I'll tell you one day.*

## ACCIONES QUE COMENZARON Y TERMINARON EN EL PASADO: VERBOS "SER" Y "ESTAR" (ACTIONS THAT STARTED AND FINISHED IN THE PAST: VERBS "SER" AND "ESTAR")

In units 30 and 31 we studied the forms and uses of the preterite. Now we will focus on the preterite of two very important verbs: **ser** and **estar**.
The preterite forms of these verbs were seen in unit 31, but we will study them in more detail in this unit.

Let's look over them again:

|  | SER | ESTAR |
|---|---|---|
| yo | fui | estuve |
| tú | fuiste | estuviste |
| usted / él / ella | fue | estuvo |
| nosotros/as | fuimos | estuvimos |
| ustedes / ellos/as | fueron | estuvieron |

As we can see, the conjugation of these verbs in the preterite is very irregular.

The preterite of the verb "ser" is used to express "permanent" states in the past, whereas "estar" refers to past "temporary" states or locations. Both are equivalent to "*was, were*" in English.

| | |
|---|---|
| Ellos **fueron** sus profesores. | *They were his teachers.* |
| **Fuimos** los ganadores de concurso. | *We were the winners of the contest.* |
| – ¿Quién **fue** el inventor de la radio? | *– Who invented the radio?* |
| – **Fue** Marconi. | *– It was Marconi. (Literally: Who was the inventor of the radio? Marconi was).* |

| | |
|---|---|
| Ella **estuvo** enferma la semana pasada. | *She was ill last week.* |
| ¿**Estuvieron** ellos en la fiesta? | *Were they at the party?* |
| No **estuviste** con ella. Fuiste a otro lugar. | *You weren't with her. You went somewhere else.* |

In the last example, the verb "fuiste" is the preterite of "ir" (*to go*). Remember that the preterite of "ser" and "ir" is exactly the same.

## EL VERBO "DAR" [THE VERB "DAR"(TO GIVE)]

This verb has a special feature: although it ends with "-ar", in the preterite it is conjugated as verbs ending with "-ir". It is equivalent to "**gave**" in English.

| | DAR |
|---|---|
| yo | **di** |
| tú | **diste** |
| usted / él / ella | **dió** |
| nosotros/as | **dimos** |
| ustedes / ellos/as | **dieron** |

| | |
|---|---|
| Ellos nos **dieron** este libro. | *They gave us this book.* |
| ¿Qué te **dio** ella? | *What did she give you?* |
| No le **di** (a él) los regalos. | *I didn't give him the presents.* |
| ¿Cuánto dinero le **diste** a ella? | *How much money did you give her?* |

## EL VERBO "TENER" *[THE VERB "TENER"(TO HAVE)]*

The verb "**tener**" is also very irregular in the preterite and is conjugated in a similar way to the verb "estar". This tense corresponds to "**had**" in English, but we know that the verb "tener" is equivalent to "*to be*" in many expressions, so this tense could also mean "*was/were*".

| | TENER |
|---|---|
| yo | tuve |
| tú | tuviste |
| usted / él / ella | tuvo |
| nosotros/as | tuvimos |
| ustedes / ellos/as | tuvieron |

| | |
|---|---|
| Mis abuelos **tuvieron** muchos hijos. | *My grandparents had a lot of children.* |
| Él no **tuvo** tiempo libre. | *He didn't have any free time.* |
| ¿**Tuviste** frío anoche? | *Were you cold last night?* |
| No **tuvimos** suerte y perdimos el partido. | *We weren't lucky and lost the match.* |

## ¿CUÁNDO FUE LA PRIMERA/ÚLTIMA VEZ QUE......?
### *(WHEN DID YOU FIRST/LAST ...?)*

This question is almost always made in the preterite and refers to the first or last time that somebody did something.

¿Cuándo **fue** <u>la primera vez</u> que **fuiste** a EEUU?
¿Cuándo **fuiste** a EEUU <u>por primera vez</u>?
*When did you first go to the USA?*

¿Cuándo **fue** <u>la última vez</u> que **compraste** el periódico?
¿Cuándo **compraste** el periódico <u>por última vez</u>?
*When did you last buy the newspaper?*

¿Cuándo **fue** la primera vez que ustedes **vinieron** aquí? *When did you first come here?*

¿Cuándo **fue** la última vez que ella **hizo** un pastel de manzana? *When did she last make an apple pie?*

## VOCABULARIO:

**Delitos** *(Crimes)*

**robar:** *to steal, to rob*
**ladrón:** *thief, robber*
**ladrón (callejero):** *pickpocket*
**arrestar, detener:** *to arrest*
**escapar:** *to escape*
**peligroso:** *dangerous*
**cárcel, prisión:** *jail, prison*

**robo:** *theft, robbery, burglary*
**ladrón (en una tienda):** *shoplifter*
**ladrón (en una casa):** *burglar*
**testigo:** *witness*
**armado:** *armed*
**detective:** *detective*
**policía:** *police, policeman, policewoman*

Hubo un **robo** en el Banco Central.
El **ladrón** estaba **armado**.
Un **ladrón** me **robó** la billetera.
La **policía arrestó** a ese peligroso **ladrón**.
No hubo **testigos** del **delito**.

*There was a robbery at the Banco Central.*
*The thief was armed.*
*A pickpocket stole my wallet.*
*The police arrested that dangerous burglar.*
*There weren't any witnesses of the crime.*

**In this unit we will learn:**
. The past imperfect: forms and uses.
. Elements to join sentences: "mientras" and "cuando".
. Vocabulary: Objects on the street.

## Unit
# 33
**Days 65 & 66**

**Diálogo** / *Dialog*

Pedro habla con Rita y le pregunta acerca de lo que hizo el domingo anterior.

*Pedro is talking to Rita and asks her about what she did last Sunday.*

P: El domingo pasado **quería** verte pero no te encontré en casa. ¿**Estabas** con tu familia?
R: No. Salí por la mañana y no volví hasta la noche.

P: ¿Qué hiciste todo el día?
R: Como **era** un buen día y **hacía** sol decidí ir al campo, pero allí **llovía**. Entonces volví a la ciudad y fui al museo de ciencias naturales.

P: ¿Es un museo interesante?
R: Muy interesante. Allí **había** animales, plantas, minerales, fósiles.... **Mientras veía** todo eso **me acordaba** de mi madre. A ella **le gustaba** mucho ese museo. **Pasaba** horas allí. Luego quise volver a casa pero el auto no **arrancaba**. **Eran** las 5:30 y decidí tomar el autobús. **Cuando** llegamos a la parada cerca de mi casa, **había** niebla y no **veía** nada. No **había** nadie en la calle. Bueno, yo no **podía** ver a

P: *Last Sunday I wanted to see you but you weren't at home. Were you with your family?*
R: *No. I went out in the morning and didn't come back until the evening.*

P: *What did you do all day long?*
R: *Since it was sunny and a nice day I decided to go to the country, but it was raining there. Then I came back to the city and went to the museum of natural science.*

P: *Is it an interesting museum?*
R: *Very interesting. There were animals, plants, minerals, fossils... While I was looking at all that I remembered my mother. She liked that museum a lot. She spent hours there. Then I wanted to go back home but the car didn't start. It was 5:30 and I decided to take the bus. When we reached the bus stop near my house, it was foggy and I couldn't see anything. There was nobody on the street. Well, I couldn't see*

nadie. No **veía** ni la **valla publicitaria** que hay allí. Sólo **veía** la **farola**. Era un poco peligroso.

P: ¿Y qué hiciste?

R: Me fui a casa, pero **mientras iba** a casa **oía** pasos detrás de mí. Empecé a correr y choqué contra el **buzón** que hay en la **acera**. Me asusté un poco.

P: ¿Y qué pasó?

R: Pude llegar a casa pero, **cuando** entré, alguien llamó a la puerta. Entonces me asusté mucho.

P: ¿Quién **era**?

R: **Era** una vecina. **Quería** contarme algunas cosas.

*anybody. I couldn't even see the billboard there. I could only see the lamppost. It was a little dangerous.*

P: *And what did you do?*

R: *I started home but, while I was on my way home, I could hear steps behind me. I started to run and bumped into the mailbox that is on the sidewalk. I got a little frightened.*

P: *And what happened?*

R: *I was able to get home but, when I came in, someone knocked at the door. Then I got scared.*

P: *Who was it?*

R: *It was a neighbor. She wanted to tell me some things.*

## EL PRETÉRITO IMPERFECTO *(THE IMPERFECT)*

With the preterite we can't express all the actions and events that took place in the past. We also use the imperfect, which is a very common tense. Fortunately, the conjugation of this verbal tense is very easy.

As with every tense, we have to know the endings for each person. Let's study them with practical examples. Ex: **hablar** (*to speak*), **aprender** (*to learn*), **escribir** (*to write*).

| | -AR<br>HABL**AR** | -ER<br>APREND**ER** | -IR<br>ESCRIB**IR** |
|---|---|---|---|
| yo | habl**aba** | aprend**ía** | escrib**ía** |
| tú | habl**abas** | aprend**ías** | escrib**ías** |
| usted / él / ella | habl**aba** | aprend**ía** | escrib**ía** |
| nosotros/as | habl**ábamos** | aprend**íamos** | escrib**íamos** |
| ustedes / ellos/as | habl**aban** | aprend**ían** | escrib**ían** |

We can take note that the endings for "-er" and "-ir" verbs are exactly the same.

All the verbs in Spanish follow this pattern*. We only have to use the right endings according to the verb (infinitive) ending.
(*) The only exceptions are "**ser**" (*to be*), "**ir**" (*to go*) and "**ver**" (*to see*).

We already know that the imperfect in Spanish (the same as the preterite) is also equivalent to the past simple in English, but it is important to notice that the imperfect is frequently translated in ways other than the past simple in English.

¿Qué **hacía** Guadalupe? (Ella) **navegaba** por internet.
*What was Guadalupe doing? She was surfing the internet.*

¿Dónde **estabas**? **Estaba** en la cocina.
*Where were you? I was in the kitchen.*

¿Con quién **hablaban** ustedes? **Hablábamos** con nuestra vecina.
*Who were you talking to? We were talking to our neighbor.*

The impersonal form "**hay**" belongs to the verb "**haber**", so its imperfect form is "**había**" (*there was/there were*).

Hace veinte años no **había** tantos celulares como hoy.
*Twenty years ago there weren't as many cell phones as today.*

## And we use the imperfect:

**a) To describe a state or a situation in the past:**

| | |
|---|---|
| Susana **estaba** cansada cuando llegó a casa. | Susana was tired when she got home. |
| Aquí **había** un cuadro antes. | There was a picture here before. |

**b) To express habits or repeated actions or facts in the past:**

| | |
|---|---|
| A menudo **jugábamos** en la plaza. | We often played in the square. |
| Hace mucho tiempo me **gustaba** comer caramelos. | I liked eating sweets a long time ago. |

**c) To refer to past actions or events that occurred over an unspecified time:**

| | |
|---|---|
| Los alumnos **salían** de la escuela. | The pupils left the school. |
| ¿Dónde **vivías**? **Vivía** en Londres. | Where were you living? I was living in London. |

**d) To indicate time or age in the past:**

| | |
|---|---|
| **Eran** las 6 de la tarde. | It was 6:00 p.m. |
| Ella **tenía** veinticinco años. | She was twenty-five years old. |

The verbs "**ser**" (to be), "**ir**" (to go) and "**ver**" (to see) are the only verbs that follow different patterns:

| | SER | IR | VER |
|---|---|---|---|
| yo | era | iba | veía |
| tú | eras | ibas | veías |
| usted / él / ella | eran | iban | veían |
| nosotros/as | éramos | íbamos | veíamos |
| ustedes / ellos/as | eran | iban | veían |

| | |
|---|---|
| Brenda **era** muy tímida. | Brenda was very shy. |
| – ¿Dónde **ibas**? | – Where were you going? |
| – **Iba** a tu casa. | – I was going to your house. |
| Había niebla y no **veíamos** nada. | It was foggy and we couldn't see anything. |

## ELEMENTOS PARA UNIR FRASES: "MIENTRAS" Y "CUANDO"
### *(ELEMENTS TO JOIN SENTENCES: "WHILE" AND "WHEN")*

There are times when we need to say several things or refer to several actions in the same sentence. Thus, we make a longer sentence including these ideas, but we need an element to join them. In this unit we will work on two of these linking words: **mientras** (*while*) and **cuando** (*when*).

**Mientras** (*while*) can be defined as "during the time that". It means that the two actions joined in the same sentence by "**mientras**" are simultaneous, that is, they are happening at the same time. **Mientras** is generally placed at the beginning of the sentence or in a middle position.

Yo leía **mientras** mi padre cocinaba.
**Mientras** mi padre cocinaba, yo leía.

*I was reading while my father was cooking.*

Sonó el teléfono **mientras** tú te duchabas.
*The phone rang while you were taking a shower.*

Voy al gimnasio **mientras** mis hijos están en la escuela.
*I go to the gym while my children are at school.*

"**Mientras**" or "**mientras tanto**", as adverbs of time, are equivalent to "*meanwhile*", "in the *meantime*".

Voy de compras. **Mientras (tanto)**, tú puedes lavar el auto.
*I'm going shopping. Meanwhile, you can wash the car.*

**Cuando** (*when*) means "at the time that". It is similar to the interrogative "¿cuándo?" (*when?*) but without the graphic accent. It is also placed in an initial or middle position.

> **Cuando** los niños salieron de la escuela, sus padres los recogieron.
> *When the children went out of the school their parents picked them up.*

> Me despierto **cuando** suena el despertador.
> *I get up when the alarm clock rings.*

> ¿Qué haces **cuando** no puedes dormir?
> *What do you do when you can't sleep?*

## VOCABULARIO:

**El mobiliario urbano** *(Objects on the street)*

**banco:** *bench*
**papelera:** *waste basket*
**fuente:** *fountain*
**buzón:** *mailbox*
**caseta del autobús:** *bus shelter*
**semáforo:** *traffic lights*
**farola:** *lamppost*
**estatua:** *statue*
**monumento:** *monument*
**acera:** *sidewalk*
**valla publicitaria:** *billboard*
**jardinera:** *garden bed*

Ellos están sentados en un **banco** de madera. — *They are sitting on a wooden bench.*
Hay muchas **papeleras** en esta zona. — *There are a lot of waste baskets in this area.*
Había una **fuente** cerca de la **jardinera**. — *There was a fountain near the garden bed.*
El camión chocó contra la **caseta del autobús**. — *The truck crashed into the bus shelter.*
La **valla publicitaria** estaba delante de la **estatua**. — *The billboard was in front of the statue.*

**In this unit we will learn:**

. To express durative actions in the past.

. Different meanings of the same words in different Spanish-speaking countries.

# Unit
# 34

**Days 67 & 68**

## Diálogo / *Dialog*

Mauricio y Carlota hablan sobre el español que se habla en diferentes países.

*Mauricio and Carlota are talking about the Spanish spoken in different countries.*

M: ¡Hola, Carlota!

C: ¡Hola!

M: ¿Quieres **tomar** algo?

C: No, gracias. No tengo sed.

M: Bueno, no sólo me refería a una bebida. ¿Quieres comer algo?

C: No, tampoco tengo hambre, gracias.

M: Yo soy español y, en España, el verbo **"tomar"** se puede referir a comidas o bebidas. Por cierto, estás muy **guapa**.

C: No, ¿por qué dices eso?

M: Porque te veo linda.

C: Bueno, para nosotros, **"estar guapo"** es estar enfadado.

M: [Risas] Para nosotros, "estar guapo" significa algo diferente.

C: Sí. Una amiga **estuvo practicando** español en algunos países latinoamericanos y también notó diferencias con el español que ella

M: *Hello, Carlota!*

C: *Hello!*

M: *Would you like to have something?*

C: *No, thank you. I am not thirsty.*

M: *Well, I didn't refer only to a drink. Would you like something to eat?*

C: *No, I am not hungry either, thank you.*

M: *I am Spanish and, in Spain, the verb "tomar" can refer to both food and drink. By the way, you look very pretty.*

C: *No. Why do you say that?*

M: *Because you look beautiful.*

C: *Well, for us "estar guapo" means to be annoyed.*

M: *[Laughs] For us, "estar guapo" means some thing different.*

C: *Yes, a friend of mine was practicing Spanish in some Latin American countries and she also noticed some differences with the Spanish that*

hablaba. Por ejemplo, en algunos países dicen "**carro**" o "**coche**" cuando hablan de un auto.

M: Sí, hay muchas palabras y expresiones diferentes. Tú **estabas estudiando idiomas**, ¿no?

C: Sí, **estuve estudiando** inglés y francés durante tres años, pero lo tuve que dejar.

M: ¿Por qué?

C: Porque necesitaba dinero y tuve que trabajar. Y mientras **estuve trabajando**, no tenía tiempo para estudiar. Por cierto, ¿qué **estabas comiendo** cuando llegué?

M: **Estaba tomando** una "tapa". Otra costumbre española.

*she spoke. For example, in some countries they say "carro" or "coche" when they speak about a car.*

M: *Yes, there are many different words and expressions. You were studying languages, weren't you?*

C: *Yes, I was studying English and French for three years, but I had to stop.*

M: *Why?*

C: *Because I needed money and I had to work. While I was working I didn't have time to study. By the way, what were you eating when I arrived?*

M: *I was having a "tapa". It's another Spanish custom.*

## ACCIONES DURADERAS EN EL PASADO *(PAST DURATIVE ACTIONS)*

To express a durative action in the past we can use two tenses: the preterite and imperfect, but in a continuous or progressive way. In this case, both tenses are equivalent to the past continuous in English (*was/were + gerund*).

**Preterite continuous** = **preterite of "estar" + gerund**

|  | **ESTAR** | |
|---|---|---|
| yo | estuve | |
| tú | estuviste | |
| usted / él / ella | estuvo | jugando |
| nosotros/as | estuvimos | |
| ustedes / ellos/as | estuvieron | |

When we use this tense we want to indicate that the action was durative but it was completed in the past.

Nosotros **estuvimos jugando** al tenis ayer.
*We were playing tennis yesterday.*

Ellos **estuvieron trabajando** para esa empresa hace dos años.
*They were working for that firm two years ago.*

**Estuve cenando** en ese restaurante la semana pasada.
*I was having dinner in that restaurant last week.*

| Imperfect continuous | = imperfect to "estar" + gerund |
| --- | --- |

|  | **ESTAR** |  |
| --- | --- | --- |
| yo | estaba | |
| tú | estabas | |
| usted / él / ella | estaba | jugando |
| nosotros/as | estábamos | |
| ustedes / ellos/as | estaban | |

Él **estaba jugando** al tenis cuando se cayó.
*He was playing tennis when he fell down.*

¿Qué **estaba haciendo** ella? Ella **estaba nadando**.
*What was she doing? She was swimming.*

Yo **estaba hablando** con ella cuando alguien la llamó por teléfono.
*I was talking to her when somebody phoned her.*

By using this tense we refer to a durative action in progress (Él estaba jugando al tenis) in a certain moment in the past (cuando se cayó), but, in fact, the action was not completed.

This "certain moment" in the past may not appear explicitly, but it is understood in context.

¿Qué **estaba haciendo** ella (cuando la viste)?
(Cuando la vi) Ella **estaba nadando.**

*What was she doing (when you saw her)?*
*(When I saw her) She was swimming.*

This tense is also used when we refer to two durative past actions happening simultaneously.

Yo **estaba leyendo** mientras ellos **estaban haciendo** sus deberes.

*I was reading while they were doing their homework.*

Or when a single action "interrupted" another one in progress. In this case, the action that "interrupts" is expressed in the preterite.

**Estábamos viendo** la televisión cuando alguien **llamó** a la puerta.
*We were watching television when somebody knocked at the door.*

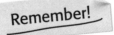
## Remember!

In continuous tenses we <u>never</u> use the verb "ser", but "estar".
Also remember that, in many cases, you can use the simple form of the imperfect to refer to a durative action. Therefore it would be translated as a past continuous in English:

Ella **leía** mientras yo **limpiaba** la casa.
*She <u>was reading</u> while I <u>was cleaning</u> the house.*

## DIFERENTES SIGNIFICADOS DE LAS PALABRAS EN DIFERENTES PAÍSES
### (DIFFERENT MEANINGS OF WORDS IN DIFFERENT COUNTRIES)

As it happens with English, many words or expressions have different meanings depending on the country where they are used. In this unit we will look at a few of them, but this is something we always have to pay attention to when we speak.

The verb **"tomar"** (*to take*) is used in many Latin American countries as a synonym of **"beber"** *[to drink (alcoholic drinks)]*:

Ayer no **tomé** nada.    *I didn't have a drink yesterday.*

The verb **"manejar"** (*to handle, to manage*) is used in some countries for **"conducir"** (*to drive*).

¿Sabes **manejar**?    *Can you drive?*

The pronoun **"ustedes"** (*you*), when used informally, corresponds to **"vosotros, vosotras"** in Spain.

**Ustedes** son españoles = **Vosotros** sois españoles..
*You are Spanish.*

The word **"auto"** (*car*) is used in some countries, but in some others it is **"carro"** or **"coche"**.

Mi **auto** no arranca.    *My car doesn't start.*

The adjective "angry" is equivalent to "bravo", "guapo" or "enfadado", depending on the country.

Tu padre está **bravo**. ¿Qué hiciste?    *Your father is angry. What had you done?*

As we have said, "guapo" means "*angry*" in some countries, but it means "*handsome*" in Spain.

Juan está **guapo** hoy.    *Juan is angry today.*

Juan está **guapo** hoy.    *Juan looks handsome today. (in Spain)*

There are also many anglicisms in Spanish, mainly in the Spanish spoken in Mexico, Central America and the Caribbean, which are not so common in other countries, such as:

**cloche** *(from clutch)*        embrague
**troque** *(from truck)*        camión
**aplicación** *(from application)*    solicitud
**overol** *(from overall)*        mono, traje de faena

These are just a few examples of the differences that we may find when talking to Spanish-speaking people from different countries. Of course there are many more, so we will we have to pay attention to different possible meanings in the different countries.

<table>
<tr><td>

**In this unit we will learn:**

. To express past actions: the preterite versus the imperfect.

. Expressions when asking someone out on a date and impressing the other person.

</td><td>

**Unit**

**35**

**Days 69 & 70**

</td></tr>
</table>

## Diálogo / Dialog

Guillermo ve a una muchacha (Rosalía) mirando un plano de la ciudad y le pregunta:

*Guillermo sees a girl (Rosalía) looking at a map of the city and asks her:*

G: ¡Hola! ¿Puedo ayudarte?
R: Sí, por favor. ¿Dónde está la escuela de arte?
G: ¿Eres nueva en la ciudad?
R: Sí. Llegué la semana pasada, pero todavía no la conozco bien.
G: ¿Te gusta?
R: Sí, es muy bonita.
G: ¿Dónde vivías antes?
R: En España.
G: Yo soy de aquí. Me llamo Guillermo.
R: ¡Encantada! Yo me llamo Rosalía.
G: **Tienes una sonrisa muy bonita**, Rosalía.
R: ¡Gracias!
G: Mira, la escuela de arte está allí mismo. La puedes ver desde aquí.
R: Muy bien. Muchas gracias. Yo **estuve** aquí hace muchos años, pero no me **acordaba** de muchos sitios.
G: ¿Conoces el Café Central?
R: Sí.
G: ¿**Quieres ir**? Podemos tomar algo y hablar un poco.
R: Mmm. No sé.....¡Está bien!
G: Pues vamos. Es por allí.

*G: Hello! Can I help you?*
*R: Yes, please. Where is the art school?*
*G: Are you new in town?*
*R: Yes, I arrived last week but I don't know it well yet.*
*G: Do you like it?*
*R: Yes, it is beautiful.*
*G: Where were you living before?*
*R: In Spain.*
*G: I'm from here. My name is Guillermo.*
*R: Pleased to meet you! My name is Rosalía.*
*G: You have a very nice smile, Rosalía.*
*R: Thank you.*
*G: Look! The art school is right there. You can see it from here.*
*R: Ok. Thank you very much. I was here many years ago but I didn't remember many places.*
*G: Do you know the Café Central?*
*R: Yes.*
*G: Would you like to go? We can have a drink and talk a little.*
*R: Mmm... I don't know..... Alright!*
*G: Then, let's go. That way.*

Guillermo y Rosalía llegan al Café Central.

*Guillermo and Rosalía are now in the Café Central.*

G: ¿Tu abuelo **vino** a América en 1920? ¿Por qué?

R: Sí. Él **vivía** en España, en un pueblo pequeño. Sus padres no **tenían** dinero. Eran muy pobres. Por eso **decidió** emigrar a Argentina.

G: ¿Cómo **fue** allí?

R: **Tomó** un barco y, después de un viaje de 55 días, **llegó** a Buenos Aires. Allí **encontró** trabajo como camarero. **Fueron** unos años duros, pero **pudo** ahorrar algo de dinero y **compró** el bar donde **trabajaba**.

G: ¿Qué **hizo** después?

R: **Se quedó** en Argentina durante 20 años. Luego, **volvió** a España. Entonces **conoció** a mi abuela, **se casaron**, y nunca más **volvió** a América. **Estaba** muy enamorado de ella.

G: Bueno, es muy interesante pero, ¿**qué tal si** bailamos?

R: Estoy con un hombre muy apuesto. No puedo negarme....

G: Oye, Rosalía, ¿**tú crees en el amor a primera vista**?

R: Err... ¿**Te apetece** un trago?

---

G: *Did your grandfather come to America in 1920? Why?*

R: *Yes. He was living in Spain, in a little village. His parents didn't have any money. They were very poor. That's why he decided to emigrate to Argentina.*

G: *How did he get there?*

R: *He went by ship and, after a 55-day journey he arrived in Buenos Aires. There he got a job as a waiter. Those years were very hard but he managed to save some money and bought the bar where he was working.*

G: *What did he do after that?*

R: *He stayed in Argentina for 20 years. Afterwards he went back to Spain. Then he met my grandmother, they got married and he never came back to America. He was very much in love with her.*

G: *Well, it's very interesting but....how about dancing now?*

R: *I am with a very handsome man. I can't say no.*

G: *Listen, Rosalía. Do you believe in love at first sight?*

R: *Err... Do you feel like a drink?*

## UNA ACCIÓN EN PASADO: ¿QUÉ TIEMPO USO?
### (A PAST ACTION: WHAT TENSE DO I HAVE TO USE?)

So far we have studied two past tenses: the preterite and the imperfect. Let's see some important differences between them that may help us use these tenses properly.

**a)** When we use the imperfect we are placed "within" a past fact or event and describe an unfinished process at that moment.

**Hacía** mucho frío.                                   *It was very cold.*

But using the preterite we are placed "after" a past fact or event and describe a process already finished or completed.

**Hizo** mucho frío (ese día).                          *It was very cold (that day).*

**b)** By using the imperfect we refer to a fact that has not finished at a specific moment in the past. We describe a momentary situation.

Ayer, a las 8, yo **estaba visitando** a mi tía.       *Yesterday at 8:00 I was visiting my aunt.*

Cuando llegaste yo **estaba haciendo** un ejercicio.
*When you arrived I was doing an exercise.*

But the preterite shows an action that has already been finished at a specific moment in the past. We refer to a completed fact.

Ellos **estuvieron trabajando** hasta las 5.           *They were working until 5.*
**Hice** el ejercicio en dos minutos.                   *I did the exercise in two minutes.*

For this reason, when we refer to the "total duration" of an action (two years, an hour, all morning, until 5:00, twice, a long time, etc.) we have to use the preterite, not the imperfect.

La semana pasada **trabajé** todos los días.            *Last week I worked everyday.*

**Estuvimos** en México durante tres meses.             *We were in Mexico for three months.*

Ellos **estuvieron conversando** mucho tiempo.          *They were talking for a long time.*

**c)** We use the imperfect to indicate features of objects or people:

| | |
|---|---|
| Tu hermana **era** muy simpática. | *Your sister was very friendly.* |
| Los gatos **eran** negros. | *The cats were black.* |
| El vaso **estaba** lleno de agua. | *The glass was full of water.* |

But the preterite when we refer to features of a process or activity:

| | |
|---|---|
| La reunión **estuvo/fue** interesante. | *The meeting was interesting.* |
| La fiesta **estuvo/fue** divertida. | *The party was fun.* |

**d)** You also have to take into account the following differences between these two tenses:

| | |
|---|---|
| **Conocí** a tu padre. | *I met your father. (We were introduced)* |
| **Conocía** a tu padre. | *I knew your father. (It was a past fact)* |
| Ellos **traían** regalos. | *They used to bring some presents.* |
| Ellos **trajeron** regalos. | *They brought some presents (that time).* |
| Él **tenía** un hijo. | *He had a son. (It was a past fact)* |
| Él **tuvo** un hijo. | *He had a son. (His son was born)* |

Cuando **iba** al cine compraba palomitas.
*When I would go to the movies, I bought some popcorn.*

Cuando **fui** al cine compré palomitas.
*When I went to the movies I bought some popcorn (after getting there).*

## LAS FECHAS *(DATES)*

To say the date in Spanish is very easy. We simply use cardinal numbers, the preposition "**de**" (*of*) introducing the month, the month, the preposition "**de**" introducing the year, and the year.

Remember that, unlike in English, dates are expressed with cardinal numbers and not ordinal ones.

12 **de** febrero **de** 2003      *February 12th, 2003*

Hoy es 24 **de** mayo **de** 2009      *Today is May 24th, 2009*

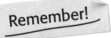

**Remember!**

In Spanish we always follow this order: **day / month / year**. Besides this order, there are some other differences with English:

**a) In Spanish the months are written in lowercase letters:**
    **f**ebrero       **m**ayo

**b) The years are always read as a quantity:**
    2009 dos mil nueve
    1966 mil novecientos sesenta y seis (NOT diecinueve - sesenta y seis)

But if we want to say the date when something occurs, we need to add "**el**" before the number:

Mi cumpleaños es **el** 15 (quince) de agosto.
*My birthday is on August 15th.*

El examen es **el** 3 de abril.
*The exam is on April 3rd.*

El hombre llegó a la luna **el** 20 de julio de 1969.
*Man landed on the moon on July 20th, 1969.*

## TOP VOCABULARY AND EXPRESSIONS

### LOS DÍAS DE LA SEMANA *(The days of the week)*

| | |
|---|---|
| **lunes** | *Monday* |
| **martes** | *Tuesday* |
| **miércoles** | *Wednesday* |
| **jueves** | *Thursday* |
| **viernes** | *Friday* |
| **sábado** | *Saturday* |
| **domingo** | *Sunday* |

In unit 15 we learned the days of the week listed above and now we are going to focus on their uses and expressions.

The days of the week are preceded by "**el**" (except when we refer to the day today, yesterday, tomorrow, etc.).

| | |
|---|---|
| Tengo una cita **el** <u>jueves</u>. | *I have a date on/next Thursday.* |
| Él vino **el** <u>domingo</u>. | *He came on/last Sunday.* |
| Hoy es <u>martes</u>. | *Today is Tuesday.* |
| Ayer fue <u>lunes</u>. | *Yesterday was Monday.* |

When we use the days of the week in plural, we only change the article "el" for "**los**", except for "sábado" and "domingo", which have plural forms (sábados, domingos).

| | |
|---|---|
| No me gustan **los** <u>lunes</u>. | I don't like Mondays. |

Ellos tienen clases de español **los** <u>miércoles</u> y <u>viernes</u>.
*They have Spanish lessons on Wednesdays and Fridays.*

| | |
|---|---|
| Ella va al teatro **los sábados**. | *She goes to the theater on Saturdays.* |

For "*next + day*" we say "**el próximo + day**" and for "*last + day*" we use "**el pasado + day**".

**El próximo** <u>sábado</u> voy a un concierto.
**El** <u>sábado</u> **próximo** voy a un concierto. ⎤ *Next Saturday I'm going to a concert.*
**El** <u>sábado</u> **que viene** voy a un concierto. ⎦

Tuve un examen **el pasado** <u>jueves</u>. ⎤ *I had an exam last Thursday.*
Tuve un examen **el** <u>jueves</u> **pasado**. ⎦

The parts of the day may also be added to the days of the week. In this case we have to say:

**el / los** + <u>día</u> + **por la +** ⎡ **mañana** ⎤    *on + day +* ⎡ *morning(s)* ⎤
                       **tarde**                           *afternoon(s)*
                       **noche** ⎦                      *evening(s)* ⎦

Ustedes están cansados **los lunes por la mañana**.
*You are tired on Monday mornings.*

Vuelo a Nueva York **el jueves por la tarde**.
*I'm flying to New York on Thursday afternoon.*

Ella va a bailar **los martes por la noche**.
*She goes dancing on Tuesday evenings.*

## LAS CONJUNCIONES "PERO" Y "SINO"
### [THE CONJUNCTIONS "PERO" AND "SINO" (BUT)]

Both **"pero"** and **"sino"** are conjunctions that indicate <u>contrast</u>. They are equivalent to "*but*" in English.

- **Pero** introduces an idea that contrasts with the previous one:

Sé manejar **pero** no tengo auto.
*I can drive but I don't have a car.*

Tus padres no vienen **pero** tu hermano sí.
*Your parents are not coming but your brother is.*

No teníamos café, **pero** teníamos té.
*We didn't have any coffee but we had some tea.*

- **Sino** introduces an idea that corrects something previously said, that is, we negate an element and replace it for another.

No hablo francés, **sino** español.
*I don't speak French, but Spanish.*

Él no tiene 42 años, **sino** 48.
*He isn't 42 years old, but 48.*

Ellos no venían de Argentina, **sino** de Chile.
*They didn't come from Argentina, but from Chile.*

There is a common mistake that English speakers make:

          **sino**
No soy Juan, ~~pero~~ Pedro.       *I'm not Juan, but Pedro.*

**Sino** can go before an infinitive or a gerund, but, if the verb is conjugated, **sino** changes for **sino que**.

No quieren cantar, **sino** <u>bailar</u>.     *They don't want to sing, but to dance.*
No estamos comiendo, **sino** <u>viendo</u> la TV.   *We aren't eating, but watching TV.*
Ella no aprobó el examen, **sino que** lo <u>suspendió</u>.
*She didn't pass the test. She failed it, instead.*

## In this unit we will learn:
. To ask for details about people, things and places.
. Diacritical signs.
. Vocabulary: Months and seasons.

## Unit
# 37
**Days 73 & 74**

### Diálogo / Dialog

Raúl y Josefina hablan sobre sus vacaciones.

*Raúl and Josefina are talking about their vacations.*

R: El pasado **septiembre** fui a París. Es una ciudad preciosa.
J: ¿Viste la Torre Eiffel?
R: ¡Por supuesto!
J: ¿**Cuánto mide de altura**?
R: Mide 330 metros.
J: Es un monumento muy original. ¿**A qué distancia** está París de Londres?
R: A menos de 500 kilómetros. En Londres también hay monumentos interesantes, como el Puente de la Torre.
J: Sí, lo he visto en una foto. ¿**Cuánto mide de largo**?
R: No lo **sé** exactamente, pero mide unos 250 metros de largo.
J: Yo no estuve en Europa. El **verano** pasado fui a Perú y Bolivia y pude ver el lago Titicaca.
R: Creo que es un lugar muy bonito. ¿**Qué profundidad tiene**?
J: Me dijeron que más de 350 metros.

R: *Last September I went to Paris. It's a beautiful city.*
J: *Did you see the Eiffel Tower?*
R: *Of course!*
J: *How high is it?*
R: *It's 360 yards high.*
J: *It is a very original monument. How far is Paris from London?*
R: *Less than 310 miles. In London there are interesting monuments as well, like the Tower Bridge.*
J: *Yes, I have seen it in a picture. How long is it?*
R: *I don't know exactly, but it is about 270 yards long.*
J: *I wasn't in Europe. Last summer I went to Peru and Bolivia and I was able to see lake Titicaca.*
R: *I think it is a very nice place. How deep is the lake?*
J: *They told me it is more than 1,150 feet deep.*

R:  ¿Está caliente el agua? **¿A qué temperatura** está?
J:  No está muy fría. Está templada.
R:  Viajar es maravilloso. El **otoño** próximo
    quiero ir a Italia. Es otro país muy interesante.
J:  Me encantaría ir a Italia. ¡Qué suerte tienes!

R:  *Is the water hot? How hot is it?*
J:  *It isn't very cold. It is warm.*
R:  *Traveling is marvelous. Next fall I want to go to
    Italy. It's another interesting country.*
J:  *I'd love to go to Italy. You are so lucky!*

## PEDIR DETALLES ACERCA DE GENTE, COSAS Y LUGARES
### *(ASKING FOR DETAILS ABOUT PEOPLE, THINGS AND PLACES)*

When we are interested in knowing details about measures, distances, prices, sizes, etc., we can
ask questions like these:

**Tamaño** *(size):*

**¿Cómo es de grande** la casa?   *How big is the house?*

**¿Cómo es de largo/ancho** el pasillo?
*How long/wide is the corridor?*

**¿Cuánto mide de ancho/largo** el pasillo?
*How wide/long is the corridor?*

**Altura** *(height)*:

**¿Cuánto mides?**     *How tall are you?*

**¿Qué altura** tiene ese edificio?
*How tall is that building?*

**Peso** *(weight)*:

**¿Cuánto pesa** Ramón?
*How much does Ramón weigh?*

**Precio (price):**

**¿Cuánto cuesta** esto?
*How much is this?*

**Distancia** *(distance)*:

**¿A qué distancia** está tu oficina de tu casa?
*How far is your office from your house?*

**Profundidad** *(depth)*:

**¿Qué profundidad** tiene el lago?
*How deep is the lake?*

**Temperatura** *(temperature):*

**¿A qué temperatura** está?  *How hot is it?*

**¿Qué temperatura** tiene?  *What temperature is it/he/she?*

**¿Cuál es la temperatura?** = **¿Qué temperatura hace?**
*What temperature is it?*

**Velocidad** *(speed):*

**¿A qué velocidad** va el auto?
*How fast is the car?*

**Edad** *(age):*

**¿Qué edad tiene** ese árbol?
*How old is that tree?*

**Tiempo** *(time):*

**¿Cuánto (tiempo)** tardas* en llegar a casa?
*How long does it take you to get home?*

---

*) The verb **"tardar"** has different meanings:

**a)** To take a period of time (to do something):
    Ella **tarda** dos horas en vestirse.    *It takes her two hours to get dressed.*

**b)** To be late:
    ¡Date prisa! ¡No **tardes**!    *Hurry up! Don't be late!*

Take note that in English we use the interrogative *"how?"* for almost all these questions, but in Spanish there are three different interrogatives: **¿qué?**, **¿cuánto?** and **¿cómo?**

In the questions with **¿cómo?**, the structure can be:

| **¿Cómo + "ser" + de + adjective?** | or | **¿Cómo + de + adjective + "ser"?** |
|---|---|---|

| | |
|---|---|
| ¿Cómo <u>es</u> de caro? | *How expensive is it?* |
| ¿Cómo de fuerte <u>es</u>? | *How strong is it?* |

**Qué**, **cuánto** and **cómo** also have something else in common: they are written with a graphic accent but none of them should have it, according to the rules that we learned in unit 8. The fact is that they need this diacritical sign for being questioning words.

## LA TILDE DIACRÍTICA *(THE DIACRITICAL SIGN)*

One-syllable words never have a written accent in Spanish, except when we use the diacritical sign. The diacritical sign (mark or accent) is used to differentiate words with the same spelling but different meanings.

We have already seen many of them:

| | |
|---|---|
| **tú** (subject pronoun) | **tu** (possessive adjective) |
| **él** (subject pronoun) | **el** (article) |
| **mí** (personal pronoun) | **mi** (possessive adjective) |
| **sé** (verb) | **se** (pronoun) |
| **té** (tea) | **te** (pronoun) |

**Qué, cuál, quién, cuánto, cuándo, dónde** and **cómo** have the written accent when they are used in questions or exclamations. Otherwise they do not have it.

**Éste, ése, aquél**, etc. have the accent mark when they function as pronouns, but they do not have it when they go before a noun.
There are some more words that need the diacritical sign, but we will learn them as they come up.

## TOP VOCABULARY AND EXPRESSIONS

### LOS MESES Y LAS ESTACIONES *(The months and the seasons).*

**Los meses** *(The months)*

| | |
|---|---|
| **enero:** *January* | **julio:** *July* |
| **febrero:** *February* | **agosto:** *August* |
| **marzo:** *March* | **septiembre:** *September* |
| **abril:** *April* | **octubre:** *October* |
| **mayo:** *May* | **noviembre:** *November* |
| **junio:** *June* | **diciembre:** *December* |

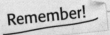

---

**Remember!**

The months are written in lowercase letters in Spanish.
The preposition that almost always goes before the months is **"en"** *(in)*.

| | |
|---|---|
| Yo nací **en** <u>septiembre</u>. | *I was born in September.* |
| El curso comienza **en** <u>agosto</u>. | *The course starts in August.* |
| Ellos se casaron **en** <u>abril</u>. | *They got married in April.* |

---

**Las estaciones** *(The seasons)*

 **primavera** *spring*    **verano** *summer*    **otoño** *fall / autumn*    **invierno** *winter*

| | |
|---|---|
| En **primavera** hace buen tiempo. | *It's good weather in spring.* |
| El próximo **verano** voy a Panamá en vacaciones. | *Next summer I'm going to Panama on vacation.* |
| Hace un poco de frío en **otoño**. | *It's a little cold in fall.* |
| El **invierno** pasado aprendí a esquiar. | *Last winter I learned to ski.* |

As we can see, **"en"** is the preposition that precedes the seasons as well.

In the examples, notice that the seasons can also be introduced by "el próximo" *(next)* or "el pasado" *(last)*, and you can say both "<u>el próximo</u> **verano**" and "<u>el</u> **verano** <u>próximo</u>", or "<u>el pasado</u> **otoño**" and "<u>el</u> **otoño** <u>pasado</u>".

**In this unit we will learn:**
. The preposition "de".
. To describe objects: materials and uses.
. "Ser" de + material.
. "Servir" para + infinitive.
. Vocabulary: Materials and shapes.

## Unit
# 38
**Days 75 & 76**

### Diálogo / Dialog

Soraya y Alberto hablan sobre los usos de algunas cosas.

*Soraya and Alberto are speaking about the usefulness of certain things.*

| | |
|---|---|
| S: ¿Sabes, Alberto? Ayer compré una mesa. | *S: Did you know, Alberto? I bought a table yesterday.* |
| A: ¿Cómo? | *A: What?* |
| S: Digo que ayer compré una mesa. | *S: I said that I bought a table yesterday.* |
| A: No, pregunto que cómo es la mesa. | *A: No, I am asking what is the table like.* |
| S: ¡Ah! [Risas] Es **rectangular**. No es muy grande. | *S: Ah! [Laughs] It is rectangular. It isn't very big.* |
| A: **¿De qué está hecha?** | *A: What is it made of?* |
| S: **Es de madera.** | *S: It's made of wood.* |
| A: ¿Y **para qué** la necesitas? | *A: And what do you need it for?* |
| S: La necesito para poner encima la computadora. Tenía otra mesa, pero estaba vieja y era demasiado pequeña. Ahora estoy buscando una mesa **de** jardín, pero la quiero **redonda** y **de plástico**. | *S: I need it to put the computer on. I had another table, but it was old and too small. Now I am looking for a patio table, but I want it round and plastic.* |
| A: Yo no uso mucho la computadora. **¿Para qué** la usas tú? | *A: I don't use the computer much. What do you use it for?* |
| S: Pues yo la uso todos los días. Escribo correos electrónicos, busco información, leo las noticias, chateo con los amigos.... | *S: I use it everyday. I write emails, look for information, read the news, chat with friends...* |
| A: Sí, **sirve para** muchas cosas. Con una computadora uno está conectado al mundo. | *A: Yes, it is useful for a lot of things. With a computer you are connected to the world.* |
| S: La mía es un poco antigua. Era **de** mi hermana. Ahora necesito una nueva, más moderna y potente. | *S: Mine is a little old. It was my sister's. Now I need a new one, more modern and powerful.* |
| A: ¿Pero tendrás suficiente dinero para comprala después **de** pagar las dos mesas? [Risas] | *A: But, will you have enough money to buy it after paying for the two tables? [Laughs]* |

## LA PREPOSICIÓN "DE" *(THE PREPOSITION "DE")*

As we know, **"de"** indicates a starting point or origin:

| | |
|---|---|
| Ella es **de** Bogotá. | *She is from Bogota.* |
| – ¿**De** dónde vienes? | *Where are you coming from?* |
| – Vengo **de** mi casa. | *I'm coming from my house.* |

But **"de"** also introduces an element to specify or identify another element. Thus **"de"** shows:

**a) Material, substance** or **content**:

| Un anillo **de** oro. | Una gota **de** agua. | Un cartón **de** leche. |
|---|---|---|
| *A golden ring.* | *A drop of water.* | *A carton of milk.* |

**b) Possession.** "De" is used when both the possessor and the possession appear in the sentence. In Spanish the possession is placed first, then "de" and after that, the possessor (it can be a person or an object).

| El hermano **de** Juan está ahí. | *Juan's brother is there.* |
|---|---|
| El celular **de** mi primo no funciona. | *My cousin's cell phone doesn't work.* |
| Una pata **de** la mesa está rota. | *One of the table legs is broken.* |

**c) A reference to locate something.** In this case it usually appears after adverbs and prepositions of place or time.

| Mi casa está <u>cerca</u> **de** la estación. | *My house is near the station.* |
|---|---|
| Sus hijos están <u>lejos</u> **de** aquí. | *Her children are far from here.* |
| El gato está <u>debajo</u> **de** la mesa. | *The cat is under the table.* |
| <u>Después</u> **de** la clase ella se fue a casa | *After the class she went home.* |
| Ellos llegaron <u>antes</u> **de** las 3. | *They arrived before 3:00.* |

**d) A kind of object:**

| | | |
|---|---|---|
| Un auto **de** carreras. | Ropa **de** verano. | Un libro **de** español. |
| *A race car.* | *Summer clothing.* | *A book of Spanish.* |

We can also indicate the starting point and the end of a period of time or a space with "**de**" and "**a**":

**De** mi casa **a** la estación hay 100 metros. = Desde mi casa hasta la estación hay 100 metros.

*There are 100 metres from my house to the station.*

Tengo vacaciones **de** lunes **a** viernes.   *I'm on vacation from Monday to Friday.*

Don't forget that   **de + el = del**

| | |
|---|---|
| Ése es el libro **del** niño. | *That is the boy's book.* |
| Estamos lejos **del** pueblo. | *We are far from the village.* |

Some common expressions with the preposition "**de**":

| | |
|---|---|
| **¡De acuerdo!:** *Ok! All right!* | **de día:** *by day, in the daytime* |
| **de noche:** *by night, at night* | **de esta manera:** *(in) this way* |
| **de hoy en adelante:** *from today on* | **de nuevo:** *again* |
| **de buen/mal humor:** *in a good/bad mood* | **de memoria:** *by heart* |
| **¡De nada!:** *You're welcome!* | **de pie:** *standing* |
| **de pronto, de repente:** *suddenly* | **de vez en cuando:** *from time to time* |

## DESCRIBIR OBJETOS: MATERIALES Y UTILIDADES
### (DESCRIBING OBJECTS: MATERIALS AND USES)

**a)** To ask about the material an object is made of we say:

| | |
|---|---|
| **¿De qué material es?** | *What material is it?* |
| **¿De qué material está hecho?** | *What material is it made of?* |

And to answer or describe an object we use <u>the verb "ser"</u> + **de** + <u>material</u>:

**Es** una mesa **de** madera.
*It's a wooden table.*

La cuchara **es de** plástico.
*The spoon is plastic.*

**Son** figuras **de** cristal.
*They are glass figures.*

**b)** When we refer to uses, we can ask:

| | |
|---|---|
| **¿Para qué?** | *What for?* |
| **¿Para qué sirve\*?** | *What is it used for?* |
| **¿Para qué se usa?** | *What is it used for?* |

(*) Amongst the meanings of the verb "servir", one of them is "to be used".

And to answer we can use several sentences: **"para + infinitive"**, **"servir para + infinitive"** or **"usarse para + infinitive"**.

Necesito un sacacorchos **para abrir** una botella.
*I need a corkscrew to open a bottle.*

– ¿**Para qué sirve** una llave?  — *What's a key used for?*
– **Sirve para** abrir puertas.  — *It's used for opening doors.*

– ¿**Para qué se usan** los relojes?  — *What are watches used for?*
– (Los relojes) **Se usan para** saber la hora.  — *They are used to know the time.*

## TOP VOCABULARY AND EXPRESSIONS

## MATERIALES Y FORMAS *(Materials and shapes)*

**Materiales *(Materials)***

**(de) plástico:** *plastic*
**(de) metal:** *metal*
**(de) vidrio/cristal:** *glass*
**(de) algodón:** *cotton*

**(de) madera:** *wood (wooden)*
**(de) hierro:** *iron*
**(de) papel:** *paper*
**(de) lana:** *wool (woolen)*

| | |
|---|---|
| Yo necesitaba <u>una pieza</u> **de metal**. | *I needed a piece of metal.* |
| Ella compró <u>una camisa</u> **de algodón**. | *She bought a cotton shirt.* |
| <u>Las puertas</u> **de hierro** pesan mucho. | *Iron doors are very heavy.* |

## Formas *(Shapes)*

**redondo:** *round*
**ovalado:** *oval*
**cuadrado:** *square*
**rectangular:** *rectangular*
**triangular:** *triangular*
**cilíndrico:** *cylindrical*

There are some other shapes that can be expressed as follows:

**tener forma de ...... / con forma de ......:** *(to be) ......-shaped*
**tener forma de rombo:** *(to be) rhombus-shaped*
**tener forma de L:** *(to be) L-shaped*

| | |
|---|---|
| El espejo es **ovalado**. | *The mirror is oval.* |
| Me gustan las mesas **redondas**. | *I like round tables.* |
| Esta calle **tiene forma de U**. | *This street is U-shaped.* |

Ellos necesitaban un trozo de madera **con forma de L**.
*They needed an L-shaped piece of wood.*

<table>
<tr><td>

**In this unit we will learn:**

. To express opinions.

. Verbs that introduce opinions: creer, pensar.

. Adverbs of time: después (de), antes (de)

(*after, before*).

. Vocabulary: Natural disasters.

</td><td>

# Unit
# 39

**Days 77 & 78**

</td></tr>
</table>

### Diálogo / *Dialog*

Luis y Catalina dan sus opiniones sobre distintos temas.

*Luis and Catalina are expressing their opinions about different topics.*

| | |
|---|---|
| L: | Catalina, ¿**qué piensas** tú **de** los ovnis? ¿**Crees que** existen? |
| C: | No. **Creo que** no existen. Puedo comprender que hay fenómenos extraños pero no **creo en** los ovnis. ¿Y tú? ¿**Qué piensas**? |
| L: | No lo sé. Tampoco estoy seguro. Pero **después de** ver alguno, puedo cambiar de opinión. [Risas] |
| C: | ¿Y **crees** tú **que** hay vida en otros planetas? |
| L: | Sí, **creo que** hay vida en otros planetas. Puede ser cualquier forma de vida, no particularmente con forma de marciano. ¿**Cuál es tu opinión**? |
| C: | Yo también **pienso que** hay vida en otros planetas. De hecho, los científicos ya descubrieron agua en Marte. Y el agua significa vida. |
| L: | Bueno, el agua puede causar muchas desgracias también: **inundaciones, maremotos**… |
| C: | Sí, cada día vemos estos **desastres** en algún lugar del mundo pero no podemos hacer nada por evitarlos. |
| L: | Bueno, no lo sé. Podemos prevenirlos **antes de** que causen graves **daños, muertos** o **heridos**. |
| C: | Sí. **Después** la situación es siempre dramática. |

| | |
|---|---|
| L: | *Catalina, what do you think about UFOs? Do you think they exist?* |
| C: | *No. I don't think they exist. I can understand that there are strange phenomenons but I don't believe in UFOs. And you? What do you think?* |
| L: | *I don't know. I am not sure, either. But after seeing one, I may change my mind. [Laughs]* |
| C: | *And do you think there is life on other planets?* |
| L: | *Yes, I think there is life on other planets. It can be any form of life, not particularly in the shape of a martian. What's your opinion?* |
| C: | *I also think there is life on other planets. In fact, scientists already discovered water on Mars. And water means life.* |
| L: | *Well, water can also cause many disasters: floods, tidal waves…* |
| C: | *Yes, we see these disasters somewhere in the world everyday, but we can't do anything to avoid them.* |
| L: | *Well, I don't know. We can prevent them before they cause serious damage, and fatal or serious casualties.* |
| C: | *Yes. Afterwards the situation is always dramatic.* |

## EXPRESAR OPINIONES *(EXPRESSING OPINIONS)*

When we express an opinion about any matter, we usually start with the words "**Creo que**" (*I think that...*), which introduce our real thought.

| | |
|---|---|
| **Creo que** ella es mejicana. | *I think (that) she is Mexican.* |
| **Creo que** hace frío fuera. | *I think (that) it is cold outside.* |
| **Creo que** ellos leyeron el periódico. | *I think (that) they read the newspaper.* |

But we can also express somebody else's opinions or thoughts. In this case we start the sentence saying:

| | |
|---|---|
| **Tú crees que** yo no tengo razón. | *You think (that) I'm wrong.* |
| **Él cree que** tú eres estadounidense. | *He thinks (that) you are American.* |
| **Ellos creen que** Silvia es mi hermana. | *They think (that) Silvia is my sister.* |

There are some other ways to introduce someone's opinion. One of them is with the verb "**pensar (que)**" [*to think (that)*] such as:

| | |
|---|---|
| **Pienso que** esta reunión es aburrida. | *I think (that) this meeting is boring.* |
| Él **piensa que** Picasso fue un gran pintor. | *He thinks (that) Picasso was a great painter.* |
| **Pienso que** es muy simpática. | *I think (that) she is very friendly.* |
| **Pensamos que** es una buena idea. | *We think (that) it is a good idea.* |

And to ask somebody for an opinion:

| | |
|---|---|
| **¿Qué crees?** | *What do you think?* |
| **¿Qué cree usted?** | *What do you think?* |
| **¿Qué piensa de/sobre/acerca de...?** | *What do you think about....?* |
| **¿Cuál es su opinión sobre.....?** | *What is your opinion about....?* |

| | |
|---|---|
| **¿Qué piensas de** Lucy? | *What do you think about Lucy?* |
| **¿Cuál es tu opinión sobre** este tema? | *What is your opinion about this matter?* |

## TOP VOCABULARY AND EXPRESSIONS

### ADVERBIOS DE TIEMPO: ANTES (DE), DESPUÉS (DE), MÁS TARDE, LUEGO. *[Adverbs of time (before, after, later, then)]*

**antes:** *before*

**después:** *afterwards, after that*
**luego:** *after*
**más tarde:** *later*

These expressions have the same meaning, so they are interchangeable.

Estuve jugando al tenis **antes**.
*I was playing tennis before.*

¿Vas **luego** al cine?
*Are you going to the movies later?*

¿Viste a mi prima **antes**?
*Did you see my cousin before?*

Me levanté temprano, **después** fui a trabajar y **más tarde** llamé a Juan.
*I got up early, after that I went to work and later I phoned Juan.*

These adverbs stand alone but "antes" and "después" can also go before a noun or an infinitive, but, in these cases we need the preposition "de" in between.

**antes de:** *before*
**después de:** *after*

**antes de:**
**después de:** ⎤ + *determiner + noun*

Quiero estudiar un poco **antes de** <u>la clase</u>.    *I want to study a little before the lass.*
Nos fuimos a casa **después de** <u>la reunión</u>.    *We went home after the meeting.*

**antes de:**
**después de:** ⎤ + *infinitive*

Yo tenía un perro **antes de** <u>comprar</u> este gato.    *I had a dog before buying this cat.*
**Después de** <u>ver</u> la televisión se fue a la cama.    *After watching television he went to bed.*

Be careful because in English the present participle is used in these expressions, instead of the infinitive.

## VOCABULARIO:

**Desastres naturales *(Natural disasters)***

| | |
|---|---|
| **huracán:** *hurricane* | **muertos:** *dead people* |
| **ciclón:** *cyclone* | **heridos:** *injured people* |
| **terremoto:** *earthquake* | **daño:** *damage* |
| **temblor:** *earth tremor* | **desastre:** *disaster* |
| **maremoto:** *tidal wave* | **catástrofe:** *catastrophe* |
| **inundación:** *flood* | **rescate:** *rescue* |
| **incendio:** *fire* | **la Cruz Roja:** *the Red Cross* |
| **devastar, arrasar:** *to devastate* | **causar daños:** *to cause damage* |

In the case of a natural disaster, we unfortunately may hear any of these expressions asking for help:

**¡Socorro!**
**¡Auxilio!**     *Help!*
**¡Ayuda!**

El **huracán** arrasó la ciudad.
*The hurricane devastated the city.*

El año pasado hubo un **terremoto** en Asia.
*Last year there was an earthquake in Asia.*

¿Hubo muchos **heridos**?
*Were there many injured people?*

Después del **incendio** reconstruimos la casa.
*After the fire we rebuilt the house.*

## Unit

# 40

**Days 79 & 80**

**In this unit we will learn:**
. Uses of the preposition "en".
. The past participle.
. Participles as adjectives.
. Vocabulary: Food and drinks.

**Diálogo / *Dialog***

Silvia le cuenta a Leonardo sus planes para vacaciones.

*Silvia tells Leonardo her plans for her vacation.*

L: ¿**En** qué piensas, Silvia?

S: **Pienso en** las próximas vacaciones.

L: ¿Estás hablando **en serio**?

S: ¡Claro! Ayer me dijeron que puedo tener vacaciones en julio. ¿Qué tal si pasamos unos días **en** Disneylandia?

L: ¿**En** Disneylandia? No sé. Yo tengo mucho trabajo **en** verano. Soy un hombre muy **ocupado**, pero estoy **sorprendido** por tu proposición.

S: Tenemos que tomar una decisión **en** unos días y reservar los billetes con antelación. Tengo ganas de ver a personajes **conocidos**.

L: Sí, a Mickey y a Donald. [Risas]

S: No, me refería a personajes famosos, cantantes, actores.... Ellos también suelen ir allí **en** verano. De todas formas, Mickey y Donald son mis personajes **preferidos**. Por cierto, ¿por qué tienes la mano **vendada**?

L: Bueno, tengo que decirte algo. Entra **en** el baño. La puerta está **abierta**. Tuve un pequeño accidente y el espejo está **roto**.

S: ¿Un pequeño accidente? ¿Qué ocurrió realmente?

L: *What are you thinking about, Silvia?*

S: *I am thinking about my next vacation.*

L: *Are you talking seriously?*

S: *Of course! Yesterday I was told that I can take vacation in July. What about spending a few days in Disneyland?*

L: *Disneyland? I don't know. I have a lot of work in summer. I am a very busy man, but I am surprised by your proposition.*

S: *We have to make a decision in a few days and book the tickets in advance. I feel like seeing familiar characters.*

L: *Yes, Mickey and Donald [laughs].*

S: *No, I referred to famous people, singers, actors... They usually go there in summer as well. Anyway, Mickey and Donald are my favorite characters. By the way, why is your hand bandaged?*

L: *Well, I have to tell you something. Go to the bathroom. The door is open. I had a little accident and the mirror is broken.*

S: *A little accident? What happened really?*

## USOS DE LA PREPOSICIÓN "EN" *(USES OF THE PREPOSITION "EN")*

Basically, the preposition **"en"** indicates that something is inside a place or object, but it is better to consider it as "within the limits" of an object, a place, a period of time, etc.

**"En"** is one of the most usual prepositions in Spanish and may be used in many and very different situations. That is why it has several equivalents in English: *in, on, at, by,* etc.

| | |
|---|---|
| **en** la mesa: | *on the table* |
| **en** casa: | *at home* |
| **en** Nueva York: | *in New York* |
| **en** vacaciones: | *on vacation* |
| **en** el centro: | *in the center* |
| **en** el trabajo: | *at work* |
| **en** el sofá: | *on the couch* |
| **en** la gaveta: | *in the drawer* |
| **en** la estación: | *in/at the station* |

| | |
|---|---|
| Los documentos están **en** la gaveta. | *The documents are in the drawer.* |
| Ellos viven **en** La Habana. | *They live in Havana.* |
| Ella está sentada **en** el sofá. | *She is sitting on the couch.* |
| Dejé mi celular **en** la mesa. | *I left my cell phone on the table.* |

## We use "en" when we refer to:

**a) Some periods of time:**

**en** enero: *in January*    **en** verano: *in summer*
**en** 1978: *in 1978*    **en** este momento: *in this moment*
**en** Navidad: *at Christmas*

**b) Means of transport:**

**en** coche: *by car*    **en** autobús: *by bus*    **en** tren: *by train*
**en** avión: *by plane*    **en** barco: *by ship*    **en** taxi: *by taxi*
**en** bicicleta: *on a bicycle*    **en** elefante: *on an elephant*

But: **a** caballo *(on a horse)* **NOT** en caballo
**a** pie *(on foot)* **NOT** en pie

Voy al centro de la ciudad **en autobús**.
*I go downtown by bus.*

Ella vino **en taxi**.
*She came by taxi.*

**c) The way we do some things:**

    **en** privado: *privately*    **en** secreto: *secretly*
    **en** público: *in public*    **en** general: *in general*
    **en** particular: *in particular*    **en** serio: *seriously*
    **en** resumen: *in brief*

**d) The time it takes us to do something:**

    **en** dos días: *in two days*
    **en** diez minutos: *in ten minutes*

Anoche cenamos **en diez minutos**.
*Last night we had dinner in ten minutes.*

---

## Some expressions with the preposition "en":

**en broma:** *in fun*    **en caso de:** *in case of*    **en medio de:** *in the middle of*
**en vez de:** *instead of*    **en ningún lugar:** *nowhere*
**en punto:** *sharp (with time expressions)*

---

## Some verbs commonly followed by "en":

**confiar en:** *to trust, to rely on*    **consistir en:** *to consist of*
**entrar en:** *to enter*    **fijarse en:** *to notice*
**insistir en:** *to insist on*    **meterse en:** *to get into*
**pensar en:** *to think of/about*

    El conductor no se fijó **en** el semáforo.    *The driver didn't notice the traffic light.*
    Estoy pensando **en** mis padres.    *I am thinking of my parents.*

## EL PARTICIPIO *(THE PAST PARTICIPLE)*

The past participle will be studied and practised in depth in future units, as its basic function is in the formation of perfect tenses with the auxiliary verb "haber", as well as to express the passive voice. Past participles are formed by dropping the infinitive ending (-ar, -er, -ir) and adding **"-ado"** to the infinitive stem of "-ar" verbs and **"-ido"** to the stems of "-er" and "-ir" verbs.

**Ex:**

| -AR verbs | -ER verbs | -IR verbs |
|---|---|---|
| hablar – habl**ado** | correr – corr**ido** | vivir – viv**ido** |
| *to speak – spoken* | *to run – run* | *to live – lived* |

A group of common verbs and their compounds have irregular past participles:

| | |
|---|---|
| abrir – **abierto** | *(to open – opened)* |
| cubrir – **cubierto** | *(to cover – covered)* |
| decir – **dicho** | *(to say – said)* |
| escribir – **escrito** | *(to write – written)* |
| describir – **descrito** | *(to describe – described)* |
| freír – **frito** | *(to fry – fried)* |
| hacer – **hecho** | *(to do/make – done/made)* |
| deshacer – **deshecho** | *(to undo/unmake – undone/unmade)* |
| morir – **muerto** | *(to die – died)* |
| poner – **puesto** | *(to put – put)* |
| resolver – **resuelto** | *(to solve – solved)* |
| romper – **roto** | *(to break – broken)* |
| ver – **visto** | *(to see – seen)* |
| prever – **previsto** | *(to foresee – foreseen)* |
| volver – **vuelto** | *(to come back – come back)* |
| devolver – **devuelto** | *(to take back – taken back)* |

Many **past participles can be used as adjectives** and, like other adjectives, they have to agree in gender and number with the nouns they modify.

| | |
|---|---|
| El jarrón está **roto**. | *The vase is broken.* |
| Ella es una actriz muy **conocida**. | *She is a well known actress.* |

Estamos **cansados** y ellos están **aburridos**.
*We are tired and they are bored.*

La puerta estaba **cerrada** pero las ventanas estaban **abiertas**.
*The door was closed but the windows were open.*

## Remember!

For "–er" and "-ir" verbs, if the stem ends in a vowel, an accent mark will be required, except for those verbs ending in "-uir" (construir, seguir, huir, etc.).

**Ex:** creer – creído *(to believe – believed)*; oír – oído *(to hear – heard)*; poseer – poseído *(to possess – possessed)* but construir – construido *(to build – built)*.

## TOP VOCABULARY AND EXPRESSIONS

### COMIDAS Y BEBIDAS *(Food and drinks)*

**beans:** *habichuelas, frijoles*
**puré de patatas:** *mashed potato*
**salsa de tomate:** *tomato sauce*
**mostaza:** *mustard*
**soup:** *sopa*
**agua:** *water*
**vino:** *wine*
**té:** *tea*
**comer:** *to eat*
**desayunar:** *to have breakfast*
**cenar:** *to have dinner/supper*

**bocadillo:** *sandwich*
**helado:** *ice cream*
**chocolate:** *chocolate*
**galletas:** *cookies, biscuits*
**ensalada:** *salad*
**cerveza:** *beer*
**refresco:** *soft drink*
**agua mineral:** *mineral water*
**beber:** *to drink*
**almorzar:** *to have lunch*

No me gusta la **mostaza**.
*I don't like mustard.*

Ayer almorcé **habichuelas** y **ensalada**.
*Yesterday I had beans and salad for lunch.*

Me encanta el **helado** de **chocolate**.
*I love chocolate ice cream.*

¿Quieres **vino**? No, gracias,
prefiero **agua mineral**.
*Would you like some wine? No, thanks,
I prefer mineral water.*

In this unit we will learn:
. The present simple of the verb "haber".
. The present perfect.
. Vocabulary: Leisure activities.

## Unit
# 41

**Days 81 & 82**

### Diálogo / Dialog

Olivia se encuentra a su amigo Roberto en la calle cuando volvían a casa.

*Olivia meets her friend Roberto on the street as they were coming back home.*

| | |
|---|---|
| O: | ¡Buenas noches, Roberto! Pareces contento. ¿Dónde **has estado**? |
| R: | ¡Buenas noches! Sí, estoy contento. **He estado** con los amigos. **Nos hemos divertido mucho.** |
| O: | ¿Sí? ¿Qué **han hecho**? |
| R: | **Hemos paseado** por el centro de la ciudad; **hemos ido** a un bar español, **hemos comido** unas "tapas" y, mientras, **hemos contado** muchos chistes. **Nos hemos reído** mucho. |
| O: | ¿Y después? ¿**Han ido** a tomar un trago? |
| R: | Sí, **hemos ido** a la discoteca, pero la música no era buena y no estuvimos allí mucho tiempo. ¿Y tú? ¿Qué **has hecho**? |
| O: | Yo **he estado** en una fiesta de cumpleaños. **He pasado** toda la tarde allí. También lo **he pasado** muy bien. **He visto** a muchos amigos, **he bailado** e incluso **he practicado** el portugués con un chico brasileño. |
| R: | Estupendo. Juntarse con los amigos es siempre agradable. Por cierto, ¿**has visto** a Pedro en la fiesta? ¿Sabes? Él y su esposa **se han separado.** |
| O: | ¿Sí? No lo sabía. Sí lo he visto en la fiesta, pero no **he hablado** con él. |
| R: | Bueno, me alegro de verte, Olivia. Ahora me voy para casa porque estoy un poco cansado. |
| O: | Sí, yo también estoy cansada. Te acompaño hasta la esquina.... |

| | |
|---|---|
| O: | *Good evening, Roberto! You look happy. Where have you been?* |
| R: | *Good evening! Yes, I am happy. I was with my friends. We had a nice time.* |
| O: | *Yes? What did you do?* |
| R: | *We went walking through downtown, we have been to a Spanish bar, we have eaten some "tapas" and, meanwhile, we have told many jokes. We have laughed a lot.* |
| O: | *And then? Have you gone for a drink?* |
| R: | *Yes, we went to the disco, but the music wasn't good and we weren't there for long. And you? What have you done?* |
| O: | *I have been to a birthday party. I have spent the whole afternoon and evening there. I also had a nice time. I have seen many friends, I have been dancing and I have even practiced Portuguese with a Brazilian guy.* |
| R: | *Great! Meeting your friends is always nice By the way, did you see Pedro at the party? Do you know? He and his wife have split up.* |
| O: | *Have they? I didn't know. I have seen him at the party, but I haven't talked to him.* |
| R: | *Well, glad to see you, Olivia. Now I have to go home because I am a little tired.* |
| O: | *Yes, I am tired too. I'll walk to the corner with you....* |

In this unit we will start to study the perfect tenses. They are compound tenses, that is, they are formed by two words: the auxiliary verb "haber" *(to have)* and the past participle of the main verb.

## PRESENTE DEL VERBO "HABER"
### *(PRESENT SIMPLE OF THE VERB "HABER")*

The present simple of the verb **"haber"** *(to have)* is conjugated as follows:

| | | |
|---|---|---|
| yo | **he** | *I have* |
| tú | **has** | *you have* |
| usted | **ha** | *you have* |
| él | **ha** | *he has, it has* |
| ella | **ha** | *she has, it has* |
| nosotros/as | **hemos** | *we have* |
| ustedes | **han** | *you have* |
| ellos/as | **han** | *they have* |

We have to learn these forms very well, as we need them to express the present perfect.

## EL PRETÉRITO PERFECTO *(THE PRESENT PERFECT)*

The present perfect is expressed by combining the present simple of the verb "haber" with the past participle of the main verb.

> Subject + **present of "haber"** + **past participle**

We have to keep in mind that "haber" is the verb that we conjugate, as the past participle is invariable for every person.

| | |
|---|---|
| yo | **he** |
| tú | **has** |
| usted | **ha** |
| él | **ha** |
| ella | **ha** |
| nosotros/as | **hemos** |
| ustedes | **han** |
| ellos/as | **han** |

**+ comprado** un diccionario bilingüe.

| | | |
|---|---|---|
| I | have | |
| you (informal) | have | |
| you (formal) | have | |
| he | has | |
| she | has | + bought a bilingual dictionary. |
| we | have | |
| you | have | |
| they | have | |

| | |
|---|---|
| Yo **he comido** paella. | I have eaten paella. |
| Tú **has traído** ese paquete, ¿verdad? | You have brought this package, haven't you? |
| Ellos **han estudiado** francés. | They have studied French. |
| Mi abuela **ha venido** desde Europa. | My grandmother has come from Europe. |

Be careful not to mistake the Spanish "has" (tú has) for the English "has" (he/she/it has).
They are written the same in both languages, but, as we can see, these forms correspond to different persons.

In unit 40 we already learned that the past participle is formed by dropping the infinitive ending and attaching "-ado" (-ar verbs) or "-ido" (-er, -ir verbs) to the verb stem. But remember that some participles are irregular.

| | |
|---|---|
| Él ha **pagado** mucho dinero. | He has paid a lot of money. |
| Usted ha **bebido** mucho. | You have drunk a lot. |
| Nosotros hemos **hecho** nuestros deberes. | We have done our homework. |

**Some of these irregular participles are:**

| | | | | |
|---|---|---|---|---|
| **ABRIR** | → abierto | | **DECIR** | → dicho |
| **ESCRIBIR** | → escrito | | **DESCUBRIR** | → descubierto |
| **HACER** | → hecho | | **MORIR** | → muerto |
| **RESOLVER** | → resuelto | | **ROMPER** | → roto |
| **VOLVER** | → vuelto | | | |

The present perfect, like any other tense, can be expressed with no explicit subjects, as the verb "haber" shows the person we are referring to. They are only used in cases of ambiguity.

| | |
|---|---|
| (yo) <u>He jugado</u> al ajedrez. | *I have played chess.* |
| (tú) <u>Has escrito</u> una carta. | *You have written a letter.* |
| **Él** <u>ha escuchado</u> la radio. | *He has listened to the radio.* |
| **Usted** <u>ha explicado</u> la lección. | *You have explained the lesson.* |
| (nosotros) <u>Hemos estado</u> en Brasil. | *We have been to Brazil.* |
| **Ustedes** <u>han hablado</u> con el encargado. | *You have spoken to the manager.* |
| **Ellas** <u>han visto</u> esa película. | *They have seen that film.* |

The verb "haber" and the past participle are inseparable. It means that, in order to make negative sentences, we have to place "no" before the verb "haber":

| | |
|---|---|
| **No** <u>he comprado</u> el periódico. | *I haven't bought the newspaper.* |
| Ella **no** <u>ha venido</u>. | *She hasn't come.* |
| Ustedes **no** <u>han comido</u> pizza. | *You haven't eaten pizza.* |

As the two words that form this tense are inseparable, if we use direct or indirect object pronouns in the sentence, they must be placed just before the verb "haber".

| | |
|---|---|
| Él **la** ha besado. | He has kissed **her.** |
| Ellos **lo** han hecho. | They have done **it.** |
| Tú **me** has dado mil pesos. | You have given **me** one thousand pesos. |

But if we find any of these pronouns and the negative "no" in a sentence, we have to use "no" before the pronoun:

Él **no** la ha besado.
*He hasn't kissed her.*

Ellos **no** lo han hecho.
*They haven't done it.*

Tú **no** me has dado mil pesos.
*You haven't given me one thousand pesos.*

And to ask questions, again the verb "haber" and the past participle are inseparable (be careful, because in English the order is different):

| | |
|---|---|
| ¿**Han pintado** ellos la habitación? | *Have they painted the room?* |
| ¿**Has escrito** un libro? | *Have you written a book?* |
| ¿No **ha llegado** ella? | *Hasn't she arrived?* |
| ¿Qué **has hecho**? | *What have you done?* |

With reflexive verbs, the pronouns also precede the verb "haber" in affirmative, negative and interrogative sentences:

| | |
|---|---|
| **Me** he lavado la cara. | *I have washed my face.* |
| Ellos no **se** han ido a la playa. | *They haven't gone to the beach.* |
| ¿Qué **te** has comprado? | *What have you bought for you?* |

## TOP VOCABULARY AND EXPRESSIONS

### ACTIVIDADES DE OCIO *(Leisure activities)*

**ir de compras:** *to go shopping*
**ir al gimnasio:** *to go to the gym*
**ir a tomar un trago:** *to go for a drink*
**ir a bailar:** *to go dancing*
**reunirse con los amigos:** *to meet one's friends*
**ir a nadar:** *to go swimming*
**ir a un concierto:** *to go to a concert*
**escuchar música:** *to listen to music*
**practicar, hacer deporte:** *to do sports*
**hacer ejercicio (físico):** *to exercise*
**ir al cine/teatro:** *to go to the movies/theater*
**ir a un museo:** *to go to a museum*

Este mes **he ido de compras** varias veces.   This month I have gone shopping several times.
¿**Fuiste a bailar** anoche?   Did you go dancing last night?
Me encanta **escuchar música** tranquilamente.   I love listening to music quietly.
Esta semana ellos no **han hecho ejercicio.**   They haven't exercised this week.

**In this unit we will learn:**

. To express unfinished actions.

. Use of "desde", "desde que", "desde hace" and "durante".

. Verbs commonly followed by "de".

. The verb "acabar (de)".

. Vocabulary: Sitting at the table.

**Unit**

# 42

**Days 83 & 84**

## Diálogo / *Dialog*

Dalia llega a casa y ve a Antonio poniendo la mesa.

*Dalia gets home and sees Antonio setting the table.*

| | |
|---|---|
| D: ¡Hola, Antonio! | *D: Hello, Antonio!* |
| A: ¡Hola! | *A: Hello!* |
| D: Estás poniendo la mesa. ¿Ya está la comida preparada? | *D: You are setting the table. Is the meal already made?* |
| A: Bueno, yo **acabo de** llegar. No **he hecho** nada, pero hay comida en el refrigerador. ¿Puedes ayudarme? Aquí tienes los **cuchillos**, las **cucharas** y los **tenedores**. Las **servilletas** están en el cajón. | *A: Well, I have just arrived. I haven't made anything, but there is some food in the fridge. Can you help me? Here are the knives, the spoons and the forks. The napkins are in the drawer.* |
| D: Escucha. **Me he enterado de** algunas cosas esta mañana. Juan **está enamorado de** Violeta y la **ha invitado** a pasar un fin de semana en la playa. | *D: Listen. I have learned some things this morning. Juan is in love with Violeta and has invited her to spend a weekend at the beach.* |
| A: ¡Puff! **Hace mucho tiempo que** no voy a la playa. | *A: Puff! I haven't been to the beach in a long time.* |
| D: Yo tampoco. No **he ido durante** los últimos dos años. También **he oído** que Lelia **ha dejado de** trabajar. Ella **ha trabajado desde que** tenía 18 años. No sé qué hará ahora. | *D: Neither have I. I haven't been there for the last two years. I have also heard that Lelia has given up working. She has been working since she was 18. I don't know what she will do now.* |
| A: Bueno, eso **depende de** ella. ¿Está todo en la mesa? Vamos a comer. | *A: Well, it's up to her. Is everything on the table? Let's eat.* |
| D: ¿Y el pan? | *D: And the bread?* |
| A: ¡Ay! **Me he olvidado de** comprar pan. | *A: Ah! I forgot to buy bread.* |
| D: No importa. No **he comido** pan **desde hace** días. Quiero perder peso. | *D: It doesn't matter. I haven't eaten bread for days. I want to lose weight.* |
| A: Yo no. Prefiero **disfrutar de** una buena comida. | *A: I don't. I prefer to enjoy a good meal.* |

We already know how the present perfect is formed and now we will study its different uses. They will be studied throughout this unit and the following ones.

## EXPRESAR ACCIONES NO ACABADAS
### *(EXPRESSING UNFINISHED ACTIONS)*

The present perfect tense is frequently used for <u>actions that started in the past and still continue into the present</u>, that is, for <u>unfinished actions</u>.

**Hemos vivido** en Miami los últimos dos años.
*We have lived in Miami for the last two years.*

**He trabajado** para esta empresa durante mucho tiempo.
*I've worked for this firm for a long time.*

If you remember, in unit 31 we learned some uses of **"desde"**, **"desde que"** *(since)* and **"durante"** *(for)*. These expressions are very common together with the present perfect.

He <u>tenido</u> este trabajo **desde** enero.
*I have had this job since January.*

Ella <u>ha sido</u> mi novia **desde que** me conoció.
*She has been my girlfriend since she met me.*

Ustedes <u>han manejado</u> **durante** dos horas.
*You have been driving for two hours.*

Another expression with "desde" is **"desde hace"** *(for)*, which has the same meaning as "durante" *(for)*.

> He vivido en Bogotá **desde hace** dos años.
> *I have lived in Bogota for two years.*

In this case, as Spanish is so flexible, we can use a different tense to express "the idea" of the present perfect: the present simple.

> **Vivo** en Bogotá desde hace dos años  =  **He vivido** en Bogotá desde hace dos años.

We can also place "desde hace dos años" at the beginning of the sentence, but, in this case, the action is frequently expressed in present simple and not in present perfect (although it is still correct):

> <u>Desde hace dos años</u> **vivo** en Bogotá.

But **"desde hace + period of time"** can also be expressed:

> **Hace + period of time + que**

This common expression is normally used at the beginning of the sentence with the present simple, not the present perfect.

**Hace dos años que** <u>vivo</u> en Bogotá.
*I've been living in Bogota for two years.*

**Hace mucho tiempo que** ella <u>tiene</u> el mismo auto.
*She's had the same car for a long time.*

In unit 38 we studied the uses of the preposition **"de"**. Now we will focus on some verbs that require this preposition.

## Some verbs commonly followed by "de":

| | |
|---|---|
| **acordarse de:** *to remember* | **cambiar de (ropa, tema):** *to change (clothes, subject...)* |
| **cansarse de:** *to get tired of* | **cuidar de:** *to take care of* |
| **dejar de:** *to stop, to give up* | **depender de:** *to depend on* |
| **despedirse de:** *to say goodbye to* | **disfrutar de:** *to enjoy* |
| **enamorarse de:** *to fall in love with* | **enterarse de:** *to find out about, to learn* |
| **fiarse de:** *to trust* | **olvidarse de:** *to forget* |
| **preocuparse de:** *to worry about* | **quejarse de: to complain about** |
| **reírse de:** *to laugh at* | **servir de:** *to serve as, to be used as* |

| | |
|---|---|
| ¿**Disfrutaste de** la reunión familiar? | *Did you enjoy the family reunion?* |
| No me **he despedido de** tu hermana. | *I haven't said goodbye to your sister.* |
| **Depende de** ti. | *It depends on you.(It's up to you!)* |
| Él **se ha enamorado de** ti. | *He has fallen in love with you.* |
| **Estamos cuidando del** perro de Juan. | *We are taking care of Juan's dog.* |

When you use any preposition that depends on a verb, we have to place the preposition before the interrogative in questions with interrogative pronouns (qué, quién, etc.).But be careful because in English it is placed at the end:

¿**De** <u>qué</u> te estás riendo?
*What are you laughing <u>at</u>?*

¿**De** <u>quién</u> cuidaste?
*Who did you take care <u>of</u>?*

¿**De** <u>qué</u> se ha quejado él?
*What has he complained <u>about</u>?*

If the preposition "de" is followed by a verb, this verb is almost always an infinitive (be careful as in English it is usually a present participle):

Ellos **han dejado de** <u>fumar</u>.
*They have stopped <u>smoking</u>.*

Me **he cansado de** <u>vivir</u> en la ciudad.
*I have got tired of <u>living</u> in the city.*

Ella **se olvidó de** <u>cerrar</u> la puerta.
*She forgot to <u>close</u> the door.*

There are many other verbs that follow this pattern, but now we will pay attention to one of them in particular, as in English you need the present perfect to express it:

**acabar de** + **inf**   *to have + just + past participle*

We use this verb to refer to an action that has just taken place. The present simple of this verb in Spanish corresponds to the present perfect form plus "just" in between "have" and the participle in English.

**Acabo de** llegar a casa.
*I have just got home.*

Ustedes **acaban de** recibir un mensaje.
*You have just received a message.*

Él **acaba de** colgar el teléfono.
*He has just hung up the phone.*

Ellos **acaban de** elegir a un nuevo presidente.
*They have just elected a new president.*

Besides this kind of expressions, the verb "acabar" (with no "de") means *"to finish, to end"* It's a synonym of "terminar".

**He acabado** este trabajo = **He terminado** este trabajo

*I have finished this work.*

But if we mean that an activity is over and this activity is a verb, we also use the above structure (but the equivalent in English is different).

**acabar de** + **infinitive** = **terminar de** + **infinitive**   *to finish + present participle (gerund)*

**Acabé de** estudiar a las 9.
**Terminé de** estudiar a las 9.
*I finished studying at 9:00.*

**¿Has acabado de** limpiar?
**¿Has terminado de** limpiar?
*Have you finished cleaning?*

## TOP VOCABULARY AND EXPRESSIONS

### SENTADOS A LA MESA *(Sitting at the table)*

**poner la mesa:** *to set the table*
**mantel:** *tablecloth*
**plato:** *dish, plate*
**plato hondo:** *soup dish*
**cuchillo:** *knife*
**cuchara:** *spoon*
**wine glass:** *copa de vino*
**coffee cup:** *taza de café*
**salero:** *salt shaker*
**pimentero:** *pepper shaker*
**cucharilla de postre:** *dessert spoon*

**quitar la mesa:** *to clear the table*
**servilleta:** *napkin*
**vaso:** *glass*
**plato llano:** *shallow dish*
**tenedor:** *fork*
**platillo:** *saucer*
**botella:** *bottle*

**In this unit we will learn:**

. To express past and recent actions.

. The present perfect + "alguna vez"/ adverbs of frequency.

. The present perfect + "ya", "todavía" and "aún".

. Vocabulary: Celebrations.

**Unit**

# 43

**Days 85 & 86**

## Diálogo / Dialog

Félix y Rosaura hablan sobre distintos países.

*Félix and Rosaura are talking about different countries.*

F: Rosaura, ¿**has estado alguna vez** en China?

R: No, **nunca he estado** en China, pero es un país que quiero visitar. Estoy muy interesada en la cultura china.

F: Bueno, hay otros lugares que también son interesantes. Yo quiero volver a la República Dominicana.

R: ¿**Ya has estado** allí?

F: Sí, estuve allí hace tres años. Me encantó. Los dominicanos son muy alegres y las playas son maravillosas. También me gustan sus **celebraciones**. El 27 de febrero es el **Día de la Independencia** y hay música por todas partes. A ellos les gusta mucho bailar. También hay **fuegos artificiales** por la noche. ¿**Has bailado** merengue **alguna vez**?

R: ¡Claro que sí! ¿Y tú? ¿**Has aprendido ya**?

F: Err..., bueno, no, no **he aprendido todavía**, pero yo no dejo de moverme cuando suena la música.

R: Bueno, eso es importante. A mí también me gustan esas **celebraciones**. Por cierto, el próximo viernes voy a una **fiesta de los 15 años**.

F: **Nunca he asistido** a esas fiestas.

R: Pues tienes que ir alguna vez. Se celebran en muchos países.

F: Sí, lo sé.

F: Rosaura, have you ever been to China?

R: No, I have never been to China, but it is a country I want to visit. I am very interested in Chinese culture.

F: Well, there are also other places which are interesting. I want to go back to the Dominican Republic.

R: Have you already been there?

F: Yes, I was there three years ago. I loved it. The Domincans are very cheerful and the beaches are wonderful. I also like their celebrations. On February 27th, it is the Independence Day and there is music everywhere. They like dancing very much. There are also fireworks at night. Have you ever danced merengue?

R: Yes, of course! And you? Have you already learned?

F: Err..., well, no, I haven't learned yet, but I don't stop moving when the music plays.

R: Well, that's important. I also like those celebrations. By the way, next Friday I'm going to a girl's 15th birthday party.

F: I've never been to those parties.

R: Then you have to go some time. They are celebrated in many countries.

F: Yes, I know.

## EXPRESAR ACCIONES PASADAS Y RECIENTES
### (EXPRESSING PAST AND RECENT ACTIONS)

We have already learned some ways to express past actions (preterite, imperfect, past continuous), but, if we refer to a past action as a past experience <u>not stating when this experience occurred</u>, we use the present perfect.

| | |
|---|---|
| **He leído** "Guerra y Paz". | *I have read "War and Peace".* |
| Él **ha trabajado** como pintor. | *He has worked as a painter.* |
| **Hemos limpiado** la casa. | *We have cleaned the house.* |
| Ellos **han estado** en Europa. | *They have been to Europe.* |

### If we say when these actions took place, we use the preterite instead of the present perfect:

**Leí** "Guerra y Paz" hace muchos años.
*I read "War and Peace" many years ago.*

Él **trabajó** como pintor cuando tenía 25 años.
*He worked as a painter when he was 25 years old.*

**Limpiamos** la casa ayer.
*We cleaned the house yesterday.*

Ellos **fueron** a Europa en 2003.
*They went to Europe in 2003.*

## The present perfect is also used when we refer to how often a past experience has occurred.

In this case we use **"alguna vez"** when we make questions (generally at the beginning or at the end of the sentence). It is the equivalent to "ever" in English.

| | |
|---|---|
| ¿**Alguna vez** ha llegado usted tarde a una reunión? | *Have you ever been late for a meeting?* |
| ¿Ha comido María caracoles **alguna vez**? | *Has María ever eaten snails?* |
| ¿Han perdido ellos el tren **alguna vez**? | *Have they ever missed the train?* |
| ¿Ha tenido él pesadillas **alguna vez**? | *Has he ever had a nightmare?* |

To answer these questions we use adverbs of frequency:

**Nunca** he llegado tarde a una reunión.
*I have never been late for a meeting.*

María ha comido caracoles **muchas veces**.
*María has eaten snails many times.*

Ellos **a veces** han perdido el tren.
*They have sometimes missed the train.*

Él ha tenido pesadillas **a menudo**.
*He has often had nightmares.*

## With regard to recent actions, they can also be expressed with the present perfect:

**a) When the period of time in which the action takes place is not over:**

No **he leído** el periódico <u>hoy</u>.
*I haven't read the newspaper today.*

¿Qué **has hecho** <u>esta semana</u>?
*What have you done this week?*

<u>Este año</u> **he escrito** dos novelas.
*This year I have written two novels*

As we can see in these examples, we have used the present perfect because "hoy", "esta semana" and "este año" are periods of time that are not over yet.

**b) When we refer to actions that could have happened by the time they are expressed.**
In this case we almost always use the adverbs "ya", "todavía" and "aún" *(already, still, yet)*.
In unit 24 we studied some of their uses, but now we will see some more.

**"Ya"** means "by that moment" or "at an unspecified time before now" and is equivalent to *"already (yet)"*. It is used in affirmative sentences and questions.
In questions, "ya" may be placed in different positions: before or after the verb, or in the final position.

¿**Ya** ha llegado la carta?
¿Ha llegado **ya** la carta?
¿Ha llegado la carta **ya**?

*Has the letter already arrived?*
*Has the letter arrived yet?*

In affirmative sentences, "ya" can also be placed before or after the verb or at the end of the sentence, although it is more frequent to find it before the verb.

**Ya** ha llegado la carta.
*The letter has already arrived.*

Hemos terminado **ya**.
*We have already finished.*

"**Todavía**" has a negative connotation when it occurs with the present perfect. It is used in negative sentences and placed before the negative "no", after the verb, or at the end of the sentence. It is equivalent to *"yet"* in English.

**Todavía** no se han comido el bocadillo.
No se han comido **todavía** el bocadillo.
No se han comido el bocadillo **todavía**.

*They haven't eaten the sandwich yet.*

La carta no ha llegado **todavía**.
*The letter hasn't arrived yet.*

**Todavía** no hemos terminado.
*We haven't finished yet.*

No me han dicho sus nombres **todavía**.
*They haven't told me their names yet.*

In this context, **"aún"** is a synonym of "todavía" and can be used in the same cases.

| | |
|---|---|
| La carta no ha llegado **aún**. | *The letter hasn't arrived yet.* |
| **Aún** no hemos terminado. | *We haven't finished yet.* |
| No me han dicho sus nombres **aún**. | *They haven't told me their names yet.* |

## TOP VOCABULARY AND EXPRESSIONS

### CELEBRACIONES *(Celebrations)*

**Semana Santa:** *Holy Week*
**Navidad:** *Christmas*
**Nochebuena:** *Christmas Eve*
**Año Nuevo:** *New Years Eve*
**Día de Reyes (Magos):** *Twelfth Day, Epiphany*
**Día de la Madre:** *Mother's Day*
**Día de los Muertos:** *Day of the Dead*
**Día de la Independencia:** *Independence Day*
**fuegos artificiales:** *fireworks*
**petardo:** *firecracker*
**feria:** *fair*

**fiesta religiosa:** *religious celebration*
**procesión:** *procession*
**peregrinación:** *pilgrimage*
**peregrino:** *pilgrim*
**santuario:** *sanctuary*
**celebración de una boda:** *wedding celebration*
**celebración de un bautizo:** *baptism celebration*
**aniversario:** *anniversary*
**fiesta de cumpleaños:** *birthday party*
**Quinceñera/ Celebración de los 15 años:** *Girl's 15th birthday*

## Unit
# 44
**Days 87 & 88**

**In this unit we will learn:**
. The present perfect continuous.
. Form and uses.
. Use of pronouns and reflexive verbs in the present perfect continuous.
. Vocabulary: Dwellings.

**Diálogo / Dialog**

Violeta llega a casa y habla con su marido, Adalberto.

*Violeta gets home and is speaking to her husband, Adalberto.*

A: ¡Buenas, Violeta!

V: ¡Muy buenas! ¡Por fín en casa!

A: Pareces aliviada. ¿Qué has hecho hoy?

V: Sí, estoy cansada. **He estado limpiando** el **apartamento**, que estaba un poco sucio. Luego he almorzado y **he estado trabajando** toda la tarde. ¿Y tú?

A: Pues también **he estado trabajando**. A las 8 recogí a Carlos y **hemos estado pintando** un condominio, pero no **hemos terminado** todavía. A las 6 me vine a casa y **he estado descansando** hasta ahora.

V: ¡Ah! También **he estado hablando** con los profesores de Miguel. Me han dicho que necesita estudiar más.

A: Esta tarde **él ha estado estudiando**. Ahora está durmiendo.

V: Creo que mañana tiene dos exámenes.

A: Bueno, Violeta, **he estado pensando**.... ¿qué tal si nos compramos un televisor nuevo? Éste no funciona bien.

V: Pero no tenemos suficiente dinero.

A: **Hemos estado ahorrando** durante meses. Sí tenemos dinero.

V: No, Adalberto. Necesitamos ese dinero para pagar deudas. ¿Las has olvidado?

---

A: Hello, Violeta!

V: Hello! Home at last!

A: You look relieved. What have you done today?

V: Yes, I am tired. I have been cleaning the apartment, which was a bit dirty. Then I have had lunch and I have been working all afternoon. And you?

A: I have also been working. At eight I picked Carlos up and we have been painting a condominium, but we haven't finished yet. At six I came home and I have been resting until now.

V: Ah! I have also been talking to Miguel's teachers. They have told me that he needs to study harder.

A: He has been studying this evening. He is sleeping now.

V: I think he has two exams tomorrow.

A: Well, Violeta, I've been thinking... what about buying a new television set? This one doesn't work properly.

V: But we don't have enough money.

A: We have been saving for months. We do have money.

V: No, Adalberto. We need that money to pay debts. Have you forgotten them?

## ACCIONES DURADERAS: PRETÉRITO PERFECTO CONTÍNUO
### *(DURATIVE ACTIONS: THE PRESENT PERFECT CONTINUOUS)*

In Spanish, like in English, the present perfect continuous is formed with the present simple of "haber" followed by the past participle of the verb "estar" (estado) and the present participle of the main verb.

> **present of "haber" + estado + present participle of main verb (-ando, -iendo)**
>
> *have/has + been + present participle*

| | |
|---|---|
| **He estado estudiando** español. | *I have been studying Spanish.* |
| Él **ha estado durmiendo**. | *He has been sleeping.* |
| Ustedes **han estado viendo** la televisión. | *You have been watching television.* |
| **Hemos estado nadando.** | *We have been swimming.* |
| **Ha estado ladrando** (el perro). | *It has been barking.* |

The verbs that can be conjugated in continuous forms are those that imply duration, that is, durative activites.

## The present perfect continuous is used in the following situations:

**a) To show that something started in the past and has continued up until now.**

Ellos **han estado hablando** durante dos horas.
*They have been talking for two hours.*

**He estado trabajando** en España desde junio.
*I have been working in Spain since June.*

**b) Without expressions that show duration, this tense has the meaning of *"lately"* (últimamente) or *"recently"* (recientemente):**

**Me he estado sintiendo** muy cansado (<u>últimamente</u>).
*I have been feeling really tired (lately).*

**Ella ha estado descansando** (<u>recientemente</u>).
*She has been resting (recently)*

c) **To show the present result of a past action.**

Estoy sudando porque **he estado corriendo**.
*I'm sweating because I have been running.*

Tenemos las manos sucias porque **hemos estado trabajando** en el jardín.
*Our hands are dirty because we have been gardening.*

d) **It may refer to a repeated action, whereas the present perfect (simple) makes reference to a single action.**

Ellos **han estado cortando** madera.     *They have been cutting wood.*
Él **se ha cortado**.     *He has cut himself.*

- **Negative sentences and questions follow the same pattern as with the present perfect simple (see unit 41).**

Él **no** ha estado pintando esta tarde.     *He hasn't been painting this afternoon.*
**No** hemos estado haciendo nada interesante.     *We haven't been doing anything interesting.*
¿Has estado tocando el piano?     *Have you been playing the piano?*
¿Dónde han estado viviendo ellos hasta ahora?     *Where have they been living until now?*

- If there are direct and indirect object pronouns in the sentence, they can be placed either before the verb "haber" or after the present participle of the main verb, attached to it.

Mi jefe **me** ha estado aconsejando todo este tiempo.
*My boss has been advising me all this time.*

Ustedes han estado enseñándo**nos** español.
*You have been teaching us Spanish.*

---

**Los** hemos estado haciendo
Hemos estado haciéndo**los**.
— *We have been doing them.*

**La** he estado escuchando
He estado escuchándo**la** (la sinfonía).
— *I've been listening to it.*

**¿Las** has estado limpiando?
¿Has estado limpiándo**las**?
— *Have you been cleaning them?*

Ella **me** ha estado mintiendo
Ella ha estado mintiéndo**me**.
— *She's been lying to me.*

- With reflexive verbs, the pronouns can also be placed in those same positions:

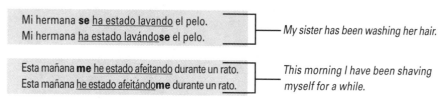

Mi hermana **se** ha estado lavando el pelo.
Mi hermana ha estado lavándo**se** el pelo.
— *My sister has been washing her hair.*

Esta mañana **me** he estado afeitando durante un rato.
Esta mañana he estado afeitándo**me** durante un rato.
*This morning I have been shaving myself for a while.*

Notice that when the pronoun is attached to the present participle, the word has a graphic accent.

## TOP VOCABULARY AND EXPRESSIONS

### VIVIENDAS *(Dwellings)*

**apartamento:** *apartment*
**piso:** *flat*
**condominio:** *condominium*
**rascacielos:** *skyscraper*
**rancho, hacienda:** *ranch*
**cabaña:** *cabin*
**choza:** *hut*
**castle:** *castillo*
**palacio:** *palace*
**posada:** *inn*
**motel:** *motel*
**cueva:** *cave*
**hostal:** *hostel*
**albergue:** *youth hostel*
**mansion:** *mansión*
**casa:** *house*

## Unit
# 45

**Days 89 & 90**

## In this unit we will learn:
. Time expressions with the present perfect continuous.
. The verb "llevar".
. "Hace + period of time + que".
. Vocabulary: The garden.

### Diálogo / *Dialog*

Clara va camino del supermercado y ve a Luis trabajando en su jardín.

*Clara is going to the supermarket and sees Luis working in his garden.*

C: ¡Hola, Luis!

*C: Hello, Luis!*

L: ¡Hola, Clara! ¿Cómo estás? **¡Hace mucho tiempo que no** nos vemos!

*L: Hello, Clara! How are you? We haven't seen each other in ages!*

C: Sí. Estoy muy bien, gracias. Ya veo que tú estás trabajando.

*C: Yes. I am very well, thank you. I see that you are working.*

L: Sí, **llevo trabajando** en el **jardín toda la mañana. He estado cortando** el césped por allí, cerca de la **barbacoa.**

*L: Yes, I have been working in the garden all morning. I have been mowing the lawn over there, near the barbecue.*

C: Ya veo. Pero esas **flores** están un poco secas.

*C: I see. But those flowers are a bit dry.*

L: Sí, **hace una semana que no las riego.**

*L: Yes, I haven't watered them for a week.*

C: Y esa **hierba** está muy alta.

*C: And that grass is very high.*

L: Así es. **Llevo un mes sin chapearla,** pero pronto estará perfecta.

*L: Yes. I haven't cut it for a month, but it will be perfect soon.*

C: Bueno, después podrás descansar y tomar el sol tranquilamente. **Hace mucho tiempo que yo no** tomo el sol en el **jardín.**

*C: Well, later you will relax and lay in the sun quietly. I haven't been sunbathing in the garden for a long time.*

L: La **reposera** está en el **cobertizo.** Puedes sacarla y tumbarte en ella.

*L: The chaise lounge is in the shed. You can take it out and lie on it.*

C: [Risas] Muchas gracias, pero ahora no puedo. Tengo un poco de prisa. Quiero comprar algunas cosas para la comida.

*C: [Laughs] Thank you so much, but I can't now. I am in a bit of a hurry. I want to buy some things for lunch.*

L: Muy bien. Entonces, que tengas un buen día.

*L: OK, have a nice day, then.*

C: Igualmente. ¡Hasta pronto!

*C: Same to you! See you soon!*

L: ¡Adiós, Clara!

*L: Goodbye, Clara!*

As we saw in the last unit, there are some time expressions that are very common when we use the present perfect continuous:

**He estado haciendo** ejercicio <u>durante media hora</u>.
*I have been exercising for half an hour.*

**Hemos estado esquiando** <u>por la mañana temprano</u>.
*We have been skiing early in the morning.*

Ella **ha estado cocinando** <u>desde hace dos horas</u>.
*She has been cooking for two hours.*

El teléfono **ha estado sonando** <u>(durante) un rato</u>.
*The phone has been ringing for a while.*

## - When we refer to a long time we can say:

| | |
|---|---|
| **desde hace .....:** | *for......* |
| **durante mucho tiempo:** | *for a long time* |
| **(durante) un rato:** | *for a while* |
| **todo el día:** | *all day (long)* |
| **toda la mañana:** | *all morning* |
| **toda la tarde:** | *all afternoon* |
| **toda la noche:** | *all night (long)* |
| **todo este tiempo:** | *all this time* |

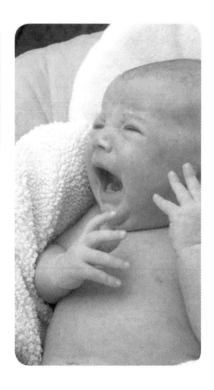

El bebé ha estado llorando **toda la noche**.
*The baby has been crying all night long.*

He estado esperándote **toda la mañana**.
*I've been waiting for you all morning.*

Hemos estado viendo la televisión **(durante) un rato**.
*We have been watching television for a while.*

The present perfect continuous can be replaced by other structures with the same meaning. Let's see some of them:

**a) In Spanish there are some verbs that can be used both in the present perfect simple and continuous with the same meaning.**

**He dormido** toda la mañana = **He estado durmiendo** toda la mañana

*I have been sleeping all morning*

| Ella **ha trabajado** en esa empresa durante años | = | Ella **ha estado trabajando** para esa empresa durante años |
|---|---|---|

*She has been working for that firm for years.*

**b) The concept of the present perfect continuous can also be expressed by means of the verb "llevar", which we are going to review next.**

## EL VERBO "LLEVAR" *(THE VERB "LLEVAR")*

The verb "llevar" has several meanings. It may be equivalent to *"to take"*, *"to wear"*, *"to carry"*, *"to imply"*, etc. But in this unit we are going to study it in some structures, as another way to express a durative action that started in the past and still continues at present.

One of them is:

**llevar + period of time + present participle (-ando, -iendo)**

| | |
|---|---|
| **Llevo** <u>dos años</u> **viviendo** en esta ciudad. | *I've been living in this city for two years.* |
| Ella **lleva** <u>dos horas</u> **durmiendo**. | *She has been sleeping for two hours.* |
| Ellos **llevan** <u>diez minutos</u> **hablando**. | *They have been talking for ten minutes.* |

But the "period of time" can also be placed <u>after the present participle</u>:

**Llevo viviendo** en esta ciudad <u>dos años</u>.
Ella **lleva durmiendo** <u>dos horas</u>.
Ellos **llevan hablando** <u>diez minutos</u>.

As we can see, this expression is equivalent to the present perfect continuous in English.

So far we have learned how to express the time that someone has been doing something, but let's see now how to express what someone hasn't been doing.

> **llevar + period of time + sin + infinitive**

| | |
|---|---|
| **Llevamos** <u>dos días</u> **sin comer**. | *We haven't eaten for two days.* |
| **Llevas** <u>tres meses</u> **sin fumar**. | *You haven't smoked in three months.* |
| **Llevo** <u>una semana</u> **sin ver** a Clara. | *I haven't seen Clara for a week.* |

**We can also express the period of time after the infinitive:**

**Llevamos sin comer** <u>dos días</u>.
**Llevas sin fumar** <u>tres meses</u>.
**Llevo sin ver a Clara** <u>una semana</u>.

**To ask about the "period of time" that the action is taking:**

| | |
|---|---|
| <u>¿Cuánto tiempo</u> **llevas estudiando** español? | *How long have you been studying Spanish?* |
| <u>¿Cuánto tiempo</u> **lleva** él **sin manejar** un auto? | *How long hasn't he driven a car?* |

If we use object pronouns or reflexive pronouns, they are usually placed after the gerund or the infinitive, attached to them.

| | |
|---|---|
| Llevo 20 minutos <u>esperándo**la**</u>. | *I have been waiting for her for 20 minutes.* |
| Llevamos un mes sin <u>ver**nos**</u>. | *We haven't seen each other for a month.* |

All these sentences can also be expressed in a different way:

> **Hace + period of time + que + (no) + present of the main verb**

Hace dos años que vivo en esta ciudad.
Llevo dos años viviendo en esta ciudad.    *I have been living in this city for two years.*
He estado dos años viviendo en esta ciudad.

Hace tres meses que no fumas.
Llevas tres meses sin fumar.    *You haven't smoked for three months.*
Has estado tres meses sin fumar.

If we use object or reflexive pronouns, they must be placed just before the present of the main verb, as it is a conjugated tense. But remember that they follow a gerund or an infinitive.

Hace 20 minutos que **la** espero.
Llevo 20 minutos esperándo**la**.    *I have been waiting for her for 20 minutes.*
He estado 20 minutos esperándo**la**.

Hace un mes que no **nos** vemos.
Llevamos un mes sin ver**nos**.    *We haven't seen each other for a month.*
Hemos estado un mes sin ver**nos**.

## TOP VOCABULARY AND EXPRESSIONS

### EL JARDÍN *(The garden)*

| | | |
|---|---|---|
| **barbacoa:** *barbecue* | **arbusto:** *bush* | **planta:** *plant* |
| **árbol:** *tree* | **arriate, jardinera:** *flower bed* | **valla:** *fence* |
| **flor:** *flower* | **invernadero:** *green house* | **manguera:** *hose* |
| **regar:** *to water* | **tumbona, reposera:** *chaise lounge* | **hamaca:** *hammock* |
| **césped:** *lawn* | **cortacésped:** *lawn mower* | **hierba:** *grass* |
| **estanque:** *pond* | **piscina:** *swimming pool* | **cobertizo:** *shed* |

# Unit
# 46
**Days 91 & 92**

**In this unit we will learn:**
. Present perfect or preterite?
. "Ha habido" and "hubo".
. Expressions showing disgust and repugnance.

**Diálogo / *Dialog***

Adriana y Nelson van a empezar a cenar cuando...

*Adriana and Nelson are about to start having dinner when...*

| | |
|---|---|
| A: | ¡Argh! ¡Una cucaracha! |
| N: | ¿Qué? |
| A: | ¡Allí! ¡Allí está! ¡Argh! ¡**Me dan asco** las cucarachas! |
| N: | Ya **se ha ido**. Cálmate. |
| A: | Son unos bichos **repugnantes**. Siempre me **han dado asco**. Aquí nunca **ha habido** cucarachas. ¿Qué hacía ésta aquí? |
| N: | Adriana, es normal que aparezcan cuando hace calor. |
| A: | ¡Pero no en esta casa! |
| N: | [Risas] Ya se **fue**. Venga, vamos a comer. ¿Qué **has preparado**? |
| A: | **He frito** pescado. Lo **compré** esta mañana temprano. Está muy fresco. |
| N: | Mmmm. Tiene un aspecto delicioso. |
| A: | ¿Qué es esto? ¡Argh! ¡Una mosca en mi pescado! ¡Las moscas son **asquerosas**! |
| N: | No te preocupes, cielo. No hacen nada. |
| A: | Pero son **desagradables**. [Oliendo alrededor] Oye, aquí **huele mal**. |
| N: | ¡Puff! ¡Vaya día! |

| | |
|---|---|
| A: | *Argh! A cockroach!* |
| N: | *What?* |
| A: | *There! There it is! Argh! Cockroaches disgust me!* |
| N: | *It's already gone. Calm down!* |
| A: | *They are disgusting bugs. I have always loathed them. There have never been cockroaches here. What was it doing here?* |
| N: | *Adriana, it is normal that they show up when it is hot.* |
| A: | *But not in this house!* |
| N: | *[Laughs] It's gone. Come on, let's eat. What have you made?* |
| A: | *I have fried some fish. I bought it early this morning. It's very fresh.* |
| N: | *Mmmm. It looks delicious.* |
| A: | *What is this? Argh! A fly on my fish! Flies are revolting!* |
| N: | *Don't worry, dear. They don't do anything.* |
| A: | *But they are disgusting. [Smelling] Hey! It stinks here.* |
| N: | *Puff! What a day!* |

## ¿PRETÉRITO PERFECTO O INDEFINIDO?
### (PRESENT PERFECT OR PRETERITE?)

With both the present perfect and the preterite we can refer to the same situation (past and completed facts) from two different points of view.

When we use the preterite we consider the fact in itself and "the time" when this fact occurred already finished. The idea is that the situation finished "there".

**Me compré** un auto rojo. *I bought a red car.*

When we use the present perfect we relate the fact with the present and "the time" includes the space where we are. The idea is that the situation finishes "here". It gives the idea of "proximity".

**Me he comprado** un auto rojo. *I have bought a red car.*

Some of the time markers that we use or have in mind when we refer to past actions can be easily identified with each space ("here" is the space where we are now and "there" is a past space).

## Let's look at some of these markers:

When we speak about: **ayer** *(yesterday),* **el lunes pasado** *(last Monday),* **la semana pasada** *(last week),* **el mes pasado** *(last month),* **el año pasado** *(last year),* **en marzo** *(in March),* **el 8 de agosto** *(on August 8th),* **en 2005** *(in 2005),* **el otro día** *(the other day),* **ese día** *(that day),* **hace tres años** *(three years ago),* etc.,  we use the preterite because we refer to **"THERE"**, that is, a day, a date, a month, a year or a moment in the past.

When we speak about: **hoy** *(today),* **esta mañana** *(this morning),* **esta semana** *(this week),* **este mes** *(this month),* **este año** *(this year),* **este verano** *(this summer),* **esta vez** *(this time),* **hasta ahora** *(so far),* **últimamente** *(lately),* **todavía no** *(not yet),* etc., we use the present perfect because we refer to **"HERE"**, that is, the day, the date, the month, the year or the moment we are living.

Look at the examples:

> **Vi** a Ricardo el <u>mes pasado</u>.     *I saw Ricardo last month. (THERE)*
> **He visto** a Ricardo <u>esta mañana</u>.     *I have seen Ricardo this morning. (HERE)*

**When we refer to a fact that occurs very close to this moment we can use both the present perfect and the preterite, but there is a slight difference:**

- With the present perfect we show this fact as part of the present situation.
Mi madre **ha salido** <u>hace cinco minutos</u>. (Literally): My mother has gone out five minutes ago.

- With the preterite we show this fact in itself.
Mi madre **salió** <u>hace cinco minutos</u>. *My mother went out five minutes ago.*

In certain Spanish-speaking countries these differences are not so pronounced and the uses of these tenses not so limited.

## "HA HABIDO" Y "HUBO"
### ("THERE HAVE/HAS BEEN" AND "THERE WAS/WERE")

These two expressions come from the verb "haber" in its impersonal form. They indicate the presence or existence of people or things and are only used for the third person in singular, that is, **"ha habido"** and **"hubo"**.

We already know the present (hay), the preterite (hubo) and the imperfect (había). As for "ha habido", it is the impersonal form of "haber" in the present perfect. It has two equivalents in English *(there have been / there has been)*, but, in Spanish, it is only used in singular.

> **Ha habido** <u>un problema</u>.     *There has been a problem.*
> **Ha habido** <u>muchos problemas</u>.     *There have been many problems.*

With regard to its use, we have to think that it is conjugated in present perfect, so it has to be used in the cases that we already now (see units 42-43).
The differences between "ha habido" and "hubo" are also the ones that have been seen in this unit (present perfect versus preterite), so let's pay attention to the time when the actions take place.

Ayer **hubo** cinco personas heridas en el accidente.
*There were five people injured in the accident yesterday.*

Esta mañana **ha habido** cinco personas heridas en el accidente.
*There have been five people injured in the accident this morning.*

La semana pasada **hubo** algunas quejas en la reunión.
*Last week there were some complaints at the meeting.*

Hoy **ha habido** algunas quejas en la reunión.
*Today there have been some complaints at the meeting.*

## TOP VOCABULARY AND EXPRESSIONS

### EXPRESIONES DE REPUGNANCIA Y ASCO
*(Expressions showing repugnance and disgust)*

**asco:** *disgust*
**asqueroso:** *disgusting*
**dar asco:** *to feel revulsion*
**producir repugnancia:** *to disgust*
**provocar náuseas:** *to provoke nausea*
**repugnar:** *to loathe*
**oler mal:** *to stink*
**hediondo, pestoso:** *stinking*
**¡Qué peste!:** *What a stink!*

Las cucarachas **me dan asco**.    *Cockroaches disgust me.*
Esta comida está **asquerosa**.    *This meal is disgusting.*
Esos huevos **provocan náuseas**.    *Those eggs provoke nausea.*
Nos **repugna** su sabor.    *We loathe its taste.*

## Unit

# 47

**Days 93 & 94**

**In this unit we will learn:**

. To express obligation and prohibition.

. Use of "deber", "tener que", "estar obligado a", "hay que", "no se puede".

. Vocabulary: Health and illnesses

## Dialogo / *Dialog*

En el centro médico hablan el paciente y la doctora.

*The patient and the doctor are talking at the medical center.*

D: ¡Buenos días!

P: ¡Buenos días, doctora! He venido porque **estoy resfriado** y **tengo** un poco de **fiebre**.

D: ¿Cuánto tiempo **ha estado enfermo**?

P: Durante los últimos días.

D: ¿Tiene algún otro síntoma? ¿**Tos**? ¿**Vómitos**?

P: Sí, tengo **tos** también y **me duele** un poco la cabeza. En realidad, **me duele** todo el cuerpo. **No me siento bien**.

D: ¿Fuma usted?

P: Sí, cuatro o cinco cigarrillos al día.

D: Pues **tiene que** dejar de fumar. Sé que es difícil, pero hay que hacerlo. Usted **tiene gripe y debe quedarse en la cama** durante cinco o seis días.

P: ¿**Debo** tomar algún medicamento?

D: Sí. Aquí está la **receta**. **Debe** tomar estas **pastillas** cada 8 horas y también **tiene que** beber mucha agua. Pero recuerde: **está prohibido** fumar.

P: No se preocupe. En mi casa **no se puede** fumar. A mi esposa no le gusta.

D: En unos días se sentirá mejor.

P: Espero que sí. Muchas gracias.

D: De nada. Que se mejore.

*D: Good morning!*

*P: Good morning, doctor! I have come because I have a cold and a bit of fever.*

*D: How long have you been sick?*

*P: For the last few days.*

*D: Do you have any other symptoms? Cough? Vomiting?*

*P: Yes, I also have a cough and a little headache. In fact, my whole body aches. I don't feel well.*

*D: Do you smoke?*

*P: Yes, four or five cigarettes a day.*

*D: Then you must stop smoking. I know it is difficult but you have to do it. You have the flu and must stay in bed for five or six days.*

*P: Do I have to take any medicine?*

*D: Yes. Here is the prescription. You must take these tablets every 8 hours and you must also drink a lot of water. But remember: smoking is forbidden.*

*P: Do not worry. I can't smoke at home. My wife doesn't like it.*

*D: You'll feel better in a few days.*

*P: I hope so. Thank you very much.*

*D: Not at all. Get better soon.*

## EXPRESAR OBLIGACIÓN Y PROHIBICIÓN
### (EXPRESSING OBLIGATION AND PROHIBITION).

In Spanish there are many ways <u>to express obligation</u>. Let's study the most common forms.

**a) The verb "deber" + infinitive"** *(must + infinitive)*

| | |
|---|---|
| **Debes** <u>estudiar</u> más. | *You must study harder.* |
| Usted **debe** <u>dejar</u> de fumar. | *You must stop smoking.* |

**b) The expression "tener + que + infinitive"** *(have to + infinitive)*

| | |
|---|---|
| **Tenemos que** <u>levantarnos</u> temprano. | *We have to get up early* |
| **Ella tiene que** <u>alimentar</u> a sus hijos. | *She has to feed her children.* |

**c) The expression "hay que + infinitive".** This is an impersonal form that is equivalent to *"have to"* or *"it is necessary to"* but in Spanish it has no subject, although we understand that it is "we" or "everybody".

¡Fuego! ¡**Hay que** <u>salir</u> de aquí!     *Fire! We have to get out of here!*
Ahora **hay que** <u>estudiar</u> mucho porque tenemos exámenes.
*Now we have to study a lot because we have exams.*

**d) The expression "estar obligado a + infinitive"** *(be obliged/bound to + infinitive)*

| | |
|---|---|
| **Estoy obligado a** <u>asistir</u> a la reunión. | *I am obliged to attend the meeting.* |

**e) The expression "ser obligatorio + infinitive"** *(to be obligatory to + infinitive).*

**Es obligatorio** <u>rellenar</u> esa solicitud.
*It's obligatory to fill in that form.*

## And to express prohibition:

**a)** **"Estar prohibido + infinitive"**
*(to be forbidden/prohibited)*

**Está prohibido** <u>hacer</u> fotos en el museo.
*Taking pictures in the museum is forbidden.*

**b)** The expression **"no se puede + infinitive"**
*(can't + infinitive)*

**No se puede** <u>nadar</u> en ese lago.
*You can't swim in that lake.*

**c)** The expression **"no está permitido + infinitive"**
*(not to be allowed to + infinitive)*

**No está permitido** <u>poner</u> la música alta.
*It's not permitted to play loud music.*

## Let's practise with some more examples of these structures.

En el parque **no se puede** <u>jugar</u> al fútbol.
*In the park you are not allowed to play football.*

**Es obligatorio** <u>tener</u> a los perros atados.
*It is obligatory to have your dog on a leash.*

**Está prohibido** <u>pisar</u> la hierba.
*It is forbidden to step on the grass.*

Los propietarios **deben** <u>recoger</u> los excrementos de los animales.
*The owners must pick up the animal excrements.*

## TOP VOCABULARY AND EXPRESSIONS

### LA SALUD Y LAS ENFERMEDADES *(Health and illnesses)*

**salud:** *health*
**tener fiebre:** *to have a fever/temperature*
**termómetro:** *thermometer*
**tos:** *cough*
**gripe:** *flu*
**tener un resfriado:** *to have a cold*
**jarabe:** *syrup, cough medicine*
**dolor:** *pain, ache*
**dolor de cabeza:** *headache*
**romperse la pierna:** *to break one's leg*
**escayola:** *plaster cast*
**enfermera:** *nurse*
**quedarse en cama:** *to stay in bed*
**venda:** *bandage*
**tirita/curita:** *band-aid*
**remedio:** *cure*
**dolor de garganta:** *sore throat*

**enfermedad:** *illness, disease*
**tener vómitos:** *to vomit*
**tener escalofríos:** *to have the shivers*
**tener tos:** *to have a cough*
**tener la gripe:** *to have the flu*
**tener diarrea:** *to have diarrhea*
**ser alérgico a:** *to be allergic to*
**pill:** *píldora*
**tablet:** *pastilla*
**ambulancia:** *ambulance*
**doctor, médico:** *doctor*
**cirujano:** *surgeon*
**receta:** *prescription*
**calmante:** *pain killer*
**doler:** *to pain, to hurt*
**estar enfermo:** *to be ill/sick*
**concertar una cita:** *to schedule an appointment*

Antes de ir al **médico** tienes que **concertar una cita**.
*Before going to the doctor you have to schedule an appointment.*

**Tienes tos**. Debes tomar un **jarabe**.
*You've got a cough. You should take a cough syrup.*

La semana pasada tuve la **gripe** y **me quedé en cama**.
*Last week I had the flu and stayed in bed.*

Ella **se rompió una pierna**.
*She broke her leg.*

Me he cortado y necesito una **curita**.
*I've cut myself and I need a band-aid.*

**When you don't feel well you can say:**

| | |
|---|---|
| No me siento bien:<br>No me encuentro bien: | *I don't feel well* |

| | |
|---|---|
| Me siento mal | *I feel badly.* |
| Me siento fatal | *I feel terrible.* |

Before learning how to express a specific pain, let's review some different body parts, although they will be studied in greater detail later.

**cabeza:** *head*   **espalda:** *back*   **brazo:** *arm*   **rodilla:** *knee*
**barriga:** *belly*   **estómago:** *stomach*

**When we want to express that we have a certain pain, we can say:**

> **Me duele(n) + el/la/los/las + part of the body**

(A mí) **Me duele** la espalda.   *I've got a backache.*
(A mí) **Me duelen** las rodillas.   *My knees hurt.*

**If someone else has a specific pain:**

(A ti) **Te** duele la cabeza.   *You have got a headache.*
(A ella) **Le** duelen los brazos.   *Her arms hurt.*
¿**Te** duele el estómago?   *Have you got a stomachache?*

**Another way to express pain is:**

> **Tengo (un) dolor en + el/la/los/las + part of the body**

**Tengo un dolor en** el brazo.   *I've got a pain in my arm.*
**Ellos tienen un dolor en** la espalda.   *They have got a backache.*

**We can also say:**

> **Tengo (un) dolor de + part of the body**

**Tengo dolor de** barriga.   *I've got a bellyache*
**Ella tiene un dolor de** cabeza terrible.   *She has a terrible headache.*

And before ending this unit, let's learn a common idiom with the word "enfermedad".

**Es peor el remedio que la enfermedad.** *The cure is worse than the illness.*

<table>
<tr><td>

**In this unit we will learn:**
. To join sentences: Relative pronouns.
. The relative pronouns "que" and "quien".
. Vocabulary: Horoscopes and superstitions.

</td><td>

Unit

# 48

**Days 95 & 96**

</td></tr>
</table>

### Diálogo / Dialog

Carlos está leyendo el periódico.
Llega Helga y empiezan a hablar
sobre horóscopos.

*Carlos is reading the newspaper. Helga arrives and
they start talking about horoscopes.*

| | |
|---|---|
| H: ¡Hola, Carlos! ¿Qué haces? | H: Hello, Carlos! What are you doing? |
| C: ¡Hola! Estoy leyendo mi **horóscopo** para hoy en este periódico **que** me he encontrado encima del banco. | C: Hello! I'm reading my horoscope for today in the newspaper that I have found here on the bench. |
| H: ¿Qué **signo** eres? | H: What sign are you? |
| C: Nací el 16 de enero. Soy **Capricornio**. | C: I was born on January 16th. I'm Capricorn. |
| H: ¿Y qué te dicen las estrellas? | H: And what do the stars tell you? |
| C: Dicen **que** tengo que tener cuidado con los dolores de espalda y **que** será un mal día para los negocios. | C: They say that I have to be careful with backaches and that it will be a bad day for business. |
| H: ¿Y amor? | H: And love? |
| C: Mmmm. Aquí dice **que** encontraré a una persona especial. | C: Mmmm. Here it says that I will find a special person. |
| H: Será esa chica **que** trabaja en tu oficina. | H: Could it be that girl who works in your office. |
| C: No lo sé. ¿Y tú? ¿Qué **signo** eres? | C: I don't know. And you? What sign are you? |
| H: **Aries.** | H: Aries. |
| C: A ver... Salud: Excelente; Dinero: Recibirás una sorpresa de un familiar lejano; Amor: Te enamorarás de **quien** está leyendo estas palabras. | C: Let's see….Health: Excellent; Money: You will get a surprise from a distant relative; Love: You will fall in love with the person reading these words. |
| H: [Risas] Nunca cambiarás. | H: [Laughs] You'll never change. |
| C: Bueno, sé **que** hoy no es un buen día para los negocios, pero creo que no es mala idea ir a tomar algo juntos. ¿Te apetece? | C: Well, I know that today is not a good day for business, but I don't think it's a bad idea to go and have a drink together. Do you want to? |
| H: Sí, es una buena idea. | H: Yes, it's a good idea. |

There are several ways to join sentences in Spanish and, in order to do so, we make use of links. In this unit we will work on some of them: the relative pronouns.

## LOS PRONOMBRES RELATIVOS *(RELATIVE PRONOUNS)*

In this unit and the next few ones we are going to study "relative pronouns". We have to remember that a pronoun is the word that replaces a noun. And these pronouns are called "relative" because they are "related" to an element that has previously been stated.

**Let's look at two sentences that share a common noun:**

Compré <u>un helado</u>.
*I bought an ice cream.*

<u>El helado</u> estaba delicioso.
*The ice cream was delicious.*

These two sentences can be joined into one by means of the relative pronoun "que", to avoid the repetition of the common element.

El helado **que** compré estaba delicioso.   *The ice cream that I bought was delicious.*

## EL PRONOMBRE RELATIVO "QUE" *(THE RELATIVE PRONOUN "QUE")*

The most common relative pronoun is **"que"**. It can be used to refer to both people and things. **"Que"** is the Spanish equivalent of the English words: *who, whom, which,* and *that.*

Don't forget that the relative "que" has no graphic accent, not to be confused with the interrogative "¿qué?"

**"Que"** is usually followed by a verb, but it does not always function as the subject of that verb.

La película **que** (yo) vi fue interesante.
*The film that I watched was interesting.*

Las naranjas **que** (nosotros) comemos son de California.
*The oranges that we eat are from California.*

In these examples, "yo" and "nosotros" are the subjects of the verbs, although they do not appear explicitly in the sentences. But there are other sentences where **"que"** is the subject of the verb:

Las naranjas **que** están en esa caja son de California.
*The oranges that are in that box are from California.*

La música **que** suena es una ranchera.
*The music playing is a ranchera.*

In all these examples the relative pronoun **"que"** refers to things (la película, las naranjas, la música). That is why its equivalents in English are "that" and "which".
But it can also refer to people and, in this case, its equivalent in English is "who(m)":

El hombre **que** conocí es francés.          *The man whom I met is French.*
Un carnicero es una persona **que** vende carne.    *A butcher is a person who sells meat.*

The relative pronoun is often omitted in English when there is a subject after it, but it is never omitted in Spanish.

> El libro **que** estoy leyendo es muy interesante.
> *The book (that) I am reading is very interesting.*
>
> La mujer **que** viste en el parque es mi cuñada.
> *The woman (who) you saw at the park is my sister-in-law.*

## EL PRONOMBRE RELATIVO "QUIEN"
### (THE RELATIVE PRONOUN "QUIEN")

The relative pronoun **"quien"** is used when referring to people. It doesn't have a written accent, so don't mistake it for "¿quién?". **"Quien"** has a plural form: **"quienes"**.

In this unit we have seen some examples with the relative "que". When "que" refers to people, not being the subject of the verb that follows it, it can be replaced for **"a quien"**.

| | |
|---|---|
| El hombre **que** conocí es francés | = El hombre **a quien** conocí es francés |
| La mujer **que** viste en el parque es mi cuñada | = La mujer **a quien** viste en el parque es mi cuñada. |

In these pairs of sentences "que" and "a quien" are used indistinctly, but, if the relative occurs after a preposition, "que" is only used for things and "quien/quienes" for people.

Ésa es la herramienta **con** que trabajo*.
*That is the tool I work with.*

Ella es la persona **en** quien estoy pensando.
*She is the person I am thinking about.*

Éstas son las personas **con** quienes vivo.
*These are the guys I am living with.*

[The preposition is always placed before the relative and not at the end of the sentence, as often happens in English].

It is **not correct** to say:

Éstas son las personas <u>con que</u> vivo.

But it can be corrected by adding "el", "la", "los" or "las" between the preposition and "que". After any preposition, "quien" and "quienes" can be substituted for **"el/la/los/las + que"**.

Ella es la persona **en** <u>la que</u> estoy pensando.
Éstas son las personas **con** <u>las que</u> vivo.

(*) Although this sentence is correct, it is much more common to add the corresponding article just before "que".

Ésa es la herramienta <u>con **la** que</u> trabajo.

## TOP VOCABULARY AND EXPRESSIONS

### HORÓSCOPOS Y SUPERSTICIONES *(Horoscopes and superstitions)*

Signos del zodíaco: (*Zodiac signs*)

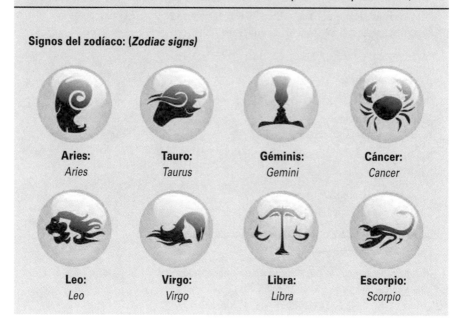

| **Aries:** | **Tauro:** | **Géminis:** | **Cáncer:** |
| *Aries* | *Taurus* | *Gemini* | *Cancer* |

| **Leo:** | **Virgo:** | **Libra:** | **Escorpio:** |
| *Leo* | *Virgo* | *Libra* | *Scorpio* |

| **Sagitario:** | **Capricornio:** | **Acuario:** | **Piscis:** |
| *Sagittarius* | *Capricorn* | *Aquarius* | *Pisces* |

**creer (en):** *to believe (in)*
**astrología:** *astrology*
**supersticioso:** *superstitious*
**traer mala suerte:** *to bring bad luck*
**cruzar los dedos:** *to cross one's fingers*
**derramar sal:** *to spill salt*
**romper un espejo:** *to break a mirror*
**pasar por debajo de una escalera:** *walking under a ladder*

**creencia:** *belief*
**astro, estrella:** *star*
**martes, 13\*:** *Tuesday, 13th*
**evitar la mala suerte:** *to avoid bad luck*
**tocar madera:** *to knock on wood*
**talismán:** *talisman*

(\*) In the Hispanic world, Tuesday the 13th is considered a very unlucky day, unlike in English-speaking cultures, where it is Friday the 13th.

¿Eres **supersticioso**?
*Are you superstitious?*

¿Qué **horóscopo** eres?
*Which sign of the horoscope are you?*

Soy **Piscis**.
*I am Pisces.*

¿Crees en la **astrología**?
*Do you believe in astrology?*

La gente **toca madera** para **evitar la mala suerte**.
*People knock on wood to avoid bad luck.*

¿Has **pasado** alguna vez **por debajo de una escalera**?
*Have you ever walked under a ladder?*

## In this unit we will learn:
. Relative pronouns when adding information.
. The relative pronouns "el que, la que, los que, las que" and "lo que".
. The relative "donde".
. The relative adjectives "cuyo, cuya, cuyos, cuyas".
. Vocabulary: Recreation and hobbies.

## Unit
# 49
**Days 97 & 98**

### Diálogo / *Dialog*

Elena y Cholo están hablando sobre sus hobbies.

*Elena and Cholo are talking about their hobbies.*

E: Cholo, ¿cuáles son tus **pasatiempos** favoritos?

C: Me gustan la **pintura**, **jugar al ajedrez** y la **jardinería**.

E: Yo creo que la persona cuyo pasatiempo es la jardinería es una persona tranquila.

C: Bueno, sí. Yo soy tranquilo. ¿Y a ti? ¿Qué te gusta hacer en tu tiempo libre?

E: A mí me gusta la **pesca**. Voy a pescar con mi padre siempre que puedo. La semana pasada pesqué una tilapia muy grande, pero **la que** pescó mi padre era enorme. Es un mundo fascinante.

C: Sí, sé **lo que** dices. ¿Dónde van ustedes a **pescar**?

E: Vamos a un río **donde** hay tilapias y carpas.

C: Cerca de la ciudad **donde** nací también hay un río **donde** la gente pesca carpas. Yo pienso que las personas **a las que** les gusta la **pesca** son muy pacientes. Demasiado pacientes. A veces estás allí durante horas y no consigues nada.

E: Bueno, siempre consigues algo. Puede ser un pescado, un tiempo de descanso, o ambas cosas.

C: Sí, tienes toda la razón del mundo.

E: *Cholo, what are your favorite hobbies?*

C: *I like painting, playing chess and gardening.*

E: *I think a person whose hobby is gardening is a calm person.*

C: *Well, yes. I am a calm person. And you? What do you like doing in your free time?*

E: *I like fishing. I go fishing with my father whenever I can. Last week I caught a very big tilapia, but the one my father caught was huge. It is a fascinating world.*

C: *Yes, I know what you mean. Where do you go fishing?*

E: *We go to a river where there are tilapias and carps.*

C: *Near the city where I was born there is also a river where people fish for carps. I think that people who like fishing are very patient. Too patient. Sometimes you are there for hours and you get nothing.*

E: *Well, you always get something. It can be a fish, time to relax, or both things.*

C: *Yes, you are quite right.*

Relative adjectives and pronouns help us join elements and make longer sentences, thus enriching our vocabulary and improving our speech.

In the last unit we studied some of the relative pronouns and, in this one, we are going to cover the rest of them.

In the sentences used as examples in unit 48, all the information given therein is necessary. But sometimes we can also **add some information** (extra information), which is not essential to understand the sentence. This "extra information" will always go between commas when written, but this does not affect the use of relative pronouns in Spanish.

Look at these sentences:

**Los marineros que estaban en el barco vieron la ballena.**
*The sailors who were on the ship saw the whale.*

**Los marineros, que estaban en el barco, vieron la ballena.**
*The sailors, who were on the ship, saw the whale.*

In the first sentence we mean that "only the sailors who were on the ship saw the whale", whereas in the second one we mean that "all the sailors saw the whale" and we add that "they all were on the ship".

**Some more examples:**

Esa mujer, a quien conocí en México, es pintora.
*That woman, whom I met in Mexico, is a painter.*

Ese anillo, que es de oro, vale una fortuna.
*That ring, which is gold, costs a fortune.*

## LOS PRONOMBRES RELATIVOS
## "EL QUE, LA QUE, LOS QUE, LAS QUE" Y "LO QUE"
### (The relative pronouns "el que, la que, los que, las que" and "lo que")

The pronouns **"el que"**, **"la que"**, **"los que"** and **"las que"** are used not to repeat the noun that has been previously said.

They are equivalent to "the one", "the ones" in English, but, in Spanish, besides singular and plural, there are also masculine and feminine forms.

Mira esos autos. **El** ~~(auto)~~ **que** me gusta es aquel.
*Look at those cars. The one I like is that one.*

Tienes varias camisas. Puedes ponerte
**la** ~~(camisa)~~ **que** quieras.
*You've got several shirts. You can put on the one you want.*

Estos zapatos son cómodos. **Los** ~~(zapatos)~~ **que** compré el año pasado son terribles.
*These shoes are comfortable. The ones I bought last year are terrible.*

Esas revistas son interesantes. **Las** ~~(revistas)~~ **que** lee mi madre son aburridas.
*Those magazines are interesting. The ones that my mother reads are boring.*

**"Lo que"** is the pronoun that we use to refer to abstract ideas. It means "the thing that" and is equivalent to *"what"* in English.

No comprendo **lo que** me estás diciendo.   *I don't understand what you are telling me.*
**Lo que** usted tiene que hacer es estudiar un poco.  *What you have to do is to study a little.*
Ella no sabía **lo que** tenía que hacer.   *She didn't know what she had to do.*

## EL PRONOMBRE RELATIVO "DONDE"
### (THE RELATIVE PRONOUN "DONDE")

The relative "donde" is used when we refer to places. It does not have a graphic accent to avoid confusion with the interrogative "¿dónde?". Its equivalent in English is "where".

| | |
|---|---|
| Es un <u>hospital</u>. Yo nací en ese <u>hospital</u>. | It is a hospital. I was born in that hospital. |
| Ese es el hospital **donde** yo nací. | That is the hospital where I was born |
| Aquel es el hotel **donde** me quedé. | That is the hotel where I stayed. |
| Miami es la ciudad **donde** ellos viven. | Miami is the city where they live. |
| Éstas son las calles **donde** él se perdió. | These are the streets where he got lost. |

In all cases we can replace **"donde"** for **"en el que"**, **"en la que"**, **"en los que"**, **"en las que"**, according to the gender and number of the noun that "donde" substitutes.

Aquel es el hotel **en el que** me quedé.
Miami es la ciudad **en la que** ellos viven.
Éstas son las calles **en las que** él se perdió.

## LOS ADJETIVOS RELATIVOS "CUYO", "CUYA", "CUYOS" Y "CUYAS"
### (THE RELATIVE ADJECTIVES "CUYO", "CUYA", "CUYOS" AND "CUYAS")

We include the relative adjective "cuyo" (and its related forms) because it relates the owner to that which is owned. Note that there are four forms to accommodate singular and plural, masculine and feminine: **cuyo, cuya, cuyos, cuyas**. Their equivalent in English is "whose".

No conozco al hombre **cuyo** apellido es Yang.
*I don't know the man whose last name is Yang.*

Fernando, **cuya** familia vive en Argentina, es muy simpático.
*Fernando, whose family lives in Argentina, is very friendly.*

Ésos son los profesores **cuyos** métodos son excelentes.
*Those are the teachers whose methods are excellent.*

La mesa, **cuyas** patas son largas, es incómoda.
*The table, whose legs are long, is uncomfortable.*

Note that the relative adjective agrees in gender and number with the thing being owned, **not** with the owner:

> No conozco al hombre **cuyo** <u>apellido</u> es Yang.
> Fernando, **cuya** <u>familia</u> vive en Argentina, es muy simpático.
> Ésos son los profesores **cuyos** <u>métodos</u> son excelentes.
> La mesa, **cuyas** <u>patas</u> son largas, es incómoda.

## TOP VOCABULARY AND EXPRESSIONS

### ESPARCIMIENTO Y PASATIEMPOS *(Recreation and hobbies)*

**billar:** *pool*
**bolos:** *bowling*
**dominó:** *dominoes*
**informática:** *computing*
**carpintería:** *carpentry*
**pintura:** *painting*
**pesca:** *fishing*
**caza:** *hunting*
**cocina:** *cooking*
**jardinería:** *gardening*

**juegos de cartas:** *card games*
**ajedrez:** *chess*
**juego de dardos:** *darts*
**juego de apuestas:** *gambling*
**dibujo:** *drawing*

## Unit
# 50
**Days 99 & 100**

**In this unit we will learn:**
. To compare things.
. The comparative of equality.
. Vocabulary: Means of transport.

**Diálogo / Dialog**

Pedro y Laura hablan sobre Ricardo, uno de los compañeros de trabajo de Pedro.

*Pedro and Laura are talking about Ricardo, one of Pedro's colleagues from work.*

P: Ricardo es un compañero de trabajo que maneja **el mismo autobús que** yo.
L: ¿Y tiene **tanta** experiencia como tú?
P: No. Él no ha manejado un **autobús** durante tantos años, pero lo hace **igual de** bien.
L: ¿Es difícil manejarlos?
P: No es **tan** difícil **como** la gente puede pensar. Sólo necesitas práctica.
L: ¿Qué hacía Ricardo antes?
P: Era taxista.
L: Yo no tengo **auto**. Voy a todos los sitios en **bicicleta** o **motocicleta**. A veces tomo el autobús, pero no **tanto como** antes.

P: *Ricardo is a colleague who drives the same bus as me.*
L: *And does he have as much experience as you?*
P: *No. He hasn't driven a bus for as many years, but he does it as well as me.*
L: *Is it difficult to drive them?*
P: *It isn't as difficult as people may think. You only need some practice.*
L: *What did Ricardo do before?*
P: *He was a taxi driver.*
L: *I don't have a car. I go everywhere by bicycle or motorcycle. I sometimes take the bus, but not as much as before.*

P: Sin embargo, a mí me dan miedo las **motocicletas**. Hace algunos años me caí de una y desde entonces nunca me he vuelto a montar en ninguna. A Ricardo le gustan mucho, pero él tampoco tiene.

L: Bueno, Ricardo ha sido taxista y es conductor de **autobús** ahora. Parece que le gusta el transporte público. En el futuro será motoconchero.

P: ¿Motoconchero?

L: Sí. Ya sabes que viví tres años en la República Dominicana. Allí el motoconcho es la motocicleta que se usa como **taxi**, y el motoconchero es su propietario. Estas **motocicletas** no son modernas, pero son muy útiles.

P: Sí, son muy buenas para evitar los atascos en las ciudades, pero ellas son muy malas cuando llueve.

L: Sí, tienes razón.

P: *Regardless, I am afraid of motorcycles. I fell off one a few years ago and I haven't ridden one since. Ricardo likes them very much, but he hasn't got one either.*

L: *Well, Ricardo has been a taxi driver and is a bus driver now. He seems to like public transportation. He will be a "motoconchero" in the future.*

P: *Motoconchero?*

L: *Yes. You know I was living in the Dominican Republic for three years. There, the "motoconcho" is the motorcycle that is used as a taxi, and the "motoconchero" is its owner. These motorcycles are not modern, but they are very useful.*

P: *Yes, they are very good to avoid traffic jams in the city, but they are very bad when it rains.*

L: *Yes, you are right.*

## COMPARAR COSAS (COMPARING THINGS)

When we want to compare two things, we can do it from different points of view. Thus, we can say that two things are equal, one superior to the other, or one inferior to the other. Therefore we will make use of the comparatives of equality, superiority and inferiority.

## EL COMPARATIVO DE IGUALDAD (The comparative of equality)

To say that two things are equal we use the following structures:

### a) With adjectives and adverbs:

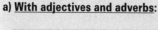

**tan** + adjective / adverb + **como**

as + adjective / adverb + as

Luis es **tan** alto **como** Miguel.
Luis no toca el piano **tan** bien **como** Miguel.

*Luis is as tall as Miguel.*
*Luis doesn't play the piano as well as Miguel.*

| igual de + | adjective / adverb | + (que) |  | as + | adjective / adverb | + as |
|---|---|---|---|---|---|---|

Luis es **igual de** <u>alto</u> **que** Miguel.
*Luis is as tall as Miguel.*

Luis no toca el piano **igual de** <u>bien</u> **que** Miguel.
*Luis doesn't play the piano as well as Miguel.*

**And also:**

Luis and Miguel son **igual de** <u>altos</u>.
*Luis and Miguel are the same height.*

Luis y Miguel no tocan el piano **igual de** <u>bien</u>.
*Luis and Miguel don't play the piano equally well.*

**b) With verbs:**

To express the same quantity:

| verb + | **tanto como** | + ..... |  | verb + | as much as | + ..... |
|---|---|---|---|---|---|---|

Esteban <u>corre</u> **tanto como** su primo.
*Esteban runs as much as his cousin.*

Jaime no <u>estudia</u> **tanto como** yo.
*Jaime doesn't study as much as me.*

To express the same quantity or manner:

| verb + | **igual que** | + ..... |  | verb + | as much as | + ..... |
|---|---|---|---|---|---|---|
|  |  |  |  | verb + | the same as | + ..... |

Esteban <u>corre</u> **igual que** su primo.
*Esteban runs as much as his cousin. (quantity)*
*Esteban runs (in) the same way as his cousin. (manner)*

Jaime no <u>estudia</u> **igual que** yo.
*Jaime doesn't study as much as me.*
*Jaime doesn't study as I do.*

**And also:**

| verb + | **igual** |  | verb + | the same |
|---|---|---|---|---|

Esteban y su primo <u>corren</u> **igual**.
*Esteban and his cousin run the same. (distance or manner)*

To express the same quantity or the same thing(s):

| **verb +** | **lo mismo** | **+ que** | | verb + | the same | + (as) |
|---|---|---|---|---|---|---|

Hoy hemos bebido **lo mismo** (que ayer)
*Today we have drunk the same (as yesterday)*

Ella estudió **lo mismo que** tú: geografía.
*She studied the same as you: geography.*

The second element of the comparison is not needed if we know what we are talking about, but with "tanto", we only omit it when the sentence is negative:

Juan es **tan** inteligente **como** Rafael e **igual de** travieso. (que Rafael).
*Juan is as intelligent as Rafael and as naughty as him.*

Mi padre come **tanto como** Miguel, pero <u>no</u> bebe **tanto**. (como Miguel).
*My father eats as much as Miguel but he doesn't drink so much.*

## c) **With nouns:**
To express the same identity or quantity:

| **el mismo/los mismos**<br>**la misma/las mismas** | **+ noun + (que)** | | the same | + noun + (as) |
|---|---|---|---|---|

Estoy leyendo **el mismo** <u>libro</u> **que** Marta.
*I am reading the same book as Marta.*

No vivo en **la misma** <u>ciudad</u> **que** tú.
*I don't live in the same city as you.*

Tienes **los mismos** <u>ojos</u> **que** tu madre.
*You have the same eyes as your mother.*

Ella hace **las mismas** <u>cosas</u> **que** su novio.
*She does the same things as her boyfriend.*

**And also:**

| | |
|---|---|
| Marta y yo estamos leyendo **el mismo** libro. | *Marta and I are reading the same book.* |
| Tú y yo no vivimos en **la misma** ciudad. | *You and I don't live in the same city.* |
| Tu madre y tú tienen **los mismos** ojos. | *Your mother and you have the same eyes.* |
| Ella y su novio hacen **las mismas** cosas. | *She and her boyfriend do the same things.* |

To express the same quantity:

| | |
|---|---|
| **tanto/ tanta** + uncountable noun + **como** | *as much + uncountable noun + as* |
| **tantos/tantas** + countable noun + **como** | *as many + countable noun + as* |

| | |
|---|---|
| No tengo **tanto** <u>dinero</u> como tú. | *I don't have as much money as you.* |
| Él bebe **tanta** <u>leche</u> como su hijo. | *He drinks as much milk as his son.* |
| Nosotros teníamos **tantos** <u>problemas</u> **como** ustedes. | *We had as many problems as you.* |
| Ella comió **tantas** <u>manzanas</u> **como** yo. | *She ate as many apples as I did.* |

<u>The second element of the comparison is not needed if we know what we are talking about, but with "tanto", "tanta", "tantos" and "tantas" we only omit it when the sentence is negative:</u>

Mira ese celular. Yo tengo **el mismo**. (celular)
*Look at that cell phone. I have the same one.*

Él tiene mucho tiempo libre, pero yo **no** tengo **tanto**. (tiempo libre)
*He has a lot of spare time but I don't have so much.*

## TOP VOCABULARY AND EXPRESSIONS

## MEDIOS DE TRANSPORTE *(Means of the transport)*

| | | | |
|---|---|---|---|
| **auto:** *car* | **taxi:** *taxi, cab* | **autobús:** *bus* | **furgoneta:** *van* |
| **camión:** *truck* | **camioneta:** *pickup truck* | **bicicleta:** *bicycle* | **motocicleta:** *motorcycle* |
| **tren:** *train* | **metro:** *subway* | **barco:** *ship* | **crucero:** *cruise ship* |
| **avión:** *plane* | **helicóptero:** *helicopter* | **tranvía:** *streetcar, trolley* | |

# Verbs at a glance

# ENDINGS OF SPANISH REGULAR VERBS

## INDICATIVE MOOD

### PRESENT

|  | **-AR** | **-ER** | **-IR** |
|---|---|---|---|
| yo | -o | -o | -o |
| tú | -as | -es | -es |
| usted, él, ella | -a | -e | -e |
| nosotros/as | -amos | -emos | -imos |
| vosotros/as | -áis | -éis | -ís |
| ustedes, ellos, ellas | -an | -en | -en |

### PRESENT CONTINUOUS

| yo | estoy | |
|---|---|---|
| tú | estás | |
| usted, él, ella | está | |
| nosotros/as | estamos | + gerund |
| vosotros/as | estáis | |
| ustedes, ellos, ellas | están | |

### PRETERITE

|  | **-AR** | **-ER** | **-IR** |
|---|---|---|---|
| yo | -é | -í | -í |
| tú | -aste | -iste | -iste |
| usted, él, ella | -ó | -ió | -ió |
| nosotros/as | -amos | -imos | -imos |
| vosotros/as | -asteis | -isteis | -isteis |
| ustedes, ellos, ellas | -aron | -ieron | -ieron |

### IMPERFECT

|  | **-AR** | **-ER** | **-IR** |
|---|---|---|---|
| yo | -aba | -ía | -ía |
| tú | -abas | -ías | -ías |
| usted, él, ella | -aba | -ía | -ía |
| nosotros/as | -ábamos | -íamos | -íamos |
| vosotros/as | -abais | -íais | -íais |
| ustedes, ellos, ellas | -aban | -ían | -ían |

# SPANISH IN 100 DAYS

## PRESENT PERFECT

| | | |
|---|---|---|
| yo | he | |
| tú | has | |
| usted, él, ella | ha | |
| nosotros/as | hemos | + past participle |
| vosotros/as | habéis | |
| ustedes, ellos, ellas | han | |

## PAST PERFECT

| | | |
|---|---|---|
| yo | había | |
| tú | habías | |
| usted, él, ella | había | |
| nosotros/as | habíamos | + past participle |
| vosotros/as | habíais | |
| ustedes, ellos, ellas | habían | |

## FUTURE

| | | |
|---|---|---|
| yo | | −é |
| tú | | −ás |
| usted, él, ella | infinitive + | −á |
| nosotros/as | | −emos |
| vosotros/as | | −éis |
| ustedes, ellos, ellas | | −án |

## FUTURE PERFECT

| | | |
|---|---|---|
| yo | habré | |
| tú | habrás | |
| usted, él, ella | habrá | |
| nosotros/as | habremos | + past participle |
| vosotros/as | habréis | |
| ustedes, ellos, ellas | habrán | |

## CONDITIONAL MOOD

### CONDITIONAL SIMPLE

| | | |
|---|---|---|
| yo | | –ía |
| tú | | –ías |
| usted, él, ella | infinitive + | –ía |
| nosotros/as | | –íamos |
| vosotros/as | | –íais |
| ustedes, ellos, ellas | | –ían |

### CONDITIONAL PERFECT

| | | |
|---|---|---|
| yo | habría | |
| tú | habrías | |
| usted, él, ella | habría | |
| nosotros/as | habríamos | + past participle |
| vosotros/as | habríais | |
| ustedes, ellos, ellas | habrían | |

## SUBJUNCTIVE MOOD

### PRESENT

| | –AR | –ER | –IR |
|---|---|---|---|
| yo | –e | –a | –a |
| tú | –es | –as | -as |
| usted, él, ella | –e | –a | –a |
| nosotros/as | –emos | –amos | –amos |
| vosotros/as | –éis | –áis | –áis |
| ustedes, ellos, ellas | –en | –an | –an |

### IMPERFECT

| | –AR | –ER | –IR |
|---|---|---|---|
| yo | –ara/-ase | –iera/-iese | –iera/-iese |
| tú | –aras/-ases | –ieras/-ieses | -ieras/-ieses |
| usted, él, ella | –ara/-ase | –iera/-iese | –iera/-iese |
| nosotros/as | –áramos/-ásemos | –iéramos/-iésemos | –iéramos/-iésemos |
| vosotros/as | –arais/-aseis | –ierais/-ieseis | –ierais/-ieseis |
| ustedes, ellos, ellas | –aran/-asen | –ieran/-iesen | –ieran/-iesen |

## PRESENT PERFECT

| | | |
|---|---|---|
| yo | haya | |
| tú | hayas | |
| usted, él, ella | haya | |
| nosotros/as | hayamos | + past participle |
| vosotros/as | hayáis | |
| ustedes, ellos, ellas | hayan | |

## PAST PERFECT

| | | |
|---|---|---|
| yo | hubiera/hubiese | |
| tú | hubieras/hubieses | |
| usted, él, ella | hubiera/hubiese | |
| nosotros/as | hubiéramos/hubiésemos | + past participle |
| vosotros/as | hubierais/hubieseis | |
| ustedes, ellos, ellas | hubieran/hubiesen | |

# IMPERATIVE MOOD

## AFFIRMATIVE

| | –AR | –ER | –IR |
|---|---|---|---|
| tú | –a | –e | –e |
| usted | –e | –a | –a |
| vosotros/as | –ad | –ed | –id |
| ustedes | –en | –an | –an |

## NEGATIVE

| | –AR | –ER | –IR |
|---|---|---|---|
| tú | –es | –as | –as |
| usted | –e | –a | –a |
| vosotros/as | –éis | –áis | –áis |
| ustedes | –en | –an | –an |

## "VOSOTROS" VERSUS "USTEDES" IN SPAIN'S SPANISH

We know that the second person plural in Spain's Spanish is different from that used in Latin America, which is the one that we have learned in this course.

The plural "you" is equivalent to "**vosotros, vosotras**" in Spain, when used informally, instead of "ustedes" (which is only used for formal treatment). The conjugation of the verbs for "ustedes" is the same as for "ellos, ellas", but it is different when we refer to "vosotros, vosotras". Here is a guide to show how to conjugate the different tenses for "**vosotros, vosotras**". The first person singular (yo) for each tense is also shown.

# INDICATIVE MOOD

## PRESENT

### REGULAR VERBS

|            | –ar (cantar) | –er (comer) | –ir (abrir) |
|------------|--------------|-------------|-------------|
| yo         | canto        | como        | abro        |
| vosotros/as | **cantáis**  | **coméis**  | **abrís**   |

### IRREGULAR VERBS

|            | ser      | estar     |          |        |
|------------|----------|-----------|----------|--------|
| yo         | soy      | estoy     |          |        |
| vosotros/as | **sois** | **estáis** |          |        |

|            | pensar     | entender    | haber     | ir       |
|------------|------------|-------------|-----------|----------|
| yo         | pienso     | entiendo    | he        | voy      |
| vosotros/as | **pensáis** | **entendéis** | **habéis** | **vais** |

## PRESENT CONTINUOUS

|            | hablar              |
|------------|---------------------|
| yo         | estoy hablando      |
| vosotros/as | **estáis hablando** |

## PRETERITE

### REGULAR VERBS

|  | -ar (hablar) | -er (aprender) | -ir (escribir) |
|---|---|---|---|
| yo | hablé | aprendí | escribí |
| vosotros/as | **hablasteis** | **aprendisteis** | **escribisteis** |

### IRREGULAR VERBS

|  | pedir | ser | estar | hacer |
|---|---|---|---|---|
| yo | pedí | fui | estuve | hice |
| vosotros/as | **pedisteis** | **fuisteis** | **estuvisteis** | **hicisteis** |

## IMPERFECT

### REGULAR VERBS

|  | hablar | aprender | escribir |
|---|---|---|---|
| yo | hablaba | aprendía | escribía |
| vosotros/as | **hablabais** | **aprendíais** | **escribíais** |

### IRREGULAR VERBS

|  | ser | ir | ver |
|---|---|---|---|
| yo | era | iba | veía |
| vosotros/as | **erais** | **ibais** | **veíais** |

## PAST CONTINUOUS

|  | hablar |
|---|---|
| yo | estaba hablando |
| vosotros/as | **estabais hablando** |

## PRESENT PERFECT

|  | comprar |
|---|---|
| yo | he comprado |
| vosotros/as | **habéis comprado** |

## PRESENT PERFECT CONTINUOUS

|  | comprar |
|---|---|
| yo | he estado comprando |
| vosotros/as | **habéis estado comprando** |

| PAST PERFECT | | FUTURE | |
|---|---|---|---|
| | *comprar* | | *comprar* |
| yo | había comprado | yo | compraré |
| vosotros/as | **habíais comprado** | vosotros/as | **compraréis** |

## CONDITIONAL MOOD

| CONDITIONAL | | CONDITIONAL PERFECT | |
|---|---|---|---|
| | *comprar* | | *comprar* |
| yo | compraría | yo | habría comprado |
| vosotros/as | **compraríais** | vosotros/as | **habríais comprado** |

## SUBJUNCTIVE MOOD

### PRESENT

#### REGULAR VERBS

| | *hablar* | *beber* | *vivir* |
|---|---|---|---|
| yo | hable | beba | viva |
| vosotros/as | **habléis** | **bebáis** | **viváis** |

#### IRREGULAR VERBS

| | *volver* | *oír* |
|---|---|---|
| yo | vuelva | oiga |
| vosotros/as | **volváis** | **oigáis** |

| | *ser* | *ver* | *estar* | *saber* | *ir* | *haber* |
|---|---|---|---|---|---|---|
| yo | sea | vea | esté | sepa | vaya | haya |
| vosotros/as | **seáis** | **veáis** | **estéis** | **sepáis** | **vayáis** | **hayáis** |

### IMPERFECT

| | *hablar* | *beber* | *vivir* |
|---|---|---|---|
| yo | hablara or hablase | bebiera or bebiese | viviera or viviese |
| vosotros | **hablarais** or **hablaseis** | **bebierais** or **bebieseis** | **vivierais** or **vivieseis** |